Doubts and Decisions
for Living

VOLUME III
The Structure of Human Life

(Enhanced Edition)

List of Books by This Author
(As of June 20, 2020)[*]

Non-fiction

The Nature of Love and Relationships 2011, **2016**
Doubts and Decisions for Living:
  Volume I: The Foundation of Human Thoughts **2014**
  Volume II: The Sanctity of Human Spirit **2014**
  Volume III: The Structure of Human Life **2014**
Relationship Facts, Trends, and Choices **2016**
The Mysteries of Life, Love, and Happiness **2016**
Relationship Needs, Framework, and Models **2016**
Gender Qualities, Quirks, and Quarrels **2016**
Marriage and Divorce Hardships **2016**
Being Better Beings **2020**

Fiction

Persian Moons 2007, **2016**
Midnight Gate-opener 2011, **2016**
My Lousy Life Stories **2014**
Persian Suns **2021 (Planned)**

---

[*] 12 older books are Enhanced Editions and printed in 2020. They were resubmitted to the Library and Archives Canada Cataloguing as well. If a book's 'print date' on the copyright page is older, the newest version is available at Amazon and bookstores.

Doubts and Decisions
for Living

VOLUME III
The Structure of Human Life

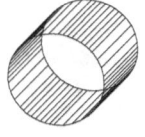

Tom Omidi, Ph.D.

Copyright © 2014 by Tom Omidi
Copyright © 2020 by Tom Omidi

All rights reserved. No part of this book may be reproduced, translated, or transmitted in any form or by any means—graphic, electronic or mechanical, including photocopying, recording, taping or information storage or retrieval systems—without the prior written permission of the publisher or author.

Omidi, Tom, 1945-, author
Doubts and decisions for living / Tom Omidi, Ph.D.

Contents: Volume I. The foundation of human thoughts
Volume II. The sanctity of human spirit
Volume III. The structure of human life.

ISBN 978-1-988351-11-7 (v. 1 : pbk.).
ISBN 978-1-988351-12-4 (v. 2 : pbk.).
ISBN 978-1-988351-13-1 (v. 3 : pbk.).

1. Conduct of life. I. Title.
II. Title: Foundation of human thoughts.
III. Title: Sanctity of human spirit.
IV. Title: Structure of human life.

Old Edition at
Library and Archives Canada Cataloguing in Publication
BJ1581.2.O45 2014   170'.44   C2014-903378-8

Cover page design by Tom Omidi

Published by Eros Books,
Vancouver, British Columbia
Canada

erosbooks2020.@gmail.com

Enhanced and Printed in 2020

For my children

"And you…!?
"With all that knowledge and education, how much have you learned about the art of living and relating?"

Table of Contents

	Page
Author's Note	1
Introduction	7

PART I: Learning and Education

Chapter One: The Role of Education	17
Education – A Basic, Structured Learning	18
Education – A Tool for Career Planning	20
The Dilemma of Education	21
The Value of Education	25
Education and Organizations	27
Chapter Two: Learning the Art of Living	29
Objectives of Learning	30
Learning about Personal Qualities	31
Learning about Life Essentialities	36
Learning about Life's Qualities	38
Learning from Our Sufferings	41
Living or Making a Living	44

PART II: Work and Organization

Chapter Three: Objectives of Working	49
Work Purposes	51
Work Philosophy	55
Aligning Our Drives for Working	58
Working for Individualism (Pride)	59
The Inherent Purpose of Work	61
The Nature and Value of Work	64
Work Contents and Conditions	66
Chapter Four: Work Environment	69
Adopting Organization Objectives	72
Personality Clashes and Moods	74

Table of Contents (Cont.)

	Page
Chapter Five: Organization Perils	77
The Organization Dependence	78
The Reality of Organization	82
Ego at Work in Organization	85
Endangered Greedy Giants	90
Chapter Six: Organization Relations	91
Remembering the Basics	92
Options for Organization Relations	96
Coping in Organizations	99
Options of Getting Absorbed	103
Organization Lessons Ignored	107
Imminent Organization Revolution	109
PART III: Companionship and Marriage	
Chapter Seven: Love and Loneliness Dilemmas	113
Motives behind Relationships	116
Irrelevant Purposes of Marriage	120
Relevant Purposes of Marriage	121
Analyzing Marriage	124
Premarital Negotiations	126
Developing a Partnership Agreement	129
Knowing Our Partner	136
Chapter Eight: Measures of Partners' Compatibility	141
(Relationships Success Factors)	
Compatibility in 'Personality Aspects'	141
Compatibility to Increase Life Enjoyments	145
Compatibility for Support and Cooperation	149
Compatibility for Building a Sensible Commitment	156
Is Compatibility a Dream?	159
Humans' Inherent Incompatibility	162
Chapter Nine: Sources of Marital Problems	165
Communication Hurdles	166
Expecting Our Partner to Change	172

Table of Contents (Cont.)

Page

Chapter Nine: (Cont.)
- Why Do We Expect Change only from others? 174
- Why Cannot We Change? 176
- The Effects of Demanding Change 178
- Blaming and Nagging Syndrome 182
- The Evil of Domination 185
- The Significance of Marriage Decision 187
- Universal Relationships Problems and Solutions 190

PART IV: Alienation and Separation

Chapter Ten: A Time for Thinking Marriage 195
- The Road to Separation 199
- The Road with No Return 201
- Revising Our Focus 202
- Alienation as a Reflection of Global Mentality 204
- Alienation Characteristics 206
- Alienation Seeds and Growth 210
- Innocent Causes of Alienation 214
- Fighting Alienation 217

Chapter Eleven: Alienation Preparedness 219
- Acknowledgment and Awareness 220
- Alienation Preparedness Factors 223
  1. Acknowledging Potential Relationship Problems ... 224
  2. Acknowledging Our Psychological Defects 226
  3. Measuring and Improving Our Tolerance 229
  4. Recognizing Our Opportunities and Fears 232
  5. Admitting, Planning, and Playing Our Roles 236
  6. Making an Objective Judgment and Decision 239

Chapter Twelve: Alienation Awareness Essentials 243
- Partners' General Recognition 243
- Coping with Human and Relationship Flaws 256
- Managing Our Tolerance Level 264

Table of Contents (Cont.)

	Page
Chapter Thirteen: Marriage Salvation	269
The Ultimate Options	269
Thinking Romance and Remarriage	272
PART V: Consciousness and Awareness	
About Part V	278
Chapter Fourteen: Learning Fundamentals	279
The Impact (and Value) of Learning	280
Learning Processes	283
Learning Sources and Factors	285
Learning through Natural Growth	286
Learning from Other Individuals	287
Learning from Other Sources	288
Learning from Personal Experiences	288
Learning from Universal Experiences	290
Learning through Objective (Focused) Thinking	294
Chapter Fifteen: Living for Learning	297
Rooted Learning Disability	299
Conscious Learning Endeavour	305
Awareness Domain and Power	308
Chapter Sixteen: Rethinking Education	313
Education-Related Social Inefficiencies	313
A Guideline for the Type and Level of Education	325
Epilogue	327

List of Tables

Table 3.1 : Types of Work	51
Table 8.1 : Compatibility Measures	144
Table 11.1: Personal Defects Causing Alienation	263

Author's Note

Doubts and Decisions for living trilogy started with my simple goal to share my thoughts about life in an organized, consistent manner with my children when they became teenagers. The first draft emerged fifteen years ago in about half its present size. Still I failed to raise my kids' interest to read it for many reasons (as explained in Volume I's Epilogue). Instead, only my hunch about parents' difficulty to communicate with their children became clearer to me. I also realized that, like most parents, I did not have a good grasp of life myself, anyway, even after many years of thinking and experimenting. Therefore, the manuscript was left alone until recently when I noticed a rising level of desperation and negativism among the youths. The gloomy trends in modern societies are hard to ignore where everybody, especially the youths, is facing all sorts of socioeconomic challenges and our relationships are drastically vulnerable.

Anyway, I felt obliged again to share my ideas with my kids as they challenged my wisdom regularly or sought my opinion accidentally. Then I found the old draft and developed it into this trilogy with the intention of drawing a general picture of life in the new era. We all know most of the facts reiterated in these three books, yet insist on ignoring them or do not quite grasp the severity of the havoc we have created. Nevertheless, a collective analysis of the main issues and thoughts about both our daunting world and existence might help us deal with the new realities of the 21st century more objectively.

The basic reality is that life has become a stressful process and all the clues show that it would only get worse in the coming years, yet we must somehow manage our lives within this chaotic environment. Despite our eagerness to be philosophical about life and develop ideal convictions, finding *practical* means of living remains a big challenge and priority. Living is a sacred, yet often scary, mission for us. All along, we should make many important decisions and choose a life path based on some form of logic, self-awareness, and facts. We must grasp our real needs, set our life priorities properly, and move forward.

Our goals for building a sound mindset (see Volume I) are to plan our lives rationally, choose a practical life path, and live as smoothly as possible. And the main purpose of sensing and strengthening our spirits (see Volume II) is to get the required energy and resilience to withstand life's hardships. We like to learn about controlling our fanciful needs and ambitions before confusion and stress overwhelms our lives. Eventually, we must accomplish all these goals or leave ourselves at the mercy of our employers, spouses, children, or maybe even healing institutions, such as a mental hospital or a penitentiary. We must make tough and tricky choices all our lives in order to stay sane and face lesser disappointments. Thus, this volume focuses on life's major decisions within a chaotic social structure.

Our mission is to somehow fit within society, most likely by getting assimilated with the mainstream—simply because most of us do no have the guts to live independently and think freely. Yet, we should at least know the kind of price we must pay for the life path we choose. We should also always remember that we had an option to live differently. While the price for a rather independent lifestyle is frequent isolation and loneliness, life in the mainstream has the higher price of hard work, humiliation, repeated failures, disappointments, and stress.

Many of us do not even realize the possibility of other ways of living, anyway. Despite our innate divine drive and intentions for individualism, we merely follow the crowd out of necessity or desperation. Our strong need for a companion by itself hinders our search for individualism. We also feel obliged to consider the needs of other people (especially our families) who demand a sense of security and optimism to stay around us. They run away if we cannot exude a great deal of passion and positive feelings regularly or do not stay within the routines of the mainstream for their convenience.

The worst scenario is when a person cannot choose a life path or philosophy for his/her existence. S/he cannot decide regarding this most important facet of his/her life, while always struggling with a huge amount of doubts. Surely, letting our doubts cripple us might ruin our lives as much as hasty and emotional decisions can. Achieving this balance and our life objectives has become extremely difficult, nowadays, however.

There is always hope that a few good things happen in our lives regardless of the path we choose. We might even get lucky and find a suitable career and a dependable companion as well. However, other than indulging our hopes and waiting, nothing can change for the better considering humans' spoiled mentality and choice of lifestyles. Only when somebody builds a strong spirit and character, s/he might develop at least some sense of contentment by pursuing a serene life philosophy fearlessly. The rest of us are eventually dragged into a lousy lifestyle due to our naivety and neediness. After all, the conventional path feels most natural to grasp, stay positive, and indulge ourselves with the possibility of finding love, fame, and pleasure.

Looking positive and hopeful is another social fad, anyway, and partially useful, too, as a kind of defence mechanism to bear life's hardships. We need a way of curbing all the negative clues surrounding our lives. We need to feel and show high hopes and optimism just to go through another day. Thus, we try to think positively, pamper our fanciful aspirations, and live in our dream world. It seems we prefer to fool ourselves and remain naive, because life is easier to bear in such an illusive world. We dislike people who remind us of our shallowness and misery, too. We would rather embrace our addictive social values and ways with a positive attitude, no matter how often we face the repercussions of our naivety and suffer deeply. We do not want to think or live differently even when our illusions and fanciful dreams lead only to more disappointments and stress. Well, maybe we have to! But that is exactly why we must at least develop a dynamic mentality to anticipate and handle all these life's challenges head-on a bit more wisely in order to survive and keep our sanity. We should contemplate our choices and decisions proactively.

Nevertheless, a major paradox overwhelms us all our lives. On the one hand, negativism is the least productive and appealing strategy for living, especially for building good relationships. We must stop being too cynical and negative to the point of crippling our brains. Negative thinking and sense of helplessness serve no purpose other than weakening our mental and physical health, while giving people more reasons to avoid us. Negativism and escaping reality merely reflect our failure to put life in a proper perspective. It shows our inability to tame our raw ambitions and live a simple life. It indicates that we have not learned how to deal with our major life decisions and doubts. Despite the evident social chaos, our negativism gives others even more ammunition to crush our spirits, instead of sympathizing or even bothering to understand our position. Subtle apathy, in spite of all the shows of empathy, is hidden in human nature and a reality that nobody can change. Giving up on life due to social pains or people's apathy provides the right justification for the whole world's view of our immaturity and vulnerability.

On the other hand, staying positive in the mainstream feels tough and stupid, nowadays, because our present social structure has very little positive features. Actually, our alluring positive thinking slogans have as many or more drawbacks as cynicism and negative thinking. We would merely hurt ourselves more by expecting lasting happiness, success, and marriage. These dreams hardly come true in life, and instead we only encounter all sorts of setbacks repeatedly. Our positive thinking motto cannot solve this conundrum, either, if we decide to become a bit realistic and honest. Living in this environment—such an imaginary positive world—only brings us more pains, the more we try to fathom life or put expectations on it. Yet, it feels necessary and wise to stay proactive and positive, while we must remain vigilant about the risks of getting absorbed in this illusive world.

A positive note about the mainstream is that, while lost in their world of illusions, at least they *feel* in control of their lives and do not keep doubting their purposes of living as often as we cynical people do. We may not understand or like their thoughts, lifestyles, and attitudes, yet, ironically, the mainstream's naivety makes them appear more realistic about the whole matter of life. They look strong enough to deal with all the nagging questions and doubts about life that a supposedly freethinker struggles with forever. After all, not standing above all the facts of life is only a sign of genetic or mental weakness.

Surely, both positive and negative thinking are risky. Thus, the ideal would be to learn *objective* thinking, instead of being merely a foolish follower or an idle idealist. 'Objective thinking' is simply a by-product of one's rising consciousness and trusting it to sail thru life. The first step is to accept the reality of the rising social chaos as a basic fact that nobody can avoid or change. Then, through self-awareness, we learn to keep our expectations from life and people very low. We must depend on some form of logic, awareness, and courage to steer our lives the best we can, and then learn to relax and take life in our strides with a sense of self-reliance and selflessness. We must build a solid foundation of thoughts and strengthen our spirits to survive and succeed as a liberated human being. Life is not a place to find happiness or indulge ourselves with pleasures, but only a venue for testing our resilience and building our identity. Why? For what end?

The short answer is that we need this radical mentality for controlling our lives within such a complex social environment—and then perhaps finding some personal purposes for living, too. We might even be lucky and find someone who likes to share the same values with us for building an easier life together. However, first, we must come to terms with ourselves regarding the path of life we can realistically pursue, even if it means living alone for the rest of our lives.

Happy reading

Tom Omidi, Ph.D.
Vancouver 2014

Introduction

We ponder and pursue two important (usually conflicting) goals throughout life according to our intelligence and knack for self-analysis. We like to:

1. Establish ourselves in society and fulfil our ambitions mainly by adopting the common life structure for reaping social rewards, including wealth, popularity, love, and sex.

2. Grasp at least some sense of our identity and soul to attain a relative peace of mind and wisdom towards self-realization in our hectic societies.

To accomplish these two goals, we draw upon many personal and social resources to educate ourselves, work, build a family, etc. These resources, activities, and their intricate interrelationships build the contemporary *structure of life*, which is discussed in this volume. We all try to maintain some kind of a logical balance between the above two decent objectives, as they often clash and stir more doubts about our identities, lifestyles, and the purposes of our struggles. However, we mostly feel *obliged* to abide by the universal life path developed around pervasive social structure and values at the cost of ignoring our needs for self-fulfilment and spiritualism. We grow up nurturing certain needs and ideals that feel normal and logical to us. We are conditioned to believe in the validity of the mainstream path and its potential to bring us success and happiness. Accordingly, we have little motivation or patience to at least study the meaning or merits of other life paths deeply. We lack enough incentive or intelligence to delve into the second objective noted above, i.e., the option of self-realization, seriously. Only rarely, someone is inspired rather mysteriously to stress on finding his 'Self.'

This book reiterates the importance of certain life decisions in line with our lingering doubts about the perils of living within the current life structure. The goal is to study peoples' attachments to, and perceptions of, prevalent life structure, as characterized by the mainstream's mentality and objectives for fitting within our societies. We might even figure out our purposes of living in search of that elusive happiness. Meanwhile, the discussions in Volumes I and II can help the readers explore the nature of less conventional paths of life in detail. Volume I gauges the perils of our uncultivated mindsets and the chance of developing a more substantive 'foundation of thoughts' to guide us through life and minimize our burdens in modern societies. Volume II suggests the means of developing our own sense of spirituality to boost our spirits, make the right decisions, and endure life.

The structure of life, as presented in this book, emphasizes on the conventional path of life that majority of people are familiar with and follow. Grasping the nature of this standard life structure is crucial, as it reveals the sources of our pains and shortfalls of our life choices and priorities. It also helps our self-awareness when we recognize our motives for following this crude social structure hypnotically. Then, we might also build an interest to study other living options, while striving to remain practical as well. The biggest challenge, especially for the youths, is to gauge the possibility of choosing a life path more in line with humans' real needs and salvation, instead of only following a formulaic lifestyle robotically to fulfil a bunch of superficial needs invented in our allegedly modern world.

Our current approach and coping mechanism could be refined somewhat at least, even if the conventional path of life still feels more realistic. After all, there is more to life than chasing some fanciful ideals blindly and always hoping to find some elusive happiness and love one day by a miracle. Even within the narrow scope of our existing social structure, we can develop healthier lifestyles, although eluding our dependence on others and society too much is unrealistic. Most importantly, we might realize that the prevalent passive form of existence cannot continue forever without severe consequences. Actually, humanity's fate depends severely on humans' interest and ability to overhaul their current doomed mentalities and lifestyles quickly.

We believe we are smart enough to build a lifestyle fitting the welfare of humanity as well as our drives for individualism and happiness. Yet, doing so is getting more fanciful in our complex societies within our crooked social values. All along, we forget that true individualism requires selflessness. We disregard that happiness can at best result only from contentment and peace of mind—the kind of mindset quite unachievable within modern lifestyles. Nonetheless, we strive to choose a practical path of life diligently, learn all its tricks, and adapt ourselves, simply because we cannot struggle with our doubts and idealism forever. Still, we should at least know about our options for choosing a lifestyle according to our personalities and the level of independence we desire and can actually handle.

Of course, choosing the mainstream's path and following the rules and mechanisms of society feels most natural, while it also maximizes people's chances of fulfilling their collective needs for pleasure, sexuality, power, and materialism. This lifestyle has evolved around some crude ideologies and unstable structure that people have historically put together recklessly and gotten used to it. We simply try to cope with common values and imitate one another in hopes of fulfilling our ambitions and needs for social acceptance and prosperity. This happens at the cost of neglecting our independence, integrity, and identity, but we usually do not mind. This phony lifestyle feels the easiest to handle for most people, anyway, as they are driven mainly by their urges for sexuality and materialism. Besides, we have been trained since childhood to follow this path. Moreover, many role models are always around to cheer one another within common values and norms. Thus, this path feels most rational to majority, even when it causes them distress and lingering doubts about 'who they are.' They merely trust this illusion of life completely as the ultimate reality of existence. Of course, the conventional path of life also demands lots of efforts, patience, dependence, and compliance. It requires hard work to survive and maybe feel a bit of success as well, yet people's fantasies about life prove to be merely a mirage —tentative and illusive.

Alternatively, we might consider building a more personal lifestyle based on our needs for independence and self-realization regardless of financial rewards. Clearly, the more freedom we seek, the more self-reliance we need, as we get a lesser chance of social integration and support—the rewards people receive for their compliance. Pursuing this rather stoic lifestyle is surely a risky task for most of us, especially in terms of communicating or relating to the mainstream deeply absorbed in a phony lifestyle. However, if we have the nerve to ignore social norms largely and accept the risks of isolation from the mainstream, we might get a chance to find our identity and soul, and to focus mainly on our passions, too. Our success in terms of wealth and power would be limited in this rather stoic lifestyle, though. We might never get enough recognition and love, while we must brace ourselves for the hardships of living with minimal subsistence and social attachment, especially in terms of finding a patient companion willing to live outside the prevalent, showy lifestyles. Besides, the notion of building a divine, stoic life path just by imagining some abstract benefits, such as tranquility, sounds ambiguous, risky, and unpopular even if we could succeed. Only few people can adopt this type of mentality and path. Not enough freethinkers are around to build their own small societies, either.

Between the above two extremes, we could always try to find the right balance that we can manage, satisfies our needs for both dependence and independence partially, and gives us a chance to pursue our passions somewhat, too. We can get a regular job and play certain idiotic roles to keep some level of social contacts and maybe build a family as well. By choosing this middle-of-the-road lifestyle, we could strive to maintain some form of control over our lives effectively. Sometimes, we might even feel happy and successful as well. Of course, sustaining even this moderate sense of freedom is hard in our society.

Another possibility when someone is too intelligent, proud, or sensitive to assimilate with the mainstream is to *adapt* himself or herself to the prevalent socioeconomic structure *rather passively*. S/he learns to play the popular games that help a person remain socially acceptable, while s/he still thinks and lives according to his/her private identity. S/he tries to maintain his/her integrity and independence as much as possible, while admitting to him/herself that playing a conforming role helps him/her live (or survive at least) better in our showy societies. Of course, our personality and genes always stand in the way of playing our roles properly and making people believe in our *tactful* pretences that might often not appear sincere enough. However, we can always do our best to fit and fight simultaneously. The trick is to stay patient and see our options for a lifestyle constructively, instead of cynically.

We should at least know the perils of living in the mainstream so eagerly and optimistically. What is really the purpose of taking all these rigorous steps in life obediently without questioning our rationality and goals? Get education, find work, make money, marry, buy a house, have children, travel, divorce, etc., all mostly in vain, as if chasing this routine life structure were ingrained in our genes. In the final analysis, it seems that all these degrading hassles, to lure and control others for more power, money, and love, are just for satisfying our primitive urges for more pleasure, companionship, and sex. *But is this all the wisdom that humans can attain and deserve after all this time?*

Ironically, the absurdity of our struggles within the existing life structure for some intangible and often frustrating outcomes is clear to us. We feel the impact of ongoing social dilemmas on our mental state as much as we strive to stay vigilant and sane. We loathe losing our integrity and pride just for the sake of fitting within our lousy lifestyles, which have proven ineffective and inefficient with no promising future for the next generations. We understand that status quo and sticking to the same principles and social mechanisms is killing our spirits. Yet, we seem trapped and forced to repeat the same routines, while hoping in vain that a miracle changes the whole world for the better. We just look for more sexuality and materialism to curb our nagging conscience.

Accepting such humiliating conditions, however, shows only our lack of initiative and spirit to study our options closer and set our life purposes as a free individual, needless of all these social superficialities. Waiting for a meaningful social structure to come around and reduce our burdens of living would also be a doomed expectation. Thus, we must plan for a more respectful existence for ourselves according to a viable personal life philosophy. We could study the viability of the existing social structure and judge its value, future, and ability to help humans. It appears extremely unlikely that our societies and cultures can succeed in defining a better life structure for us for many more millenniums at least, if ever. Therefore, our most promising option is to find our personal ways of salvation at least and attain some relative mental peace, while also cope with social pressures the best we can. Surely, we cannot abandon people and social norms, but might at least study our options for living a bit freer and the price we must pay for it.

The discussions in this trilogy reveal the extent of our niggling doubts about the validity of the contemporary life structure, while we must make many major decisions to survive within this hectic environment. These doubts and decisions overwhelm our minds a lifetime on top of the load of doubts and decisions pressing our psyches and spirits for performing our daily duties. Still, we must also do our best to keep our spirits high and build a thoughtful strategy to handle all these doubts and decisions better. We must become more realistic and assertive through self-awareness for making better decisions with utmost humility, compassion, and positivity to get along with others in society.

Book's Structure

Part I of this book discusses learning and education as two major life decisions and compares their distinct objectives in the new era. Chapter One discusses the goals and effects of education. We spend so much time at schools to train ourselves and become useful for society and ourselves. The question is how effective and relevant these processes are, nowadays. Chapter Two focuses on the means and goals of learning beyond the narrow purposes of education for living more effectively.

Part II discusses work and organization as main elements of current life structure, while a variety of essential questions about their nature and effect on our welfare boggles our minds. Chapter Three discusses the objectives of work and organizations' role, as we depend on them for making a living and keeping ourselves occupied. We all know that organization and work have become the sources of personal insecurity and stress, but cannot discover a remedy. Chapter Four studies organization environment in line with our efforts to fit within this harsh setting and cope with its demands. Chapter Five explains organization perils and suggests means of minimizing their effects on our spirits and wellbeing. Chapter Six studies the complexity of organization relationships, our roles, and our coping options.

Part III discusses companionship and marriage, which are the primary needs of humans and the main component of the present life structure. Unfortunately, however, these basic human needs have become the most troublesome social issues and the causes of deep personal suffering. Chapter Seven explores our needs and motives for building relationships, and shows how the dwindling situation in the new era can possibly be improved. We definitely need a more constructive environment for cooperation between marriage partners. Chapter Eight explains partners' compatibility measures and how they may possibly help couples. Chapter Nine discusses major sources of marital problems and reiterates the significance of marriage decisions.

Part IV discusses alienation and separation, because they have become the typical features of new lifestyles, while they cause the harshest level of disappointment and stress for most people. Considering the crucial role of companionship for keeping our mental and physical health, alienation and separation have turned into dire, unsettling features of the current life structure. Chapter Ten studies the causes of alienation in relationships. Chapter Eleven reviews our ultimate options in relationships and suggests a process of 'alienation preparedness.' Then, Chapters Twelve and Thirteen discuss alienation awareness and marriage salvation in more details.

Part V emphasizes the roles of high personal consciousness and awareness as the most effective learning mechanisms for grasping and managing our lives. Chapter Fourteen explains the learning fundamentals that can help humans gain a higher level of consciousness and wisdom thru personal initiatives and means of self-awareness—even through our sufferings—as the ultimate learning exercise about many facets of life. Chapter Fifteen delves into 'living for learning' per se with an emphasis on the means and objectives of boosting our consciousness and self-awareness through reflection and learning. Chapter Sixteen provides more hints about the shortfalls of education and a guideline for making our decisions about learning and education more objectively.

The quotes from esteemed scholars in this book are merely for reflecting worthy viewpoints on related topics without any prejudice. They are plausible opinions stated liberally in public domains regarding such philosophical topics, thus have become relevant for general review purposes. Although the author does not necessarily agree or disagree with them, they are precious points that interested readers are encouraged to check in those books for further detail and reflection.

PART I
Learning and Education

CHAPTER ONE
The Role of Education

Learning and education have found different, mostly clashing, purposes, nowadays; and sadly, we seem to have lost our wisdom on both grounds. Neither our educational systems teach us the authentic ways of living, nor do our sporadic efforts to learn help us live healthier and become a better person. Especially, over the last century, the depth and content of both education and learning have not helped us understand ourselves and our world, thus we have become less capable of relating in families, communities, and across the nations. It is just amazing and sad how cruelly the public's intelligence is kept so low intentionally, considering the long history of humanity and our eagerness to learn, relate, and be a better and smarter person. Despite the growing amount of university education throughout the world, we have become less honest and productive at both personal and social levels even in modern nations, while facing more stress every day, too. People's naivety and dogmatism is obvious in their superstitions, religious beliefs, egoism, low financial sense, greed, and high expectations from life. The irony is that we all deserve a big share of the blame for this mayhem. After all, we are the ones electing incompetent, self-serving, and hypocrite leaders to run our nations. We are the ones allowing the wicked forces in society keep us in ignorance, while we cherish our own fanciful beliefs and shallow values so much. Overall, formal education is not useful in any of the crucial areas of human concern. Instead, it has become just an instrument to exploit humans' potentialities for running our shaky societies and economies with no or very little benefit at personal level.

Learning, on the other hand, is an ongoing, automatic process that evolves according to our interests, intelligence and stamina. We usually learn a lot of useless or wicked stuff from one another and through media. However, we hardly know the processes, purposes, and values of real learning. Other than our outmoded educational processes, which we customarily pursue mostly for professional purposes, our other types of learning are random and not purposeful enough for grasping who we are and how our life plans and efforts are expected to make us happier and wiser. As noted above, the ultimate value of education itself in its present format, as a formal means of learning, is also highly questionable, even in terms of helping people for their careers. Preparing people for living per se is even a bigger responsibility ignored these days by educational systems, as explained in the next chapter.

This chapter reviews these issues and highlights the reasons for 'learning and education' being major life decisions (but also sacred purposes) of our lives, to mitigate our gullibility at least.

Education – A Basic, Structured Learning

Education is a tailored mode of learning to prepare people for social relations and jobs. Yet, it appears that it cannot fulfil even these narrow objectives, as people now have more difficulties to understand one another or find professions related to their fields of studies, nowadays. Aside from providing general knowledge for reading, writing, and math, the existing educational process appears too long and inefficient, with no tangible outcome for the welfare of humanity attached to it. Most of the materials studied are either forgotten soon or left unused for any practical purpose. Even our technical education gets obsolete within a decade at best, yet our personal and professional lives continue as if our expertise is making no real impact for us and organizations that supposedly use that knowledge. We do not even notice or care about all this waste of human potentiality and spirits.

In *Empire of Illusion*, publish by Alfred A. Knopf, Canada 2009, Chris Hedges states:

"The bankruptcy of our economic and political systems can be traced directly to the assault against the humanities. The neglect of the humanities has allowed elites to organize education and society around predetermined answers to predetermined questions. Students are taught structures designed to produce these answers even as these structures have collapsed. But those in charge, because they are educated only in specializations designed to maintain these economic and political structures, have run out of ideas. They have been trained only to find solutions that will maintain the system. This is what the Harvard Business case method is about, a didactic system in which the logic employed to solve a specific problem always, in the end, sustains market capitalism." Ibid., page 103.

The most damaging aspect of our lengthy, planned education is that it is only intended for career purposes rather than preparing people to live properly in a cooperative manner and maybe even helping them become better human beings. It does not help our social behaviour and interactions, either. Spending somewhere between 12 to 20 best years of our lives on education indicates our present wasteful method of schooling, as it teaches people very little about their being, humanity, or even basic means of relating to one another. Obviously, this amount of time and all those educational costs and efforts could be used better to prepare children for the hardships of life and relationships. Instead, we give them wrong impressions about consumerism and happiness, raise their expectations from life, and spoil and exploit them with positive psychology. Our educational and social systems seem to be conspiring to direct humans away from self-awareness and life realities. They are making people less compassionate by teaching them pomposity, competition, materialism, greed, etc. They give people, especially the youths, a wrong perspective of life, and then let them loose in a chaotic world to rip off one another under the name of freedom, capitalism, and democracy. In the end, all these struggles and confusions only lead to people's deep senses of worthlessness, abuse, humiliation, exhaustion, and defeat mostly due to people's own exaggerated expectations and ambitions not materializing.

Obviously, education has some inherent values in widening our mental capabilities and creating a knowledgebase for daily practical purposes (beyond its intended level of specialization). Some learning aspects of education help people make better judgments and decisions, enjoy life more thoroughly, and maybe earn a living, all based on hope and assumption that somebody is willing to buy our expertise. These hopes and assumptions might, however, prove increasingly unrealistic in the near future.

Education – A Tool for Career Planning

Education and career planning are major life decisions and need special attention, but not for conventional reasons. Accordingly, many essential factors addressed in this chapter need scrutiny. Everybody is rather familiar with these points, but also sceptical about his/her career options. A crucial principle that everybody is missing more every year is that a high degree of responsibility and morality should always go along with higher education. Any field of education demands honourable goals along with social responsibilities. Instead, even our physicians are getting greedier and sloppier every year. Thus, pursuing higher education would be foolish and futile, unless we are certain that our objectives are quite realistic, manageable, moralistic, and possibly in line with our potentialities. In particular, the notion of getting a degree for prestige, wealth, following the social fad for education, or just for procrastination (delaying our entry into society) is obsolete.

Education is a major life decision and making it as a young person, when we have the least experience about life, is hard and unfair. We are naive regarding job opportunities and constraints, work environments, and our real potentialities and passion. Our predictions of the future economy, job markets and demands, etc. cannot be accurate enough, either. Anyway, if we are hesitant or careless about assessing our educational needs in line with our personal temperament, the outcome of this major decision may prove disheartening and often harmful for many aspects of our lives. Thus, following some rigid guidelines is crucial for gauging our motives to choose the type and level of our education. We should also seek impartial advice, if possible, after doing a careful self-assessment to recognize our needs and potentialities. Eluding these rational thoughts and steps—because we are rigid about our choices, mistrust people's advice, or simply like to procrastinate by going to college and hoping for a miracle—could ruin our lives. If we make a wrong decision or accept a wrong advice, we simply set the scene for our first major failure in life when a job suitable to our education is not available or we abhor our career and field of education.

The Dilemma of Education

A big dilemma for most people is pursuing their passions versus doing any kind of work just to stay practical, i.e., for satisfying their financial needs and maintaining a family. Only a tiny group is brave *or naïve* enough to pursue only their passions regardless of their chances for social success. The rest of us concentrate on our careers and education for financial and social rewards. Still, we seldom analyse the relevant factors properly before choosing a field of education—not even the job market, as a moderately justifiable criterion. A large group goes to college in hopes of job availability once they graduate or only for its presumed prestige regardless of what they study and for what end. We often choose a field that feels easier to tackle or raises our curiosity. Some of us go to college or university just to procrastinate and avoid the harsh reality of work and life as long as possible. We justify our lousy education decisions, yet blame the government and society for the lack of job opportunities.

Overall, in our increasingly competitive job markets, we have three options regarding education:

1. Get out of school as soon as possible to build a career.
2. Do only specialized education related to a secure profession.
3. Do education just for the heck of it, learning, artistic interest, or prestige, regardless of its financial or social repercussions due to unemployment.

The third option does not sound practical to most of us. Thus, we usually choose options 1 or 2 rather realistically by viewing education merely a tool for making a living. Accordingly, we get upset when we cannot find a job related to our lengthy education, or any job at all. Still more shocking is the stressful and imposing work condition we face after all the hassles of education and high hopes with a positive impression about work and organizations' settings. Even when we get some kind of financial reward, the emotional price we pay for keeping those jobs is often too high.

Therefore, a right decision about education is crucial due to its long-term effect on our psyche and outlook, besides the efforts and long process of educating ourselves. On the one hand, it feels necessary to follow social trends and hope education would help us secure a good-paying job to build a happy family with a bright future. We usually have little choice, yet pursuing this familiar pattern blindly is a wasteful habit ingrained in people's minds as a main feature of the modern life structure. On the other hand, our personal and social life often suffer when we focus mainly on our decisions about education and careers, as many critical aspects of life are naively ignored, including our spirits and passions. We all seem adamant to learn only from our personal mistakes—about the fact that education hardly helps even the basic goal of making money, let alone so many essential needs, including our physical and psychological health, self-fulfilment, peace of mind, and spirituality.

We have realized the shortfalls of education systems in the present format, but we are not addressing the matter seriously yet. We are neither personally, nor collectively as a society, looking for better means of educating ourselves for proper jobs and real living. We seem unable to find better ways of satisfying both our basic and psychological needs other than following the common social patterns. Then, we get surprised when life does not feel any better even when our jobs give us some level of financial security and pride that we have sought. Only then, we realize how little role education and jobs play for reaching a relative peace of mind and building good relationships with friends and family. Sadly, the temptations for status, wealth, power, and similar incentives continue to influence our career and education decisions. These narrow motives for education are still prevalent as a firm social mentality injected in our heads since childhood, despite all the sad clues before our eyes.

Ironically, we often get bored even with a job that relates to our education. It does not feel like a real or worthy career. We feel a need to switch to a different job before we go crazy doing the same thing day after day. However, handling all the boredom and switching between jobs is not easy or necessarily a successful strategy, either. With age, the quality and quantity of our options also get more limited and complex. Accordingly, the solutions to our existing problems get more pressing and perplexing every year. Sometimes, we might even decide to re-educate ourselves, which takes extensive effort, energy, patience, money, and time that we may not have. Besides, it often proves to be another bad decision, as it often leads to another dead-end job, anyway.

At the same time, not using our education, after wasting many years of our precious lives, shows the naivety of our decisions and the ineffectiveness of job markets within the messy spectrum of socioeconomic systems. Luckily, we can save ourselves from all these hassles if only we become a bit more careful about our 'education' plans and goals. Thus, every wise high school student must assess many factors for making a decision about education.

Overall, reviewing our educational purposes more objectively is becoming more urgent, since a wrong education is one of those self-imposed limitations that lead to frustration and confusion when people cannot apply it in their jobs or for personal goals. Now, we must try to be smart and practical when pondering our desired lifestyle and the limited role of education for available jobs. Even if the cost, aptitude, and space for a desired field of study were not major obstacles, we should admit that (within the existing system) only job-related education has value. With the rising decline of reliable job opportunities and financial pressures ahead, we should now adapt to job market and choose our higher education, if any, based on plausible criteria. Meanwhile, the high volatility of job markets makes people's decisions more difficult, risky, and questionable.

Ideally, our career choices and decision criteria must reflect a balance among our passions, potentialities, and personal needs, especially psychological ones, in line with life's harsh realities. Still, our educational options usually do not match our character and talents. Naturally, discovering and implementing this balance is difficult, yet even realizing all these requirements for success might at least make us prepare ourselves more realistically from the beginning. We may never feel fulfilled, even if our education helps our subsistence at least. Or we might starve if we insist on exploring our potentialities to satisfy our self-actualization need. These harsh realities dictate our decisions about education and career regardless of our holier personal needs. Our task to make a good decision is surely cumbersome. Still, we should somehow handle this major dilemma and all our doubts and then move on. We should make a timely decision, instead of procrastinating or doing some kind of education for now because we cannot decide.

Fortunately, economic forces are gradually redefining the role of education and its relationship to the jobs of the future. Soon, mostly the level of intelligence, intuition, and basic training would prepare a person for factory and office jobs. Formal higher education in the present format would be neither affordable nor necessary for most jobs. Computers, automated systems, online education, and preset mechanisms and routines would perform the technical aspects of most jobs. Already computers can even help diagnose illnesses and prescribe preliminary treatments without the need to visit a physician. Physicians are gradually depending on these automated systems as well. The contents of future jobs would be quite different, while general intelligence and intuition become more crucial. The required training would most likely be short, on-the-job, or vocational fitted for the jobs.

The Value of Education

What is the value of education if it cannot help humanity or at least offer better ways of running our economies?

Chris Hedges states:

"Our elites—the ones in Congress, the ones on Wall Street, and the ones being produced at prestigious universities and business schools—do not have the capacity to fix our financial mess. Indeed, they will make it worse. They have no concept, thanks to the education they have received, of how to replace a failed system with a new one. They are petty, timid, and uncreative bureaucrats superbly trained to carry out systems management." Ibid., page 111.

Besides the low capacity of the educational systems these days, the value of all those efforts by professors is also highly doubtful, not to mention the purpose of incurring all the costs of running colleges and universities. These rising wastes all over the world is maddening, with no concern or action plan to reassess the effectiveness of the present format of educational systems. It is merely a prestigious habit and symbolic gesture by nations to run expensive universities and protect the interests of businesses and their needs for mentally conditioned workers. It is sad that neither the public nor governments appear to understand, or care about, the ethical demands on education to play a crucial social role for preparing people for real life. Are not we at a point in our evolution to stop and gauge the value of education in its present format? Should not we know and be concerned about its ultimate purpose for making us better human beings with a higher chance for a peaceful coexistence? Surely, it sounds outrageous to say that we still have not tackled these basic issues!

The value of education is quite low, nowadays, for personal purposes, too, (aside from its possible specialized objectives) for all the reasons noted in this chapter. Unless education is targeted in terms of its immediate application in a person's life, at least for better communication and relationships, its value is minimal. The value (impact) is actually negative due to the direct costs and the opportunity costs of human life wasted on it, not to mention the repercussions of all the erroneous personal and family values and expectations propagated through our educational systems.

Overall, the value of education must be determined solely by the validity of its 'objectives' and their relationships to a person's potentialities, besides helping him/her for real life and some form of self-realization. The professional label (degree) or the fact that one has spent so many years of one's life acquiring it (and maybe never using that expertise) is not a symbol of prestige, anymore, but actually a sign of gullibility, as it reflects a person's bad life decisions and lame mentality. It has been customary to celebrate students' graduation, rather idiotically perhaps! While respecting individuals' efforts is warranted, at that particular point we are in effect merely celebrating their abilities to endure the *most likely futile* hardships of completing a degree program. Naively, we just assume a direct relationship between education and success. We perform this charade, although we know very well that the real test of personal achievement is, of course, how and when s/he harvests the fruits of his/her education, and how society is willing and able to offer him/her a chance to do so—and most important of all, of course, for what social and personal ends?

Nevertheless, it is heartbreaking to witness how education has become a means of propagating our defective socioeconomic and political systems and expanding the public's ignorance. Chris Hedges says:

"By the time I had finished eight years in New England prep schools and another eight years at Colgate University and Harvard University, I had a pretty good understanding of the game. I have also taught at Columbia University, New York University, and Princeton University. These institutions feed students, no matter how mediocre, the comforting reassurance that they are there because they are not only the best but they are entitled to the best. You saw this attitude on display in every word uttered by George W. Bush. Here was a man with severely limited intellectual capacity and moral core. Bush, along with Scooter Libby, who attended my pre-prep school, exemplifies the legions of self-centered, spoiled, intellectually limited and wealthy elitists churned out by places like Andover, Yale, and Harvard. Bush was, like the rest of his caste, propelled forward by his money and his connections. The real purpose of these richly endowed schools is to embrace the ideology of the common man, trumpet diversity on campus, and pose as meritocracy. The public commitment to egalitarianism alongside the private nurturing of elitism creates a bizarre schizophrenia." Ibid., page 98.

Education and Organizations

Nobody has a priori sense of job peculiarities in organizations, work pressures, and the amount of tolerance needed for earning a living this way. Especially for inexperienced youths, imagining the callousness of work environments is impossible. Naively, we believe education leads to ideal jobs in sensible settings. Self-employment may provide some independence and higher income potentials, yet not everybody has the marketing and managerial skills to succeed as an independent professional or entrepreneur. Thus, the decision about the type and level of education requires an assessment of many depressing hurdles for making a living. Accordingly, the big headaches related to organization relations and politics will be addressed vastly in Part II due to its growing role within social structure and for humans' welfare, nowadays.

Considering all the facts reiterated in this chapter, educational systems should soon change their curriculum drastically, too, because:

1. The sooner students get out of school and enter the job market, the higher would be their chances of finding jobs and getting on-the-job experience, which are many folds more crucial than current form of education per se.
2. The vast amount of money spent annually on wasted education can be used for more efficient national economic purposes.
3. Doing more education merely for prestige has already lost its appeal, if not considered obsolete and foolish.
4. Holding students back in our outmoded educational systems is an added cause of their frustration and a disservice to society.
5. Unless one's job prospects for a particular college education is rather definite, schooling would only hurt one's morale and psyches more than help. The justification for any non-technical education would decline vastly in the future.
6. The intensity of competition for good jobs and career planning would soon force even high school students to look for some form of training or employment to get into job markets faster.
7. The length of primary education must be drastically reduced in the future, too, maybe to nine or ten years maximum, in order to accommodate students and raise both the effectiveness and efficiency of educational systems.

Chapter Sixteen provides more details about education shortfalls and rethinking this important, ignored concept.

CHAPTER TWO
Learning the Art of Living

For making many major life decisions reiterated in this book, we need a special wisdom that can be acquired only through diligent learning, self-awareness, and a high level of consciousness about major life decisions and realities. A proactive mindset and lots of sacrifice are needed to grow this wisdom and learn many secrets about existence. Only then, some of us might eventually arrive at the intersection of wisdom paths when we grasp the absurdity of our routines, and thus seek a more divine philosophy of life for ourselves. Accordingly, we try to learn the art of living for both our worldly affairs and spiritual needs.

Overall, though, 'learning for living' is the most essential life decision for everybody, as this chapter will demonstrate. Some people might even reach such a high degree of divinity to adopt the extreme, rather stoic lifestyle of 'living for learning' per se, as discussed in Chapter Fifteen. However, for most of us mediocre human beings, even learning how to live properly is becoming too hard and confusing in our modern societies. More and more every day, our educational achievements appear to be misleading humans in terms of their real needs, while we try to celebrate our superficial achievements absurdly. Meanwhile, humans' capacity and opportunities for learning the art of living has diminished.

Objectives of Learning

Learning certain disciplines (e.g., science) in customary fashion (e.g., college education) raises our life opportunities and social standing. This common objective of learning is mostly for career purposes, which usually makes us feel important and smart, too. Yet, this narrow means and objective of learning does not offer a chance to explore our essential life purposes, if not limit our span of attention about our being altogether. While education helps us earn a living, living demands a special type of learning. Only learning about 'self' and means of finding a soul-satisfying life path, mostly through self-awareness, might provide tranquility, and thus be considered the ultimate objective of learning. Only this kind of learning can support our psychological growth and offer us a truthful perspective of life. However, we usually ignore this type of endeavour due to our preoccupation with education or preference to devote ourselves to work and pleasures.

Actually, since education distracts everybody from essential learning, 'learning' per se now requires an even higher emphasis, as the main device for enhancing our grasp of reality *directly and deeply*. Instead of treating 'learning' as general knowledge on a random basis, it should be embraced as a major life decision in itself—along with its big demands for special interest and efforts. Only by recognizing 'learning' as a crucial aspect of existence, we might focus on the sources of real learning more consciously, do enough self-analysis, and learn about our spirits. 'Leraning' per se has a sacred value with a direct impact on our lives, including a role for choosing the right career and lifestyle in line with the chance to explore our innate potentialities and self-esteem.

Then again, sadly, this book's long discussions about learning would sound foolish in a world where most people do not even know what learning is or requires, let alone devote a good portion of their times and minds to it. Still, it must be discussed as both a crucial social discipline and a necessity for any intelligent being who values learning for self-assessment and likely salvation.

Overall, learning can improve our lives by, i) pinpointing our inspirational life purposes and finding tranquility, and ii) coping somewhat easier with the stress of our socioeconomic needs and aspirations. Thus, our mission is to gauge whether our learning efforts are aligned with our professional training and education, for what end, and at what price—more stress or tranquility. A big dilemma about *happiness* is that it requires plenty of sacrifice and work, mostly in the form of learning the right stuff about life. In fact, a vital objective of learning and self-awareness is to find that mysterious happiness in the depth of a stoic contentment.

Besides learning the right stuff about life, we should build the capacity to gauge the validity of our judgments and criteria for making our major life choices and interpretations. We must also reassess our preliminary interpretations of life's facts and myths through conscious learning, especially about happiness and love myths. Most of all, we should remember that true learning does not make anybody more dogmatic or certain about life realities or divine myths, but rather more thoughtful and humble.

'Conscious learning' is discussed in Part V. The remainder of this chapter, however, discusses some main areas of learning that require diligent attention based on the general learning techniques and principles noted in Part V. These special topics, such as our personality and potentialities, can also help us with our major life decisions and 'learning for living.'

Learning about Personal Qualities (Potentialities, Needs, and Personality Aspects)

Exploring our varied potentialities is an exhilarating challenge. Our minds and potentialities flourish during our life experiences somewhat, but mostly when we delve into our 'self' and possibly even reach the outer realms of the universe to create the greatest thoughts and divine feelings. Not only the joy of learning about our unique talents and nature, but mostly our growing wisdom to develop extraordinary thoughts, things, and feelings make these learning experiences exciting and crucial for our psychological health and existence.

Of course, we cannot tap our potentialities easily, nor can we do everything as perfectly as somebody else might do, but we can generate our own unique thoughts and feelings that might enrich our lives more than any popular life pleasure. The experiences of self-actualizers, who do not mind dying during such exhilarating moments, offer ample clues about the scope and interconnectivity of human mind, spirit, and spiritual capacity, as we learn about and activate our potentialities. Especially, the power and beauty of spirituality attained during this process are enlightening for choosing a more suitable path of life. We are not talking about religions or shallow rituals, but rather our inherent resources, our souls, that connect us to our 'self' and our creator. Only those spiritual dimensions bring us a sacred vision to see the intricacies of each unit of life in its detail and feel the glory of every plant, creature, and Nature as a whole.

Then there is the challenge of learning about our needs. We are born with *authentic* needs that we often ignore, and we have invented many *artificial* needs that we have become addicted to due to social conditioning. We can learn to distinguish these two conflicting sets of needs and analyse each with proper mindset. For example, we can apply Maslow's personal needs tree to do two things. First, we can assess the values of each level of needs in this hierarchy (e.g., food and shelter, security, belongingness and love, status, self-actualization) in terms of their life-boosting potentials. We can try to learn how, in our opinion, each one of these needs might affect our mental growth and life quality if we stopped dreaming, e.g., about love, happiness, or other myths. Second, we could try to determine the level of our needs within the 'needs hierarchy' at the present time, and perhaps the level of needs that our aspirations are pointing to. For example, are we planning to satisfy our self-actualization needs or are just happy focusing only on our social status or love needs forever?

Learning about our needs is a deep psychological exploration. It reveals our inner urges and external incentives that goad those needs, mostly for soothing our insecurities and Egos. However, studying our needs also helps us learn about our suppressed and hidden potentialities. We need not be a psychologist to study our needs, personality, and potentialities. All we need is a cultured commonsense and objectivity. Sometimes, we might ask a friend or counsellor to hear our thoughts and plans in order to sharpen our values and objectivity.

Our needs are obviously a reflection of our personality. Thus, learning about our needs would also reveal a lot about who we are and why. Conversely, learning about our personality usually gives us good clues about the authenticity of our needs. We also learn to look for our 'self.'

With our unique personalities and eccentricities, we dwell on satiating certain shallow medium-range needs all our lives rather contrary to Maslow's theory that suggests people usually have the urge to move up the needs hierarchy. Instead, most of us stop, very abruptly in fact, when we reach one of the medium level needs, such as need for socializing. Therefore, we never mature psychologically, nor find our sense of spirituality.

Learning about the three aspects of our personality (explained in Volume I in simple terms) can also provide a refreshing insight about our thoughts and deeds. Once we grasp the characteristics of each aspect of our personality, we can detect and distinguish them in our actions and attitude. We can notice how Ego, Model, and Self aspects of our personalities emerge and dominate our thoughts and decisions regularly. They represent us at different situations and settings based on our needs at that moment, though usually in line with our value systems. Observing our personality aspects in action offers a great platform to learn about ourselves in general. We can evaluate our weaknesses and strengths by witnessing the peculiar manifestations of Ego, Model, or Self in various circumstances. Quite often, we recognize the dominating personality aspect rather easily, but sometimes we need more time and patience to detect the inner workings of our personality. Anyway, with a refined, conscious evaluation of our thoughts, attitudes, actions, and reactions, we can learn a lot more about ourselves and humans in general. We can become quite at ease with this self-assessing and self-developing process, to the point where it becomes a second nature and a natural routine.

Particularly, learning about our personality aspects gives us the opportunity to observe how our Self is being undermined by our Ego and Model constantly as a matter of lifestyle or for social adaptation. This learning might goad us eventually to nurture the neglected 'self' to play a stronger role in our lives. The state of awareness about our personality aspects is not as complex or a myth as many of us might envision it. If only our curiosity is aroused to study our own, or someone else's, personality aspects, we can learn to distinguish them quickly and easily. However, we should avoid making hasty judgments. We should refrain from attributing our flaws to either Model or Ego and moving on. We should also try to understand the motives behind our own or other people's thoughts and actions. As we learn about the dire forces behind people's moods and reactions, we develop a fairer sense of assessment and judgment along with lots of compassion.

Learning about our personality aspects reveals *the process* of satisfying our various needs as well. We learn about not only the *nature* of our needs, but also our methods and schemes to satisfy or control them. Sometimes, we can sense that our interpretations of personal needs get ambiguous by our unauthentic or unethical desires. Are these desires, e.g., lust, real needs or only unleashed psychological defects? We are often unclear about the domain of psychological needs and defects. For example, if we agree that sex is a basic psychological need and useful for our health, what ethical boundaries are necessary, if any, to control its abuse. Must self-control play any role? In all, since we accept sex as a basic need, we face many dilemmas. For example, since marriage and companionship commitments are becoming rarer and less reliable, both engaging in, and preventing, sex outside the wedlock would somehow lead to psychological imbalance, to put it mildly.

The problem is that some of our seemingly basic needs and dilemmas can cause an entire new set of psychological imbalance when they are not brought under some personal rules of conduct and 'self'-control. When sex is freely exercised without tangible commitment and compassion, it damages personal self-image and self-esteem eventually and ruins psychological health of society. We can only personally *learn* and *decide* about this and similar dilemmas that appear like conflicts of personal needs. Only our Self can help reduce these predicaments. Our present culture and societies seem incapable of solving these dilemmas, but in fact make the situation more unsettling and complex. We have doubts about social and personal morality more every day; therefore, we should make harder decisions in this convoluted environment.

We can study another point by referring to Maslow's needs hierarchy again: While a person moves up the needs hierarchy, the consequences of satisfying some needs might affect his/her personality adversely. For instance, by attempting to satisfy his/her self-esteem need, s/he may in fact turn up the volume of Ego in hopes of improving his/her self-image and self-esteem without grasping or learning the true characteristics of these valid human attributes. Especially, for people raised with low self-esteem, it is much harder to grasp its source, learn how to boost it, or satisfy their natural needs for it. Instead, by pumping their Egos, they only make the matter worse for themselves, as they come across snobbish and immature.

Nevertheless, our attempts to satisfy some of our needs often reinforce the development of less desirable personality aspects, thus causing additional psychological defects. In effect, we may learn that our needs foster both healthy and faulty aspects of our personality. Our intrinsic and authentic needs ordinarily foster our pure potentialities and characters, while our artificial and fictitious needs lead to the misuse of our potentialities and the deterioration of our characters. And again, only learning about our Self can help us distinguish, control, and balance our needs.

By some miracle perhaps, we might finally learn that stressing on our unauthentic needs compromises our integrity, character, and life. The precious time we waste on gathering wealth, the integrity we give up by lying and cheating, the friendships we lose to satisfy our Ego and false pride, and many similar personal sacrifices are simple clues about our declining sense of 'self' and character. On the other hand, we may decide someday to give up our phony lifestyles to promote some of our authentic and innate needs. For example, we might manage our crude ambitions and free ourselves from the excessive hours of work to spend more time on exploring the values and beauties of life personally and by sharing our interest and values with family and friends.

Learning about Life Essentialities

Learning how to live requires knowing life's essentialities. How can we raise our life's quality when all our energies are wasted on activities with no real, lasting value? Or when our thoughts only focus on materialistic and soulless objectives? Or when our spirit is broken by stress, self-imposed anxiety, and endless sexuality?

Life is a perishable gift and we have a short time to unlock and enjoy it only if we grasp its finer, divine essence. Actually, these life essentialities become automatically evident once we get rid of the trivia (superficial needs and obsessions). Conversely, learning more about life essentialities would reveal our lifetime naiveté to pursue life's trivia, e.g., wealth, power, and sexuality, which we have been conditioned to embrace as living main parameters. The meaning of *life* simply manifests itself in the natural beauties and values surrounding us. Therefore, to look for life quality, we must learn about life's vanities, i.e., our crooked values and lifestyles, which have obscured our sense of reality. Our greatest challenge for discovering authentic values and beauties is to reassess the norms propagated in the perceived world. It is hard to appreciate the basic principles of a real world in which 'money cannot buy anything.' It is difficult to forego the criteria and temptation of success in the realm of the perceived world that provides satiating opportunities for competition, greed, sexuality, and arrogance. It is hard because success in the real world depends on our ability to search for and find our pure 'self,' soul, self-reliance, and divine potentialities, which all, at best, feel like some kind of intangible potentials for gratification to us trapped in the perceived world. The measure of our success in the real world is the degree of our disregard for the symbols of success in the perceived world. This is a rough concept to grasp and a tough chore to undertake!

Yet, we can learn to attain the highest measures of pleasure from the values and beauties that are both within and around us. These types of pleasures satisfy our inner needs and souls directly and do not lose their potency and relevance with time or due to other people's moods. They strengthen our feelings, creativity, and sense of attachment to aesthetic objects and ideas. A poem, a tune, a painting, the sound of water burbling in a creek, the flight of an eagle or a seagull, or the sight of a growing plant are all pleasing experiences that are divine and repeatable forever when we learn to search for and appreciate them.

Learning about life essentialities is an elaborate and ongoing process. We should learn about our real role and responsibilities within social and political systems, toward natural environments, and in our families. We should learn about our primary wisdom and *learned wisdom*, different paths of life, cultures, our body, and how to value and maintain physical fitness and health, and so much more. Then, all these life essentials become obvious to us, along with the convictions and steps needed for living peacefully, once we contemplate the basic subjects discussed in this chapter. We all have doubts about our crooked lifestyles and values, but most of us never develop enough patience and resolve to start the process of *learning* 'how to live.' 'How to live' is not a question, but rather a long learning process that beholds our sentiments and souls in line with the wisdom of simple thoughts.

Appendix C at the end of Volume II reveals the enormity of human dimensions that we have not even begun to study in the scientific world or personally. We have a chance to explore them personally at some point after building our *learned wisdom*.

Chapter Fifteen delves even deeper into this sort of analysis about the art of living. It discusses the sacred option of 'living for learning' per se that some humans choose, whereas as most of us have not even learned the basics of 'learning for living.'

Learning about Life's Qualities

Learning is not merely a mental process to know something. It requires feelings and imagination, and often it is only a feeling or impression itself. We learn about the essence of life only through inspirational sentiments. Only then, we attain self-awareness and learn about those life essentialities that make living tolerable and worthwhile. Yet, the hardest kind of learning is to learn how to control our erratic moods and mushy emotions, especially under pressure and during depression.

From experience, we have learnt, assumed, or accepted that life has two extreme sides: ups and downs, as symbolized by the feelings of joy or depression. Of course, there are also times when we are indifferent about life and what goes on around us. This kind of passive contentment or resignation is an option for living, although we normally do not accept this careless state of mind and *being* as a valid condition for increasing the quality of our lives. Unless we are in a comma or a no-thought moment, passivity reflects surrender and separation from life, which is not a dignified quality of existence for any healthy person.

The basic objective of learning is to grow psychologically and spiritually in order to improve the quality of our lives. We want to grasp our *being*, which can evolve only through our awareness about things, our moods, and our relationships with those things, people, and events. We want to make as many moments of our lives as meaningful as possible. When we are passive, indifferent, or unaware, we just bypass our chance to create enough of such exhilarating moments.

When we create our moments, e.g., through reflection, they usually stir an instance of either joy or depression. The feelings of apathy would soon move towards one of these two extremes, as we become aware and conscious of our lives and the necessity of creating our special life moments. Accordingly, the first step for self-awareness and enhancing the 'quality of life' is to inject a sense of purpose and feelings into our chronic indifference and shake our habitual passivity, without any medication, if possible. Certainly, these types of personality frailties, such as passivity, are quite intimidating and powerful to defeat easily. However, the sources of our apathy might be detected and resolved with some objectivity, activity, and perseverance.

Sometimes, indifference comes from boredom and our lack of imagination to stir challenging thoughts or feelings. Other times, indifference (or resignation) is merely a defence mechanism to subdue our anxiety or forget the world that we have given up on. The main use of 'positive thinking' is to fight off these insidious human emotions. We can monitor and control these moments of lethargy or indifference awhile. We learn eventually to master all the moments of our lives subconsciously and automatically and find something creative and interesting in every second of our waking hours. Even creating a no-thought moment is a joyous experience subsequent to our decision to defeat our bad moods and sad moments of indifference. For attaining the 'quality' of life, we cannot be passive about our moods and feelings, yet we can stay indifferent about things and people in times temporarily.

By staying conscious about our thoughts, deeds, and feelings routinely, we also study the sources of our depression, despair, or joy. However, depression and despair should be defeated only by gradual increase in personal creativity, to replace our cynicism, boredom, and negativity. This gradual transformation is a big part of self-awareness, as we learn about the roots of our thoughts and feelings, and motives behind them through self-analysis.

Still, we must also learn to, i) bear life's hardships causing our depression, and ii) remember that some depression is normal and necessary at a managed level. We must learn to accept depression only as another limitation of life, but also as a signal to attend to our spiritual needs for the benefit of our spirits. These moments of depression are the realities, and sometimes the necessities, of life, though we can learn to manage and maybe take advantage of such experiences. They stir passion and compassion along with a divine feeling and power of vision beyond normal experiences. We *learn* that bad luck is not just finding us. Rather, everybody has his/her share of hurtful events, although some people happen to have a little more or less of them to deal with. Instead, it is vital to learn the reality of hardships by recognizing their natures and sources. Our own naïve perceptions about life, superficial needs, or hasty decision stir most of our hardships. These self-imposed pains and limitations can be sensed and conquered often through personal conviction and determination.

On the other hand, common hardships, mostly resulting from social disorder and values, can only be studied and tolerated as much as our time, patience, and strength allow. We must merely build lots of resilience and wisdom to live through storms of life's erratic hardships. Life struggles are inevitable parts of existence, in particular when we prefer to adhere to the crippling values and expectations of modern societies. It is amazing how less-civilized nations feel and bear these facts naturally, when we Westerners have so much difficulty understanding social realities, nowadays, due to our irrational growing expectations from life. Constantly nagging and asking why things are so dysfunctional is just a waste of energy and focus. We lame humans have made it this bad over millenniums by our social ineptness, stupidity, and huge urge for controversy. The point now is how and if we can we really do something about this embarrassing social structure and possibly save humanity!

Moreover, we must *learn* to believe that some ultimate power or a set of complementary forces stir the laws of the universe and life. Although our perceived world obstructs our comprehension of, and connection to, the real world, we can still see enough clues to believe in this ultimate power. We can build our strength and patience by thinking about, and believing in, the fact that our destiny is mostly set by this dominant power that is responsible for the ultimate balance and laws of the universe. We can *learn* and remember that, while our existence appears like an accident, we are a living part of the universe and a part of the total energy, though stuck in the middle of a horrendous social chaos. We can *learn* to see ourselves as a vulnerable creature, yet a conscious creator of some domains within the overall spectrum for leading a relatively bearable existence.

Accordingly, we can also raise our self-awareness, patience and tolerance by learning something about the truth within the mythical real world compared to all the debilitating facts that we have accepted blindly in the wrecked perceived world. We can *learn* that our superficial distinction of facts from myths[†] is the outcome of our limited imaginations within the fast-expanding perceived world. Definitely, some vastly more tangible realities exist beyond our illusions. We can surely *learn* about our divine potentialities and spirituality, which constitute the essence of our being and fuel our spirits. *Learning* a true sense of spiritualism would unravel the futility and harms that all religions have posed upon us and humanity under the name of that mysterious power. We should accept (and rely on) the ultimate force (whatever the heck it is) that makes and defines our destiny, but we should also raise our lives' quality through objective, conscious learning.

'Conscious learning' is particularly important as an antidote to popular socially-imposed learning. We could set out to learn and practise this regimen regularly as a part of self-cleansing process and boosting our consciousness. 'Conscious learning' is discussed in Part V along with technical details about learning mechanisms and principles.

[†] Facts and myths are discussed extensively in Part II of Volume I.

Learning from Our Sufferings

Along with happy experiences and dire hopes of renewing them perpetually, we must accept, and *learn* about, our sufferings from unfavourable events or thoughts. Witnessing other people's pains and humans' wickedness in general, as well as our helplessness to do anything about rampant social conundrums, also raises our sufferings. Still, facing all those sufferings, instead of trying to suppress them is a life obligation. Drugs, alcohol, and negativism would not solve our sufferings. Instead, only through patience we can learn how to transform our anguish into compassion, creative energy, and new thoughts. When our sufferings grow, we might write an essay, ponder a pleasant experience, build something, or help someone. These are means of replacing our anxieties and negative thoughts with creative sentiments and triumph. We can *learn* to dig creativity out of our sufferings in the form of aesthetic artistry, soothing thoughts, higher compassion, and urges to help others, which could then lead to big opportunities for healing and redeeming our souls. Ironically, some sufferings ultimately might lead to genuine happiness once we learn to explore the depth of our unconscious and dig out our neglected potentialities and spirit. Our happiness actually finds a new depth, as its derivatives, e.g., cause, effect, and impact are directly attached to the feeling itself. This everlasting happiness evolves through our compassion and tangible efforts to relieve other people's miseries, while we learn about the nature of our own depression, too.

Our unresolved hurts and experiences cause depression. Thus, pinpointing the real causes of our sufferings is the main step for healing our depression. We often feel that most of our dilemmas and sufferings relate to relationship problems, personal genetic defects, or childhood traumas. Especially, our chaotic relationships with our parents, spouses, bosses, colleagues, friends, neighbours, etc., are usually the causes of our doom and gloom. Ultimately, we humans are responsible for making one another miserable intentionally or by our ignorance. We are the main culprits for the world's sufferings. At the same time, depression might be merely a symptom of our high expectations from people, society, and life, especially for happiness, which only reflects our own naiveté about humans and societies' capacities.

We get involved with many types of relationships without enough knowledge, planning, or control. We cannot choose our parents, and their shortfalls and weaknesses hurt us even though they may not harm us directly. Active relationships, e.g., when people share their sexual and emotional needs, get trickier and they affect us even more. In family and organizations, we share plenty of emotions and commotions. We receive psychological support from these relationships, but we often cause one another agony and sufferings. Our disappointments and sufferings from various relationships deflate our spirits. We extend a lot of energy to learn about their natures and impacts on us, especially during the early stages of our lives. We try to learn about human nature, relations, and personality to grasp the motives behind people's behaviour. We also learn that we should devote special attention and time to each particular relationship to learn its unique needs and meaning. Thus, with respect to relationships, in particular, we must *learn* to be a generalist as well as a specialist for interpreting the expectations, personalities, and needs of those whom we must, or choose to, have a mutually respectful relationship with. In most cases, it would not be possible to give up a relationship, or at least it might not be wise to do so. Still, for eliminating the causes of our sufferings, usually we must learn a lot about our relationships and then find plausible solutions for our unique situations. Often we must make adjustments in our own attitude and mentality.

To grasp the complications of relationships, first we must first try to learn about ourselves and the ways we judge people. This is another crucial learning, since many relationships are vital for us and we want to prevent their collapse, and because our ability to assess and judge individuals fairly indicate who we are. We must study our personal habits and psychological attributes for gauging and judging others, which are usually too hasty and tainted by our egotism and dogmatism. We should learn about our prejudices, hang-ups, communication flaws, etc. and how to manage them.

Through concerted efforts to learn about life's essentialities, values, beauties, pleasures, and sufferings, we also learn a lot about our thinking habits, logic, beliefs, dogmatism, etc. We learn to develop a philosophy of life and perhaps even discover a path of wisdom to pursue actively. We learn about the sanctity and power of our spirits and our role for keeping them happy. We learn about the strength and validity of our thoughts for building and controlling the structure of our lives. And we learn how to create no-thought moments actively and consciously to calm our minds and reach tranquillity.

All this wisdom about living becomes possible, of course, through our *conscious learning* efforts, as we focus on the variety of topics noted above with a high degree of consciousness. In return, our wisdom and mental training raises our consciousness for deciphering both our perceived and real world realities. All these learnings prepare us for living with meaningful goals and calmer mindsets.

Living or Making a Living?

Both learning and education are major decisions of life, but for different reasons. Education prepares us at best for building a career and making a living, whereas conscious learning about life's essentialities prepares us for 'living' more authentically and peacefully. This basic distinction between education and learning is important for emphasizing the ultimate objectives of each. In its literary sense, however, everything we learn is supposed to be educational. And every educational regimen must have a specific, worthwhile learning purpose. Yet, sadly, most of us fail in both grounds mostly due to social and educational systems' ineptness.

Anyway, the discussions in Part I show that we should make major mental adjustments about both education and learning. We must recognize why we educate ourselves in such a convoluted context and format, going to college and struggling for degrees and knowledge that prove hardly useful, going by the low ratio of people using their higher educations directly and fully, nowadays. We must know our education purposes and its plausible impact on our social and spiritual life, if anything at all.

Sadly, we have been conditioned to stress on education and waste most productive years of our lives on it, *ironically at the expense of losing our opportunities to learn about living itself!* How we choose and use our education is iffy and our prerogative. However, it is a major life decision, not because it might bring us more money and status, but only because it could prevent us from materializing our potentialities and freedom by learning enough about life essentialities in a timely manner.

Both the time wasted on education and the possible confusion in life as a consequence of that decision are major issues needing our careful consideration. In conjunction with the issues related to work and organization discussed Part II, particularly, we should make our decisions about education and work more thoughtfully and purposefully.

Conversely, decision about learning (not education) is crucial since it sets the direction of our lives and efforts, as well as the time we allot to enhance the quality of our lives by learning 'how to live.' Our current stress on education just for engaging in some form of work is questionable, since we never give ourselves the opportunity to even learn about the process of learning, let alone actually pursuing the rigorous learning regimen and applying our wisdom to our lives. In the present social systems, our learnings about life are left out as a side issue that we might at best attend to only if other functions of our lives are fulfilled and only if time and opportunity permit, not to mention finding a motivation to do so in the first place. Clearly, we are doing this in the wrong order. Education must be placed secondary to the initial objective of learning about life and ourselves. Thus, we need a revolutionary attitude and a more practical system to support and encourage us and our children to view learning and education in the right order and a proper perspective. If we wish to change anything about the quality of social living, life structure, crimes, people's struggles, sufferings, psychological defects and insecurities, etc., we should begin by changing our methods of education and learning. In particular, learning should become a life necessity and conscious exercise, rather than a luxury dependent upon the opportunity of time and accident, or imposed subconsciously through superficial teachings of society and religions. We should embrace 'learning' as a natural substance in our bloods to induce our creativity and reflect the meaningfulness and purposes of our lives. Only by real learning, we might free our spirits and get a chance for salvation.

The irony is that learning is much easier, cheaper, faster, and more useful than education, while it makes our lives hundred folds more meaningful and happy. Why we humans have not yet figured this simple fact about life is amazing!

While this chapter has stressed on learning for living, 'living for learning' is discussed in Chapter Fifteen along with, 'Focused Thinking,' as a special life philosophy. This conscious learning constitutes a long-term commitment to explore all aspects of life and 'self' for self-improvement and enlightenment. All the major life decisions about education, work, marriage, and other learning topics covered in this book would directly benefit from a higher level of consciousness and self-awareness. Yet, before delving into these fundamentals and mechanisms of learning in Part V, a few other major life decisions must be reviewed in the following chapters. Learning about social structure in general is crucial due to our routines and pains to cope with our societies' convoluted demands, especially in relations to work and family issues.

PART II
Work and Organization

CHAPTER THREE
Objectives of Working

> *Career (Genetic) Potentialities* discussed in Chapter Six of Volume II complements this chapter's topic. Thus, re-reading that chapter before or after this chapter will be useful.

Most of us spend all our productive years and hours looking for a job or working with mediocre motivation or fulfilment, if at all. Like everything else in modern societies, the nature of our jobs is too mechanical and overwhelmed by our egoism and insecurities. Thus, we end up working too much or too little and often wonder why making a living has become so torturous and humiliating. We pursue different types of professions, mostly in hostile and stressful settings, for mere subsistence, getting rich, or feeding our self-esteem. However, fulfilling even our moderate expectations takes massive labour. Ironically, we consider 'work' an essential part of human life, which we do for economic reasons, to avoid boredom, or merely for not being called a bum. Sometimes, we work out of a sheer sense of responsibility to self and others. For all these reasons, 'work' is a major life decision, but also because our rationale for doing all that work with so much mental and spiritual sacrifices may be questionable within the larger scheme of one's life philosophy. *Who says we must work so hard or at all, anyway, and for what end?*

Although labour feels like a natural part of life, justifying it personally is getting harder every year if no pride comes out of it, or at least some sort of appreciation, not even from our family.

Sometimes, we wonder about the purpose of our labour in such debilitating, stressful environments just to feed our addiction to extravagance. Is this kind of work habit natural? In particular, considering the growing social disorder and deteriorating family relationships, working so hard to buy more things or to become wealthy makes little sense. If it is for leading a happy life, is the prevalent 'work' format in modern societies, in fact, a relevant or distorting factor for making a living? What is work supposed to be, anyway? A career, a means of survival or building wealth, any activity, something we must do, labour, a means of filling our days and fighting boredom, a way of serving our Ego, anything that makes us tired physically or mentally, a habit, a social fad, all of these, a balanced combination of them? What? We ought to know, but most of us do not.

Overall, our lifelong niggling doubts about work and inner conflicts due to this social duty distress and confuse us, especially since we cannot readily revamp our mentality and responsibility for making money. We cannot ignore our egoism and ambitions or the pressures on us to sustain a particular lifestyle by working hard. We simply cannot think outside the box beyond the norms of the prevalent social structure. We cannot bypass the hardened social parameters about the role of work for building our phony personalities and lifestyles. Accordingly, we never get a chance to build our spirits and explore our identities as a soulful creature living for justifiable and meaningful purposes.

Nevertheless, since work occupies so much of our precious lives and minds, it makes sense to explore the value and purpose of various types of work and assess our alternatives in the light of a practical (and somewhat profound) life philosophy. We should at least convince ourselves that we know why we work so hard, instead of choosing a simpler lifestyle with less luxury and work. The again, despite all the dilemmas and pains it causes us daily, work's big effect on our spirits and humanity's survival makes it a major life decision. As a main part of economic system, in fact, 'work' and its condition need lots of personal and social scrutiny.

Work Purposes

In general, every job has its own situation and scope with specific objectives. Some jobs are interesting and joyful occasionally, but most are mundane, laborious, and lousy. The two main purposes of working are to *accomplish some personal objectives* and/or *make money*. For this book's purposes, the roles of our ambitions, egoism, boredom, or other urges for working are all considered indirect factors included in the first purpose, i.e., *personal life objectives*. For the limited goals of this book, this global view of work is sufficient without getting into too much detail about our specific personal goals for working. Accordingly, four possible working situations arise from the simple classification here, each with a specific scope and meaning, as shown in Table 3.1.

Table 3.1: Types of Work

TWO PURPOSES → ↓ OF WORK		Make Money	
		YES	NO
Accomplish Life Objectives	YES	I Ideal	II Fulfilling
	NO	III Boring	IV Slavery

Type I Work– 'Ideal'

An 'ideal' type of work satisfies our life objectives while offering good financial rewards, too. This is true, of course, as long as it does not damage our health or other aspects of our lives. This ideal situation occurs when our career matches our potentialities and temperament. We are normally satisfied with the outcome of both our work and life overall if our objectives are well defined and compatible with our potentialities. It indicates our decisions have been correct and we are not following a dead-end job.

Within this work condition, we have a good chance of eluding the psychologically harmful pressures that most work conditions cause to a large degree. This ideal situation provides a sense of financial security and freedom to make sounder decisions and look forward to continuous accomplishments. At the same time, our work also fulfills our self-actualization need. Wealth is not the incentive in this type of work, although one is often rewarded substantially. In fact, wealth, success, egoism, and power are not legitimate 'personal objectives' for making certain type of work 'ideal.' The product per se is the inherent purpose of work, and the main 'personal objective' in this class of work. This is true even when someone loves money and success and views them merely as his/her supplementary personal objectives.

Unfortunately, an 'ideal' work opportunity scarcely comes up for people, unless one becomes an established artist or researcher. This type of work is more 'ideal' than a 'fulfilling' work (Type II) only in the sense that financial worries do not block one's creativity, but not for providing a better chance of accumulating wealth. It is also 'ideal,' since the person has been able to adapt him/herself as a practical and active member of the society, as evident by the money s/he receives for his/her services, which are presumably benefiting other people as well.

Type II Work– 'Fulfilling'

We *decide actively* to pursue this type of work for self-fulfilment and achieving personal life objectives without any expectation for rewards or recognition. While our hobbies, artistic endeavours, community work, and charity are all sources of self-fulfilment, they do not necessarily result in adequate financial compensation. Our incentives are pure and unselfish, although at the end we enjoy the sense of self-fulfilment. Any financial reward would be an icing on the cake, but not an inherent aspect of the work. The work is merely fulfilling by its nature without any guarantee for financial rewards or recognition.

The only drawback of this type of work is that the person might be partly worried about his/her own and his/her family's financial needs. The causes of his/her bizarre, rather impractical, approach towards work might be of concern to him/her or others, too. It might be a clue about his/her inability to fit within normal work environments. Or it might reflect his/her resistance to work in substandard environments due to his/her strong personality and idealism. S/he apparently prefers to adopt a more independent life for him/herself, regardless of social acceptance or perhaps even losing the chance of building a family who might have obliged him/her to make more money.

Type III Work– 'Boring'

In this common work situation, we make money (or expect to do so) without any consideration to personal life objectives. We do this type of work because we have to, or we are too greedy or ambitious, often without even realizing or accepting how boring the work is, although most people feel the related stress. It is merely a matter of intelligence to realize that pursuing greed and egoism to accumulate wealth and power has no intrinsic value and it is not even a legitimate type of success for a mature person.

This type of work normally has some value for somebody or some organization, as they are willing to pay for it. Yet, for the worker, it is at best worthless for satisfying his/her psychological needs, despite the feeling of career growth and financial rewards. Furthermore, the related boredom and stress could damage other aspects of a person's life in a major way.

Type IV Work– 'Slavery'

In this type of work, neither personal objectives nor financial needs of the individual are satisfied. When the compensation is minimal or perceived inadequate, work feels like slavery. Sadly, slavery practices are still prevalent all over the world, even in the developed countries in a modern way. The form differs around the globe, but the outcome is that some people are exploited and some are exploiting. Even in developed countries, many jobs demand over 60-70 hours a week of labour and workers are made to feel that they are lucky to have those fixed-salary jobs, anyway. Most people realize how they are exploited, so, in turn, have become ineffective and inefficient in their jobs.

This kind of practice and the feeling of exploitation happen to some degree in family relationships, too, when a family member feels s/he is carrying the bulk of responsibilities and work around the household. Obviously, slavery (or even an impression of it) is the worst type of work, since no incentive or personal objectives are attached to it. We feel abused and humiliated in this type of work situation with no rewards at all.

Working under most of the above situations is humiliating and stressful, but not working feels even a lousier option for us, at least for our present mentality and within the current culture. Not working reflects our laziness, lack of ambition, and personality flaws. We feel that even our moments of relaxation should be deserved and only subsequent to tangible work, or else we are useless and ignorant. Even our no-thought moments and 'self' explorations must have some objective. Proud people feel lousy and sick without doing some kind of work, although most of the work they do has no ultimate benefit for them beyond satisfying their basic financial needs. It feels simply impractical not to work, because with some kind of work we gain at least our own respect for our existence. Only then, we feel we deserve all the leisure and pleasure that we wish to indulge ourselves with.

Apathy and laziness are incongruent with the goal of raising the 'quality' of our lives. At the same time, the quality of life commands a balance among the types of works we choose to do, relaxation, and 'self' exploration. In particular, we must strive to find means of enriching our spirits more directly, the more we feel obliged or trapped in works of types III and IV. Work has so many other critical dimensions that are explained in this chapter.

Work Philosophy

Work philosophy, thus, evolves out of its two main conflicting perspectives. The first, most prevalent, perspective relates to our obligations for supporting our financial and emotional needs. The second, less recognized, perspective relates to our innate urge to develop our identities and minds, and to support our spiritual and psychological needs. Our 'self' and spirit are highly reliant on our work's nature. Therefore, our work philosophy gets complicated, since we must satisfy both our social and spiritual needs largely through our jobs. Aligning these two perspectives of work in our psyches is both difficult and impractical in our chaotic societies.

The ideal would be to fathom a kind of profession we could pursue all our active lives for fulfilling all our needs, but mostly our spirituality. Instead, we are usually forced to labour during the most productive years of our lives merely for subsistence and then, when we get older, we are forced to retire and live idly with a shaky identity. We have no useful work to maintain our spirits when we need it the most during old age. So, in effect, we kill our spirits by both our inability to do the right work during our youth and not having something useful to do during old age when we need a fixed identity more than ever. Yet, hardly anybody gets a chance or even a mentality to define a work philosophy for him/herself, nowadays, because reconciling work's two philosophical perspectives all our lives is difficult and we must stay practical.

Still, studying and questioning our work purposes is valuable, although our chances of finding ideal works are slim, while we must stay practical. Honouring this innate human curiosity raises our self-awareness and chances to build a finer life path at least. We remember that any work tainting our individuality can become a big source of our depression. Never getting a chance to discover our potentialities and explore our 'self' develops a deep void in our psyches along with lasting stress. After all, discovering our potentialities and using them in the 'right work' are two big tasks for us on the same continuum. They must be planned together as much as possible, realistically, in the early stages of our lives to prevent lifetime disappointments, especially the burden of boring work as well as the boredom and feeling of idleness during the old age, which is just so prevalent and deplorable these days.

As part of defining our life purposes and philosophy, we must recognize these varied dimensions of work and its objectives for developing our self-image and identity. Before planning a long gloomy life in organizations, we can gauge our options and needs. We can at least study the principles of coping in organizations (as explained in Chapter Six) and keep our aspirations and Egos in check. That is one way of protecting our individuality during the power struggles of organizations. It is especially crucial to grasp both human nature and the nature of our work before planning for a career that we may end up doing and loathing a lifetime.

If work does not provide a sense of self-fulfilment, which is most likely the case, we should at least know all the reasons for doing that job and ensure they at least make sense within the overall context of our life philosophy. The fact that we are often forced to do some kind of work just to survive and stay practical is totally understandable and honourable. Beyond that, however, we must resist and refute the cultural values and criteria that view work only in terms of its financial purpose, or merely a venue for satiating our greed and ego. The two notions that cross our minds when we hear the word 'work' are *money* and *labour* (hard work and suffering). We associate work mostly with the 'work we must do,' which is expected to be laborious and stressful. This does not have to be true. We can change our mindsets to think of work more as a potent way of gaining self-fulfilment and individualism in the first place, while providing for our basic needs, too. Then again, it is only a matter of personal philosophy and how we can justify and balance our wide range of needs. It is a matter of our priority for building a private personal identity versus the option of insisting on keeping a phony personality in society.

Once we appreciate how short and unpredictable life is, it would not make much sense to waste it on unfulfilling work only for financial purposes beyond our basic needs. As a fundamental principle of our life philosophy, the purpose of work should be defined by its outcome. Work for financial rewards is justified only to the extent it serves our needs for a comfortable life. Thus, saving part of our income, by restricting useless consumption and preventing waste is crucial—to retire from unfulfilling work as soon as our financial security is guaranteed, much sooner than the official retiring age. Conversely, working long hours or at several jobs with the intention of making more money to waste on more luxury and fashion, even for making our family happy and proud, is a poor logic and invalid life philosophy. Extravagance or more pleasure to make up for the pain of our lousy jobs is an even lamer excuse, yet quite common these days.

There is no philosophical inconsistency, however, if financial rewards happen to exceed our needs, while we are doing the 'right work,' *if* we keep a balance among the time we spend on work, relaxation, family, health, and pleasures. Devoting ourselves only to work, however honourable its nature and objectives, would be against a normal person's philosophy. A unique life philosophy surely exists for selfless people like Mother Teresa and Albert Schweitzer when 'personal devotion' supersedes normal man's philosophy, including the value and balance of work.

Sometimes, we feel the inherent values of work in the way they lift our spirits. However, we normally neglect to appreciate their significance in our ways of thinking and for setting our work objectives. Even the simple awareness that 'we work because we have to, rather than want to' is a big source of relief, as we may then gauge our long-term options more wisely (not for whining more). We recognize that although 'working' reflects an inherent aspect of our individuality, only the 'right work' can truly express our identity and life objectives. We must find the 'work we want to do,' eventually, if possible, to balance the 'work we must do.'

Work stress comes from many sources and affects us based on our personalities. We might not feel it directly, or get absorbed in an organization to cope with its tyranny better, but the overall work hardships are evident in the growing stress level of office workers and society. These sufferings are also evident from the way we ruin our relationships outside of work with our families. The accelerating rate of relationship failures in the present culture is highly related to the individuals' work issues.

In all, the nature of any work stems from its role to, 1) satisfy our need for achievement, 2) support our subsistence and, 3) help us define and express our identity (outside the phony identity and individualism prevalent currently). This general picture of 'work' can enhance our perceptions of work and support our purpose of working. We need to work, but we might succeed in finding the right kind for us by considering the points raised in this chapter, or at least supplementing it with some fulfilling work on the side. We cannot avoid the need to work for subsistence, nor can we ignore the sense of failure and frustration resulting from works with superficial purposes. Still, we can give our spirits a break by exploring some self-fulfilling types of work for doing on the side according to our potentialities. Then again, most of us cannot, or resist to, even think of a fulfilling hobby or work!

Aligning Our Drives for Working

Our main drives for working to, i) make a living, and ii) achieve our life objectives hardly coincide. The crooked work and people driven by illegal and unethical goals are not even included in this book's discussions, although the number of people working a lifetime on defrauding and abusing the public has been growing. The narrow definition of personal life objectives adopted in this book comprise only of *unselfish* drive for any work that raises our spirits and is an end in itself, relative to work just for survival or selfish achievements that the majority of people customarily view as life objectives. Our greed driven efforts have their own valid objectives, too. They help us survive and feel secure. But they are mostly incongruent with the 'personal life goals' of a resourceful being. Self-gratification or pleasure from greed, power, and wealth are not authentic life objectives, as they are Ego driven goals and not an end in themselves. They only offer the tools, e.g., money, to purchase objects and pleasures that allegedly simulate self-fulfilment and happiness, or may even avail a tentative sense of success and prestige. Greed-ridden goals do not lift our spirits or soothe our psyches, though. Rather, our real life objectives must reflect our unique capacities, potentialities, and ingenious efforts and outcomes that boost our own as well as other humans' spirits. We are not here just to survive or serve our Egos!

Two questions may be raised: First, 'What kind of work we would choose to do if we were financially secure for the rest of our lives?' Second, 'Why would anybody choose to work merely out of greed when s/he is financially secure?' Logically, we must work only for achieving certain values (life objectives) if we were financially secure. Or else, we are probably incapable of, or lazy about, pinpointing our life objectives; or worse, we are simply a greedy, power-thirsty individual with no interest or capacity to imagine worthwhile life objectives for ourselves. Only making more money and exploiting (deceiving) people and society satiate these individuals' zeal for existence. The bottomline is that we can work essentially for serving either our Ego or Self. The fact that almost everybody chooses the former is amazing.

In line with these thoughts, we might also realize that a part of our life objectives should be to reach a sense of financial security as soon as possible, so that we can attend to our main personal life objectives. Accordingly, a wise person stops worrying about luxury and pretentious lifestyles that delay his/her realization of financial security. Instead, s/he strives to pinpoint his/her natural life objectives (passions) and focus on his/her higher personal needs, including spirituality and self-actualization.

Working for Individualism (Pride)

We strive to satisfy our materialistic and psychological needs through hard work, self-awareness, and our limited wisdom. The outcome—a commodity we buy with our money, a sculpture we create, or the status and recognition we earn—reflects our life objectives and success.

In a finer and deeper scope, however, only that portion of work satiating our need for achievement per se has inherent value, as it enhances our sense of individualism. Need for achievement is an innate urge in almost all humans. We hope to achieve something really worth our efforts and possibly leave a legacy. Otherwise, why would any intelligent person work so hard all his/her life for some undefined or meaningless ends, including wealth, power, or even companionships that are getting lousier these days, anyway?

Accordingly, our life objectives and the type of work we choose demonstrate our intelligence, sense of financial security, psychological needs, and individualism—the unique and inherent drive for achievement *regardless of external rewards*. This is different even from seeking achievement for social adaptation, acceptance, and approval. It is merely a 'need to achieve' solely for expressing and internalizing our deep sense of individuality. Thus, setting proper life objectives and following them become difficult. For one thing, it requires finding and pursuing the kind of work that fits our personality, aspirations, potentialities, drive for social adaptation, and ability to work for self-fulfilment per se —all at the same time. Nevertheless, a rather ideal work would fit our life objectives and reinforce our individuality by providing:

- A valuable 'product'—in line with a goal set and attained.
- A spiritual 'sense' of self-actualization.
- A psychological 'response' to our inner need for achievement.

We seek these three work attributes intuitively, yet we often bring ourselves to accept almost any job just to survive and adapt.

In all, only few of us realize, and respond to, our high 'inner need for achievement' consciously or strive for self-actualization and happiness, despite our strong common urge to explore our divine potentialities. The reasons are: 1) economic constraints debilitate us to do so, 2) we prefer to follow our greed and Ego, or 3) we do not know how to go about identifying and fulfilling our higher (inner) needs. Thus, we just try to fudge a sense of achievement in our mundane jobs. Eventually, we merely adopt organization objectives as our life objectives, since we never get a chance to identify our personal objectives based on a defined life plan. We learn to associate with, and get attached to, organization achievements as our own. We are brainwashed to feel proud and successful when the organization we work for shows large profits or attains a new milestone. In the end, it feels easier to forget our personal objectives and instead adopt organizations'.

We hope to satisfy our closely related needs for both self-actualization (spiritual) and achievement (psychological) in our organization endeavours, without realizing that the three essential attributes of work are hardly attained in organizations' substandard conditions and settings. Especially, our 'need for achievement,' which defines our individuality and identity, hardly materializes in organizations. Instead, we get more absorbed in organization objectives in hopes of satiating (actually replacing or subduing) our personal need for fulfillment and achievement.

Of course, exceptions always exist for organization work, too, where personal and organizational objectives coincide, although this is rare. For instance, a scientist or researcher identifies his work content personally and then devotes many years of his life to self-fulfilling work in an organization. Financial rewards and recognition follow as fringe benefits, but usually not as the main incentive for choosing that career or that particular organization.

Still, *working* per se (regardless of our achievements or work content) has an inherent purpose of its own, as discussed in the next section. Actually, this rather odd feature of work constitutes another crucial dimension of our individuality.

The Inherent Purpose of Work

Another peculiar aspect of work may appear rather contradictory to the discussion about work as a means of personal achievement.

That is, despite our craving for achievement, we need to work for the sake of *working* per se, without any expectation for financial or emotional rewards. Even if we had all the monies we need and had accomplished all our life objectives, we still have an urge to find something to do. This is the inherent purpose of work—to keep us amused. Most of us cannot sit idle or bear the boredom from the lack of work. We simply create any kind of work for ourselves to avoid insanity from boredom.

Why do we work just for the heck of it? **First,** we are naturally against stagnation and a state in which neither our body nor mind is functioning. This is probably one reason for the difficulty of creating no-thought moments and meditating. Of course, we have relaxation and idle times. Yet, our natural tendency is to always think (mental work) or do something physical. That is why we sometimes try to distract ourselves with more work to elude our erratic thoughts and depression. **Second,** we have a deep urge to keep testing our abilities for sustaining life. We like to gauge our stamina and strength, see their growth, or curb the speed of their depletion during old age. **Third,** our psychological health needs constant engagement in some kind of work. When we do not have much to do, or watch too much television, or even engage in excessive superficial pleasures or socializing, we get anxious and may lose our sanity eventually. In all, we have a natural tendency to work to prove our worth, indicate our liveliness, and boost our individuality at least as an able person. We seek work in the same way we are instinctually curious, always in search of knowledge. That is in fact why laziness always feels like an abnormal state of being and we feel ashamed of it frequently, too.

Working is an obligation to 'self' for building our identity. This interpretation is also evident in the foundation of our cultures, where work has become an undeniable nucleus of societies. The social structure has evolved around this personal need to work. Thank god, the urge to work seems to be inherent in humans rather than just a dire symptom of social manipulation of human mind through our long history! The need to work feels like a vital instinct engraved in our minds as a notion of being per se, and for social life and contact, even when a person has vast resources for subsistence and pleasure. Thus, both instinctually and culturally, work constitutes a vital dimension of our individuality in society, especially for personal assessment and awareness of who we are. Only as a secondary importance, we insist that our work should be valuable as well and satisfy our need for achievement in line with our artistic or scientific passions.

Thus, it seems that our individuality is highly represented by the two often opposing (but inherent) purposes of work, i.e., for 1) fulfilling ourselves (to satisfy our 'self'), and 2) validating our existence in society (to satisfy our 'ego'), including the chance for social contacts. These inherent purposes of work are ingrained in our psyches as reflections of human nature and innate needs by making money and fulfilling our personal objectives.

Our natural (opposing) drives to work (to satisfy our 'self' or 'ego') are also interesting to study for the way they push us work for organizations, for non-personal objectives, and often against our self-realization need. Keeping some kind of work nourishes our pride, thus we rush to work for organizations at the expense of delaying or undermining our life objectives (or our passions).

Of course, greed and ego further goad us to focus on finding the best paying job we can get. Yet, we mainly work to make a living, validate our existence, build social contacts, feel proud, and boost our self-image, often at the cost of jeopardizing our spiritual and psychological needs. People's zeal to embrace and personalize organizations' goals and success as their own shows how our individuality is weakened in organizations and society, nowadays—mostly as a matter of practicality, of course! We can feel how our need for achievement has been subdued due to the humiliating experiences that we endure in organization work—simply because we must work for both subsistence and pride by keeping a job. However, this puts deep psychological burdens on our psyches along with lasting hardships.

The Nature and Value of Work

The wide range of work purposes discussed above reveals both the severity and difficulty of our major decisions about education and work due to their importance for adapting to the harsh work environments prevalent in modern societies, but also boosting our individualism and identity. The value of work stems from its role to fulfil these personal purposes, i.e., adaptation, self-realization, and individualism. Any work's nature consists of 'work contents' and 'working conditions,' which are discussed briefly in the next section. Awareness about work's value and nature at office and around the house can also help us grasp, and deal better with, the causes of our stress and make long-term plans.

Our work's nature usually lies on the borderline between two or more of the four 'work situations' shown in Table 3.1 (page 51). For example, we might not like our job and it might not be fulfilling, yet it may be tolerable and not boring. Or we may get paid for our work, but so little (actually or perceptually) that it feels almost like working free. When no personal objectives are satisfied, either, work may be viewed or felt as slavery. Some homemakers feel this way, because their family do not seem to notice or value their work. They do not feel to be achieving any personal objectives by maintaining the household, either. They feel bored, and when they get tired or anxious, they claim (and believe) that they are doing slavery for the whole family.

Anyway, while our work may not be quite comparable to any of the four symbolic situations noted in Table 3.1, we associate with the related feelings of each work situation occasionally at least. At the same time, often we cannot be too fussy about the kinds of jobs we are lucky to find in our deteriorating economic conditions. Often our education goes to waste and we work in a stressful environment, because we have no choice and we should remain practical. Yet, many people who have pride and proven potentialities constantly doubt the value of wasting their lives on works that feel at best too boring and bordering slavery.

The wages often determines work's face value (importance). Yet, a work's real value transpires only in personal objectives it fulfils. This is a remarkable point about work. As soon as we take away monitory incentives, swiftly the meaning and value of work depends only on its content. For example, the work we do and the money we make by selling useless stuff or services to people has no value. When greed or even basic financial needs dominate our view of work, it turns into competition and a huge potential for stress and humiliation. The innate value of work just stems from its content, the efforts and focus that one extends in expressing his/her potentialities and thoughts, the way it affects him/her and others, plus the usefulness of the final product in general. When our ancestors laboured all day just to grow grain or wheat, their work was quite valuable, source of pride, and had real purposes. In contrast, the works most people do these days are inherently invalid and valueless due to their crooked natures and purposes.

The amount of work and talent wasted in modern societies on fashion, making foolish movies and TV programs, including dire news and games, is simply deplorable. We are wasting humanity!

It has become customary to expect work to be laborious and non-fulfilling. We accept the humiliation of work because we have learned, and been conditioned to view work, as a necessity to make the ends meet. Only seldom and by accident, we can find work a means of self-fulfilment and redeeming our potentialities. Realistically, we usually cannot limit ourselves only to fulfilling works due to tough socioeconomic conditions and our zeal to be social and have a family. Still, our awareness about the nature and quality of work, to maintain our growth and psychological health, is necessary for grasping who we are or can be. The goal is not to seek a quick solution for our career, but to transform our mentality from a state of passivity to a state of awareness and mental preparation within any work not feeling right. Surely, our mere awareness of work issues or even our passive rebellion does not solve the problem. Yet, it makes us assess our lives in general and decide about the role of work in the long run within our life philosophy more seriously. We can always remember why we do certain kind of work, for what end, and how much longer. With this mentality, we consider work an opportunity to grow mentally towards self-fulfilling works in the future, instead of merely a profession to make our subsistence, get richer, or achieve some useless, intangible objectives.

Overall, we must be conscious of the nature of the works we do and their impacts on our health. That is another reason why finding the right combination and amount of 'work' is such an important life decision. Each type of work supposedly satisfies some of our needs, or else we would not be doing it—although some futile works we cannot avoid and some we do only through coercion and intimidation. Our professions or careers are often not fulfilling, and we usually feel obliged to do lousy works. Yet, maybe we can make up for this deficiency by engaging, at least partially, in a healthier type of work related to our life objectives.

Relaxation, pleasures, or increasing sluggish time, such as watching television or socializing, cannot provide a remedy for our tensions of non-creative and non-fulfilling work. If we cannot quit working in non-fulfilling jobs, the only alternative would be to work also harder in those areas that mind can get creative and relax. The only antidote for unfulfilling work is additional work that is fulfilling. This would cause a larger workload that is often impractical, but we must at least be aware of the possible remedy for unfulfilling work. Some no-thought moments can also help relieve our tensions of non-fulfilling work tentatively, while we seek more fulfilling work or hobbies.

Work Contents and Conditions

'Work contents' reveals both the process and essence of a job for a final product. For example, carpentry consists of hammering, sawing, gluing wood, etc. However, it contains some artistic and creative efforts for making perhaps a beautiful chair or armoire. Only when individuals' potentialities and initiatives manifest in their works, the process, nature, and output become valuable and self-fulfilling. Otherwise, work remains boring and stressful, and the product itself shows no personal touch.

Meanwhile, 'work conditions' refers to one's interaction with a job setting. For example, working in a warm or stuffy office for a demanding, snotty boss makes us edgy and we lose some of our efficiency and motivation to focus on work. Although the effect of poor work conditions on productivity is by itself an important issue, its effects on physical and psychological health of workers is more of an issue in this book. Together, work contents and conditions dictate the quality and structure of our lives due to the immensity of time and energy we spend working. Especially, the work we do only for financial incentives offers much less chance for self-fulfilment, thus requires more justifications in terms of its contents and conditions at least.

Only seldom one gets a chance to be the master of the work and create the work content and conditions suitable for one. Our intuitive search for this ideal shows the difficulty and importance of our decisions about the type of works we end up doing all our lives. Last chapters' discussions about education for building our careers also show the importance of our vigilance and diligence for making these major life decisions.

Ironically, for most of us, 'organization' is synonymous with jobs and stands as the symbol of work and financial security, but it is also the source of our mental insecurity and anxiety. In fact, most of us consider ourselves lucky to have a job and work for an organization, to earn a living, or sell our services to them. Only a small group enjoys the luxury of offering its services directly as consultants or independent professionals, and thus have a bit more control over their work contents and conditions. Surely, even they have their own concerns. They carry big risks in many respects, compared with employees of established organizations with a fixed, guaranteed income. Yet, the main 'risk' separating these two work settings is the added burden on our health and integrity, with a lower chance for self-realization, since work contents and conditions in organizations often represses our real potentialities and stirs psychological imbalance and stress. Naturally, this is a harsh truth to state about organizations in our capitalistic settings!

We can master our work or be a slave to it. We should make our choices, and thus live with the consequences of our decisions about the works we spend our entire lives on. We master our work if we can control and enjoy it and get our sense of fulfilment from it, too. We become slaves to it when we accept the humiliation of coping with the harsh contents and conditions of our jobs. We become slaves when we lose our initiative and the control of our thoughts and energies. We become slaves when we strive to find and keep the jobs that provide our subsistence, but destroy our existence, while we do not realize even the sources of our stress, or merely ignore them. Work contents and conditions can ruin our spirits and the opportunity of feeling the sense of integrity and growth, which can be attained only through self-fulfilling works. 'Work' can be the source of reaching the highest level of divinity or losing our pride permanently. Thus, our position on this simple scale reflects our *relative* success in making proper, timely life decisions about education and careers. It shows our grasp and mastery of our existence, while we should remain practical for designing our life plans, too, of course.

Our level of control over work contents and conditions define the quality of our work. It reveals our success level in injecting our personal life objectives into designing our jobs. That is, the content (type) of work reflects how carefully we have planned and implemented our life objectives (especially for applying our education and potentialities). When working for an organization, or designing our jobs only for economic gains, we hardly get a chance to inject our life objectives into the job content. Work conditions also feel more stressful and less satisfactory when we are not the master of our work. Nowadays, organizations, their financial sponsors, and the agencies that provide major contracts to them mostly control work contents and conditions in society.

CHAPTER FOUR
Work Environment

This book's idealism about work being fulfilling and inspiring sounds naïve to our traditional mentality that sees work laborious, mandatory, and stressful. This general perception says a lot about our cultures even in modern, rich societies. While automation has largely mitigated the physical aspect of work, psychological and mental pressures have raised many folds. Work conditions have improved largely, we believe, but this big transition has, in fact, caused more distress and a wider sense of insecurity. Another point is that most jobs are performed by organizations, nowadays. Thus, the terms organization environment and work environment are used interchangeably in this chapter.

Criticizing organization environment is not for discouraging people or raising their cynicism regarding organization work, but rather preparing our mindsets about the poor atmosphere most of us must endure. Sadly, only a small group can find good jobs and work environments to attain at least some of the noble objectives of work, as noted in the previous chapter. Thus, we must not only find ways of dealing with the hassles and stress of work, but also compensate for the lack of fulfilling jobs to enrich our lives.

Meanwhile, we all feel like victims and assume to be the only ones suffering the perils of organizations, thus keep nagging or changing our jobs to no avail. We think that only this particular organization is contaminated by politics and Egos. That is not true, either. Thus, in the end, we should somehow learn to fit within organization environments somehow as a given fact for the time being at least. Preparing our mindsets is crucial for withstanding the hassles we must face and maybe be a productive member of these organizations, too. Realizing the universality of organization shortfalls is important.

Organization environment entails both work conditions and organization culture (values and politics). Unless we get absorbed egotistically and become the creators of those politics and values (as the main 'boss' or his/her disciples), we keep suffering from the influence and power that others impose upon us. We suffer because we find those demands and intimidations unreasonable, demoralizing, and unfair. We cannot understand, or respond to, the Egos that develop and spread crooked expectations, rules, and disrespect. Yet, we strive to tolerate the situation and play our Model to keep our faces straight. Meanwhile, we feel many types of insecurities, starting with our financial needs and uncertainty about the prospects of finding other descent jobs. Sometimes, we feel more optimistic about the job market, but then our insecurity takes over. Our rotating hopes and cynicism about job markets and our professional life crushes our spirits.

Low self-esteem is the second cause of insecurity that harms our psyches deeply. Although this is a rather self-imposed hurdle, organization environment also stirs and intensifies this source of personal insecurity many folds. When a person's self-confidence is low, 'organization culture' expedites his/her loss of confidence through regular putdowns, while raising his/her dependence on organization. Self-doubt gradually overwhelms our psyches and affects our performance. In a way, working for an organization without self-confidence is like being exposed to a deadly disease without having a strong immune system to resist and fight it off. Without ample self-confidence, we deplete our self-respect and self-image gradually and turn into a feebly absorbed employee.

All along, we do not realize what is happening to us or even the cause of our stress and confusion. At the same time, becoming more arrogant is not going to cure our low self-image, though this perception and reaction (as some kind of desperate self-defence) has vastly spread and ruined humans' characters and identities as well.

The psychological insecurity about our roles in organizations is often more stressful and damaging than job insecurity per se. Organization environment pervades workers' suspicions of one another and about their intentions. We also become suspicious of others due to our bosses and colleagues' intimidations, while we wonder how to measure our personal worth for developing our identities and dealing with family and people. Thus, we become more spiteful, arrogant, and intimidating ourselves daily to defend ourselves during our encounters with our colleagues and bosses. Yet, our self-confidence must be natural, instead of a sham!

Organization mostly refers to office work, which often means being cooped up in a cubicle or factory most of our waking hours wasting our lives on stuffs that have no intrinsic value for mind and soul. We get used to an idle lifestyle and bad diet, and soon pay for all that physical inactivity. Often we are too exhausted to exercise after work, anyway. At best, we have only enough time and energy to manage some household chores, have supper, and then possibly unwind a bit, if work related tensions and dilemmas allow. This routine causes only more depression and obesity.

Another problem with office work (and urban living) is that our contact with Nature is limited only to those rare opportunities we go to a park or beach during a weekend or vacation. Even the air we breathe all day is recycled through ineffective ventilation systems of big buildings. No windows to open for fresh air, albeit the outside air is often more polluted, anyway. Many of us whine about the poor quality of the air we breathe in offices, as well as erratic temperature changes. Overall, we work in settings void of compassion or any natural touch, even sunlight. A simple job entailing outdoor activity in the sun or walking on snow, e.g., mail delivery, offers more contact with nature than the prevalent pattern of commuting between home and office from and to our enclosed garages. The conveniences of office work and modern life in large cities have made us much lazier and eager for more automation. The poor working conditions and our obsession for convenience affect our physical and mental health. They are the causes of global stress and anxiety.

Adopting Organization Objectives

Chapter Six suggests some ideas for coping within organizations. Then again, adapting to organization environments and adopting their objectives are not easy on our psyches, either! Any kind of work at the expense of never understanding (or neglecting) our aspirations keeps us on the edge. We feel trapped and deprived of testing our real potentialities for all the reasons that make us work for an organization—which is often a lack of financial resources for subsistence or chasing our dreams. Meanwhile, organization work seems like a clear option for people without any ambitions or objectives, which is often the case for most people, nowadays. Anyway, the fact that we devote most of our time and energy to some mundane tasks, instead of our own exciting dreams, at best makes us feel passive about the welfare of organization and its objectives, yet still pressured with many tough responsibilities and deadlines to observe day after day with a shaky motivation.

The point is that unless we are running our own organizations to achieve our life plans, we are merely working for some other people's objectives, often without relating to those dreary goals. This incongruity exudes a sense of emptiness, which eventually causes boredom, stress, and loss of interest in both work and life. It feels as though our purposeless life lacks adequate scope and depth for someone who seeks happiness and life quality. In all, our dependence on organization sears our psyches subconsciously for either not having any personal life objectives, aspirations, and potentialities, or the means and guts to pursue them.

Even an 'egotistically absorbed' person feels this sense of goal incongruity. By definition, an 'egotistically absorbed' person adopts organization objectives totally and becomes committed to them fully, as if they were his personal goals. Although he might believe that his personal life objectives are the same as those of the organization, he still has some inner conflicts and urges for figuring out his innate potentialities, and for distinguishing his life objectives from those of the organization. His subconscious urges remain active, nevertheless, even when he convinces himself that organization objectives are good enough for him to adopt. He still wishes to nurture his creative aspirations and pursue his personal plans rather than solely concentrate on, and dissolve into, some tedious organization plans. Generally, however, he smothers such urges, since he is busy and tightly united with organization goals, which he has decided to give his highest priority. The rewards of compliance, including a sense of identity, power, and wealth, provide great incentives for most people to adopt organization objectives wholeheartedly and feel fulfilled.

Nevertheless, ignoring our niche (personal objectives) for any reason, even egotistical absorption in organizations, would not curb our subtle urges for independence and originality. Discovering and pursuing these urges are intrinsic needs that we might realize naturally. Deep down, however, organization objectives remain meaningless for our psyches, while we feel our inner conflicts and stress. We know all these facts, yet most of us usually feel obliged to spend a lifetime fighting for organization objectives that suffocate our authentic potentialities.

The outcome of any work (the product) reflects the level of success to fulfil personal or organization objectives. Yet most of us never see the result of our efforts; we cannot touch and feel the product of our work in the way a sculptor does. Whether we work on an assembly line or process information on a computer in an office, the product is often not a personally created output that we can relate to, although we usually invent some attachment and notions about our personal contribution, anyway. Everything these days is a product of many individuals' talents and inputs. Of course, the sense of teamwork and cooperation for making something collectively and feeling proud to contribute towards a product is precious. Yet, besides the tentative sense of gratification for being part of a team, we need our own creations to directly relate to, enjoy, and enrich our spirits. The pains of teamwork and rivalries, along with other organization pressures, often make us subconsciously resentful of organization products and creations, anyway. We are never satisfied with an organization's means of creating its products, even in organizations we wish to belong to proudly. A lot of hostility and rivalry often ruins the purpose of cooperation and the feeling of sharing.

Personality Clashes and Moods

Personality clashes and politics destroy organization morale and environment, as employees face Ego and Model personalities of their coworkers and outside contacts. Depending upon their status in organization and personalities, they should draw on their Ego and Model carefully to communicate and work with one another. Employees' moods and attitudes change erratically all the time and from person to person. Our bosses may decide to be nice to everybody one day or be intimidating the whole week with one person or everybody, etc. Their mood swings reflect how their own Egos and Models have been influenced and feel at particular times. Therefore, we keep guessing not only the expectations of our colleagues and bosses, but also the moods and behaviour that these expectations or demands are expressed in. Some bosses are mean and selfish regardless of the way an employee performs, anyway. We should guess each person's mood based on our most recent experiences with him/her. Yet, often, we find out that our guess has not been good enough. We just have to absorb another blow to our pride when we receive their orders or demands in different and bizarre behavioural contexts.

We must also always absorb many personality clashes cleverly and mitigate their effects on our lives. Then, plenty of organization politics fluctuate and agitate the overall atmosphere, relationships, and moods regularly. These organization politics are dynamic and require not only our guessing of what they are and why they are so odd, but also refine our responses and relationships according to those demented politics every day. In addition to our bosses, colleagues, and subordinates' unique demands, we must also deal with a variety of personalities of clients, customers, distributors, and suppliers who have their own special needs and agendas.

If not all these personality issues contaminate organization environment enough, add the impact of our own idiosyncrasies when communicating with a large collection of raw personalities. Handling our own personalities is indeed the most difficult task for us, even if we could learn about our flaws and find a motive to adjust our attitudes. When we get involved within organization interactions and relationships, we assess other people and their intentions too harshly. Their verbal messages and our perceptions of them agitate all aspects of our personalities somehow and to some extent. In organizations, every interaction mostly incites Ego and Model. We usually notice our Ego excited, or our Model activated and then either or both of them respond to that special interaction. Our Self is hardly active in organization, since erratic situations, interactions, and politics usually demand instantaneous responses by our Ego and Model—instead of thoughtful, patient reactions by Self. The circumstances in organizations always call for assertiveness, which often leads to aggressions. Often our Ego and Model are charged before we find a chance to really assess the situation from a 'self' viewpoint.

In organization settings, particularly, Self is usually weaker than Ego and suppressed, even when we make conscious efforts to boost it personally as much as possible. Sadly, we usually get involved with organization games quickly and feel obliged to rely on our Ego and Model, at the cost of Self, in order to survive. As the domination of one aspect of personality increases, the other aspect(s) would decline proportionately. Thus, when Ego and Model rise in an organization, we feel no choice but to let Self diminish for good, and thus our overall personality changes, too. If we want to work for an organization without allowing our Self to be suppressed, only following the 'coping mechanism,' which is discussed in Chapter Six, might help us somewhat. In general, organization setting is the most prolific place for Ego and Model to flourish; while it cannot offer any support for enhancing Self. Sometimes we feel sad and guilty about our attitudes and the way we act due to the politics and our dependency on organization. However, we usually forget and go on with our lives.

We suffer when we try hard to suppress Self just to handle the politics, personalities, and hypocrisies in organizations. We suffer from the notion of having to become one of them and acting like them in terms of promoting Ego and Model domination. We hate feeling like a puppet being played by other people's whims and wills. In all, the pressures of adjusting and responding to such deeply ego-driven relationships and interactions, while assessing and challenging our own personality aspects, place a lot of strain on our lives and contribute further to our work related stress.

Clearly, we can hardly grow psychologically under so much dependency to organization and while being subject to so much pressure at work. We get promotions and status, we gain more power, we achieve many organization objectives, and we might even make a lot of money to buy the things that make us feel good about ourselves. Yet, none of these rewards would help us achieve our life objectives, independency, and the ability to see the real values of life. Instinctually, we feel this entrapment and suffer from our weakness to break away from it.

Of course, we suffer even from the idea of having to do the work not helpful to us mentally and emotionally, but must keep doing due to financial needs and job market deficiencies. This pain is felt even more often when we educate ourselves with high hopes and expectations from work based on our (mis)perceptions of work and working conditions suitable for an educated person.

CHAPTER FIVE
Organization Perils

Humans' recurring needs for both dependence and independence probably have the severest effect on our psychological health and growth. During childhood, we rely on our parents for our needs, particularly security. Our mental growth accelerates as we learn to break away from this dependence by forming personal ideas and rejecting our parents' guidance and lifestyles, etc. Most of us succeed to gain a raw sense of independence and self-confidence. But soon, we face the responsibility of work, which brings a big wave of dependency. We become dependent on a new 'entity,' the organization, to give us not only our source of subsistence, but also our sense of security. Moreover, we try to develop our identity as a member of the organization. We adopt its objectives as our own and we hope to develop a worthwhile self-image that we have been unable to build on our own merely based on our personal attributes and personality.

Then, we become even more dependent on organization as we taste and acquire the habit of buying more personal stuff and household items. The chance to buy objects appears to satisfy our sense of gratification and partially make up for our insecurities along with organization pressures. We get addicted to our needs for more things to consume and dependent upon organizations that provide the resources to fulfil those rising superficial needs. Accordingly, organization turns into a parent-like figurehead that rules and controls our minds and energies, and punishes us quickly if we undermine its values and demand for compliance.

Without realizing how deeply we have immersed into another dependency state after our struggles to elude our parents and their demands, we build resentment—subconsciously at least—toward the entity that ignores and suppresses our need for independence and creativity. Still, we submit and get rapt in its rules, politics, and games. Without adequate self-reliance and control over our work contents and conditions, our psychological growth breaks down fundamentally, although we hardly notice it, anyway. We feel obliged to accept organization as a vital, powerful figurehead running our existence.

Then, a harsher dilemma about our needs for 'dependence and independence' besieges us when we get married, since the loss of independence accelerates in all aspects of our lives. Our rising dependency to both organization and our family along with more duties make us even more vulnerable and trapped. To maintain our family, which we need and depend on so badly, too, now we must depend even more on organization.

The Organization Dependence

Organizations control us in many ways other than satisfying our financial and security needs. They create and reinforce our sense of competition and an artificial need to climb the hierarchy of power within an organization structure. The urge for status to feed our Egos has become another superficial need that we have added to our long list of dependencies. Organization provides the opportunity to learn and enjoy the power of controlling people. It makes us feel important and secure, although we are controlled by others—our direct boss at least. We accept the humiliation of being controlled much better when we are ourselves in control of another group. The irony is that most managers secretly believe that the controlling function is most crucial at their level, while their bosses' control is so unnecessary and irrelevant. They view their bosses' control only a formality, and thus the situation feels rather tolerable and acceptable to them. This appears like a good manner of rationalizing our dependencies and fooling ourselves! Occasionally, we notice conflicting signs about control levels and mechanisms, but refuse to adjust our minds regarding the way organization works and the ways we are controlled within it. All we care for is to grab more organization power for ourselves even if a lot of personal sacrifice and hypocrisy is necessary, and even if our integrity and need for independence are jeopardized more daily. Ironically, we subconsciously sense and abhor the pressure of being controlled as much as we try to assume being in charge of things and people ourselves. Nobody has enough authority to feel independent in any organization, private or public.

Yet, we become addicted to power struggles for reaching the top echelons in the shortest time by any means available to us, including office politics, deceit, hypocrisy, favouritism, etc. Even our education (a degree, actually) is mostly for climbing up the ladder faster, which is normally linked to more financial rewards, too. Thus, the incentives for status, power, and money reinforce one another and build up a huge motivation for us to break all the perceivable hurdles, including people—as well as our own spirits—on the way up.

Dependence on this unfeeling entity—organization—makes substantial impact on our psychological health, especially since we had thought, as an adolescent, that we had learned and earned our independence and educated ourselves for a thriving future. Now, our dependence is more complex and confusing, though, with consequences much more stressful and taxing than what it had been with our parents. Parents have passion and love at least that make their type of control rather tolerable and sometimes pleasurable, in fact. Now, our idiotic dependence on organization feels cold, unnatural, and forced, with no passion, purpose, future, or commitment.

The inner conflicts due to personal search for independence, which we remember from adolescence, and the new dependence on rules and demands of organizations affect our self-image, identity, and psychological health, of course. Although our Ego might feel satisfied often during power struggles and our sporadic victories, our Self remains under constant pressure with plenty of inner conflicts. Independence is an absolute, innate state in itself as part of individualism and 'self.' Therefore, its absence is more hurtful than the urge we feel for our other unsatisfied needs. In a normal condition or state, a person must be independent and free. Thus, when it is taken away from us in some (usually harsh) way, we try hard, in any perceivable manner, to regain it to restore our self-image. Nevertheless, while we try to create some form of identity by working for a particular organization, at the end we actually lose more of our self-image and identity.

Independence resides in, and grows mostly through, Self. On the other hand, dependence is a deficiency that we must accept and learn to live with, because it may indirectly fulfil some of our elementary needs. To show our commitment to organization, we resort to our Model to parade our dependence and compliance. We pretend to like our boss, and we complement our colleagues and work rivals meaninglessly. All these shallow efforts consume our energy and spirits. Our inner conflicts mount as we attempt to build our identity as a member of a particular organization, but also as an independent individual with integrity and confidence.

All along, the conflicting needs of our Self and Model clash and stir deeper inner conflicts, while we struggle for, and miss, both independence and the supposed privileges of dependence on organization. Ego's negative role in organizations will be also noted shortly. The three aspects of personality keep competing and struggling to make their impacts for all the special needs of a person in and outside the organization. Then, more chaos erupts when each person's personality aspects try to face other people's personalities. Every two individuals communicate with certain personality aspects based on not only their moods, but also their organization status. For example, when the boss is talking thru his/her Ego, the subordinate better be listening and responding with his/her Model if s/he likes to work for the organization.

Sadly, many of the theories suggested in this trilogy are based on author's personal experiences, which might have, in fact, stirred his interest to study 'human relations' and become so fussy about the depth of these serious social issues! In fact, maybe a real and rather humorous story can depict how individuals' personality aspects interact in organizations.

In the early 1970s, I worked for a large, famous organization in Los Angeles for a few years. In my department, a 62-year-old man (Mr. S.) was assistant manager. We all reported to him as well as the manager. In those times, smoking cigarettes in the office was a normal affair. Many of us, including Mr. S., smoked liberally and rather excessively at our desks every day. For health reasons I quit smoking. The department head, who was a fanatic health-conscious, congratulated me warmly in front of the staff and supported the idea of not smoking. The very next day, Mr. S. announced that he had quit smoking, too. His incited Model had to seek the approval of the boss right away, especially after the boss's big lecture the day before. During the following months, he pretended to bask in his non-smoking self, but went to the washroom 5-6 times every day and locked himself in a stall to smoke. He found many excuses to sneak out of the office just to smoke, too. Yet, the trips to the washrooms were necessary as well. Apparently, he imagined that the smoke and scent flowing out of the stall would not raise any suspicion. Or he trusted his luck too much that nobody would visit the washroom during his mischief. Everybody, including the department manager, knew his secret and schemes, but nobody ever pointed it out. I am sure that even he realized that everybody knew about this masquerade, yet continued this degrading exercise. Maybe he even assumed that the humiliation of pretending to be a non-smoker (even when everybody knew about it) was better for his image than smoking openly. Maybe the department head valued Mr. S's self-sacrifice, too, just for keeping the boss's Ego happy. Two years after I left, I heard Mr. S. had had a heart attack and passed away at the age of 65, just a few months before his retirement. *One may wonder (in surprise or humour) whether the heart attack related more directly to the pressures of hiding this secret for so long with such tenacity than smoking itself.* He was a well-educated, diligent, healthy-looking, and bright person with a happy family, and we all respected him and his work ethics. All of us behave in almost the same manner in organizations, maybe in a more subtle way. Nevertheless, this example is a true reflection of reality in terms of our sacrifices and loss of 'self'-esteem merely for getting the approval of organization and our bosses. It is such a pity, though. Meanwhile, any strategy to fight organizations' culture, if possible, would not be wise for an intelligent person. We had better cope.

The Reality of Organization

Organizations' survival depends on their competitiveness, which leads to their uncompassionate and sometimes ruthless strategies, even if its directors and owners were not inherently too egotistical and often psychopaths. With the continuing rise of international competition and decline of profit margins, the chances are that organizations must keep cutting back expenses in any perceivable way. They must move factories and jobs to countries with cheap labour, rely more on automation, and find means of maximizing efficiencies. Still many of them cannot bear the load of pressures at some point and face bankruptcy and shutdowns. We recognize these basic facts. This gloomy picture and substantial risks in the next few decades apply even to major economies of the world, which then result in wide, global job insecurities for everybody. Therefore, employees are facing a psychologically odd dilemma, since they neither feel the security that organizations are supposed to provide, nor have learned to be independent and master their work and destiny. They just live in anxiety with cynicism about organization work's viability and their options for earning a living.

Meanwhile, organization is only interested in exploiting us, as long as we are healthy, motivated, and loyal. As soon as they do not get all that or cannot afford to pay for our services, they would not think twice before getting rid of us. Therefore, the concept of loyalty to, and dependence on, organization is only a myth at best. Ironically, despite their blunt non-committal attitude and approach toward employee security, organizations expect full dependence and loyalty from their employees. Naturally, it feels hypocritical to ask something from employees when organization itself refuses (or cannot afford) to provide in return. At best, we could possibly say that organization is offering and expecting only a 'conditional loyalty and dependence' while we work for it, and, in return, we are free to leave anytime we wish. This is just another creation of organization for exploiting employees based on some seemingly fair rules. The problem is that it is hard for employees to mentally justify this sense of conditional loyalty and dependence simply because organization thinks it is fair.

Under these circumstances, losing our jobs in organizations is a blessing perhaps, in spite of the loss of (hopefully temporary) income. Getting fired may be a benediction when the alternative is only a lifelong suffering and a constant sense of insecurity in organization. It is a kind of torture to live with constant fears of losing our jobs, while playing organizational politics and games and struggling with our pitiful self-image and confidence as an exploited, futureless employee. Alas, not everybody has grown enough self-image and inner strengths to live alone somewhat independently, even when the alternative is bearing a life with so little privileges. Realistically, fighting organizations' cultures is not a wise strategy even considering all the above points. We had better only learn how to cope.

Many of us might disagree with this negative perspective of organization and its gloomy future, because we have learned to cope with it, have mastered our compliance lessons quickly, and are now fully absorbed in it. We have become an active and loyal cell of this entity and believe in its viability, the same way we believe in the reality of our illusions about life and the perceived world. No wonder so many of us do not question, and actually deny, the futility of life we spend in organizations.

The assertions made here apply to general work conditions that are prevalent in almost all organizations. They reflect the author's personal experiences in several organizations and having the opportunity to study many more. Our attempts to elude this reality and maybe relieve ourselves from the tensions of working in organizations are futile, too, when we helplessly move from one organization to another. More or less, all of them have the same general characteristics and follow the same culture. Thus, moving from one organization to the next usually heightens our disappointment when we find out how widespread organization culture and problems are.

As said earlier, every organization is made of a collection of personalities who should interact for completing some tasks. People make organizations. They (especially those attracted to organization work) all have similar sets of needs, dependencies, and dominant personality aspects. Therefore, the atmospheres and the rules of interactions turn out to be similar with respect to most *viable* management practices and decision processes. When people move from one organization to another, they carry their management skills and mentalities with them and use them in the new ones. Therefore, the same bloods are running in the veins of all organizations, more or less.

With all the fancy theories of management techniques and human relations allegedly developed in recent decades, we keep suffering vastly from organization relationships and demands. We have apparently become a little more tactful and polite in dealing with one another in organizations, but deep down we still feel and deal with the same level of arrogance and apathy—if not more. We have learned how to hide or justify, often with proper documentation, our rigid prejudices, favouritism, discrimination, racism, and other unfair practices. Behind the masks and smiles of friendship and sincerity, we merely nurture our usual thoughts of supremacy and egotism. Management theories have taken a backseat against people's rising hypocrisy and organization's dire corruption. These theories cannot find their place in organizations except just for some prodigal show of management devotion and progress. All these management and organization educations at prominent universities have proven futile and they have hardly led to practical applications in the peculiar organization settings. They have lost their values and effects behind the rising personal evils and egoism in all organizations and government agencies. On the other hand, newer management theories, such as positive psychology, are now propagated for exploiting employees with new gimmicks that merely appear more civilized.

Ego at Work in Organization

Organization is probably the best place to cultivate our Egos and practise them freely. We notice quickly that people's Egos run the organizations and that egoism is equivalent to power, status, money, respect, and recognition. At least this is the way our bosses appear to us even if some good intentions and soft hearts existed behind those egotistic remarks and gestures. Nonetheless, arrogance is used to display confidence; aggressiveness stands for assertiveness; and superficiality rules substance and conscience. If a person wants to be logical and fair or if he does not know how to use his Ego yet, then he rather be ready for a tough ride, for a while at least until he learns his lessons to follow the herd.

Therefore, if we feel comfortable working for an organization, and if we are allowed to flourish, it means that we have the right talents and personality to become a good member of this haughty structure according to its norms. It means we feel, acknowledge, and strive for the same rotten work practices and politics that our bosses advocate. Alternatively, we might be too submissive and desperate, thus somehow survive in organization with our show of total compliance. These are the two most popular ways people use to survive and grow in an organization. Among many tricks, we learn to boost and pamper the boss's Ego all the time at all cost. In return, we are allowed to cultivate our own Egos and feed them leisurely to grow bigger daily as long as they do not interfere with, or get close to the size of, the boss's Ego.

Egoism is the reality of organization, though this might not be quite evident to us, as pretences and words are usually deceiving. They keep us confused and amused. The clever boss knows, like the rest of us, how to manipulate others by using his/her Model and hide his/her Ego with a fake show of support, promises, and phoney incentives. Yet, egoism rules in organizations as both a symbol and symptom of power and control.

In turn, we pamper our own personal Egos in organization by playing politics to receive acceptance from our staff, boss, and colleagues. To get acceptance and attract the attention of others, we also use our Model to hide our egoism and insecurity. We hide our emotions and thoughts about others and say things that they like to hear. We learn how to respond to egotistical needs of others in return for their acceptance and approval of us that their Model might disseminate generously. We know deep down how artificial all these comments and complements are, but we accept them and use them to boost our Egos, anyway. We must feed our Egos somehow, even if it means shutting our eyes and ears, and ignoring the phoniness of this baffling, brutal environment.

We enjoy the chance of pampering our egoism and controlling others. This mechanism for sensing, expressing, and fulfilling our feeling of supremacy is refreshing. It is also a means of relieving our frustration, while egoism reflects our absolute certainty about things and having solutions for all situations and problems. With egoism, we believe, and expect everybody to believe, too, that 'we are right' about everything, more like a superhuman with super intelligence, and we ensure that this message is conveyed to all staff continuously and it is properly acknowledged.

Egoism is about making people feel dumb, and for abusing our position of authority. Moreover, egoist hates being challenged or stopped. Egoist thinks only in an autocratic fashion, although he may pretend to encourage and appreciate team approach and participation. Criticism and suggestions are usually unacceptable, especially when made by employees outside the organization pack. Organization pack, of course, consists of those who have proven their loyalty and play their Models the best.

Usually the person at the top of the organization determines and propagates the characteristics and rules of the herd. S/he also selects the members of the pack from amongst those who have passed the tests of loyalty and do not challenge him/her and his/her disciples—those who feed his/her Ego the best, those who provide special services to him/her when necessary, and those who know how to use their Models to suck up and gain his/her trust. A person who shows even minimal signs of individualism, or disregards the rules of compliance, has no chance of getting in the pack. Many other interesting features of organization politics have gradually turned into inherent nature of work. For example, the level of intelligence has to be kept at a certain level suitable for the boss. Intelligence or expression of wisdom beyond the limits set by the pack would place the individual in a vulnerable position. Even the organization structure and the importance of its various departments are set according to the boss's preference and expertise. For instance, the boss's level of analytical aptitude determines the criteria applied for productivity and performance measurements with regard to organization affairs and the people allowed in the pack.

Some bosses prefer detail information and insist on technical reports and then in a few months the next boss complains about too much information. A department receives special attention or is scrutinized for downsizing depending on the boss's perception about the importance of that function based on his/her personal aptitude, or knowledge, in that field or his feelings towards that particular department head. These kinds of games are regularly played, often with little concern for organization effectiveness, efficiency, or compassion for employees who eagerly come to an organization with deep assumptions about equality and fairness.

All the rules in organization naturally reflect the desires and preferences of the head and perhaps the members of the pack. Becoming a member of the pack, or as an outside guest to receive some benefits, depends on the pack's mentality and norms, but also how nicely a person can demonstrate his/her loyalty and submissiveness. The pack controls the power and politics of the organization and distributes positions, promotions, personnel, and all the organization privileges. The rest of the work force remains second rank citizens who 'should be thankful to have a job,' as far as the members of the elite pack are concerned.

Of course, personal abilities play a role in the initial selection and progress of individuals in an organization. Organizations need expertise to run their affairs, especially the technical aspects, yet have no sense of loyalty to them. Organizations know how to satisfy their technical requirements and how to bring submissive technocrats in their service. Yet, the general rules and atmosphere revolves around the ego and model personalities that govern the organization life and employees' progress. In recent years, these technocrats have shown their frustration and power, though, often by leaking vital information. They have made big organizations and governments feel vulnerable in the hands of technocrats. So now, organizations and governments would surely invent more ways of controlling the data and expertise in organizations.

Whenever someone moves up the organization hierarchy to a new responsibility, his/her Ego rises proportionately. The newly boosted Ego quickly demands changes, not only to match his/her mindset and alleged creativity, but also to affirm his/her authority as soon as possible. Organization politics and plans also change whenever a new boss arrives and suddenly staff should adjust themselves to his/her needs. They should re-adapt themselves fast to new formats and contents of financial reports, the contents and tone of official letters, public relations' scope, etc. However, most radically, they should fathom and adjust themselves to the new boss's Ego and demands and fine-tune their Models accordingly, too. Employees may explain why things are being done in certain ways. However, suddenly all those methods and policies are no longer good, since the newly arrived Ego likes to test and solidify his/her presence. A department may even have some long-term programs and strategic plans specifically devised for boosting organization effectiveness and efficiencies, but often they do not matter any more if not fully aligned with the new boss's taste or private agenda.

Change is a vital necessity for every organization and a sign of progress with time and economic dynamics. They should, however, reflect solid goals and criteria for long-term efficiency and effectiveness. In such circumstances, change is introduced to support new organization requirements and philosophy. On the other hand, ego-driven changes that merely reflect management whims and tastes often raise only tension and conflicts, instead of improving an organization's productivity. They merely decrease employee morale that affects its effectiveness and efficiencies. It only wastes a lot of energy and time to cope with personal needs of the new boss or for justifying unnecessary projects contracted to certain favoured groups. In the process, employees face the added pressures of non-essential changes, and feel more stress and a sense of futility for all their past works. Ego-ridden changes also reflect the new boss's inflexibility or inaptitude to study and understand the way things had worked.

With their high Egos, boss's trust and confidence in others is also minimal. For a long time, often, s/he does not trust anybody, while s/he pushes to assert him/herself as the person in charge and in control of our lives. S/he monitors every detail and makes most decisions and actions in order to ensure that staff is learning and implementing his/her ideas, mostly to ensure his/her controls are in place, while his/her egotistical certitude and pride compel him/her to change the methods and practices. Staff feel powerless and humiliated regularly and still have to polish their Models more every day—to thank the boss for being such an insightful person and to tell him/her how amazingly his/her changes and policies would boost the organization performance in a huge way!

Employees notice their boss's lack of trust and still occasionally dare to declare their humble views, which the new boss often sets aside politely or reject bluntly. Yet, some of their good ideas that are rejected today may re-appear in a few days as the boss's own initiative and creativity. Egoistical bosses often take credit for the contributions of others selfishly, ruthlessly, and shamelessly in order to reinforce their powerbases.

Endangered Greedy Giants

In all, organization is an Ego-driven and soulless entity we create with our sweats and hearts at a big cost to our minds and spirits. Still, we receive more rejections from it than understanding. We do not get the love one would expect from this relationship by the virtue of our sacrifices for this monster. We see it as a creature rather than a place or people within it, because it is neither of them; it has its own life and character(istics). Organization is, in fact, a live entity that combines many individuals' eccentricities and Egos that clash and inter-activate one another around some hierarchical relationships. They intend to permeate organization objectives and culture, and work collectively and productively towards them. Yet, in reality, organization manifests more like a collection of competing personalities with unreliable objectives, incongruent motives, crooked perceptions, pathetic vanities, fears, and insecurities, desperately struggling to make the best of their limited energies and resources. An organization is supposedly an independent entity legally and inherently, but it is strained by a vast amount of dependencies it must establish with its employees, suppliers, customers, governments, etc., and it usually fails to do so effectively, too. In the end, modern organizations are turning into careless monsters damaging our cultures, human spirits, the public's basic needs, and humanity. Their struggles to align their incongruent objectives per se are also getting them entangled in big messes that would most likely lead to their hurtful demise and extinction around the globe.

CHAPTER SIX
Organization Relations

'Human relations' affect all aspects of social and organizational life. Many major decisions we should make daily also demand good knowledge of human and organization relations. The level of harm that human nature[‡] alone inflicts upon society through family and organization relations is huge. Therefore, this chapter concentrates on organization relations, while marital relations are emphasized in Parts III and IV. The pains that we cause and bear out of necessity in organizations are growing fast in line with the world's accelerating socioeconomic deficiencies, which humans seem incapable of controlling.

Discussing the intricacies and pains of organization relations takes several books, as many facets of organization environment must be assessed separately way beyond the general hurdles and sufferings noted in this part of the book. At the same time, getting cynical and pessimistic about organizations from the beginning is not useful and it is not meant to be the message conveyed in this book, either. The whole point is to remain realistic, while raising our self-awareness with an open mind about our varied personal needs besides organization work with all its tempting traps.

[‡] Human nature's vast flaws are explained in Volume II of this trilogy.

Remembering the Basics

Organization relations are quite complex, sensitive, and ominous, but remembering even some basic facts makes the task of coping in organizations somewhat easier, so Part II of this book has been designed to stress on these facts in some detail. This knowledge and foresight about organizations can somewhat mitigate people's level of initial shock and prepare them for the setbacks and stress. It might also prove helpful for self-reflection and planning about organization work if it is going to be one's lifetime engagement. If people must work for organizations, they had better have a good perception of what to expect at least.

Any setting or entity with a few chains of command is called an 'organization' for our purpose here. Not its functions or size, but rather the nature of work (employee) relationships defines an organization. The best indicator of an organization's health is the effectiveness and efficiency of staff relationships, and the degree of personal freedom given to employees to determine their work contents and working conditions. With minimal hierarchy, the nature of an organization approaches that of a self-employment. An example is the situation of physicians working for a hospital. While they belong to a large organization, their independence makes them feel more like freelance professionals. Yet, not even one in a million jobs can offer enough independence to elude the psychological pressures of working for an organization. Clearly, self-employment provides a chance to choose the contents of our work and create our working conditions. In reality, however, we must remain more practical and adapt ourselves to organization work, because self-employment is tough and insecure, too.

While we struggle with our dependence on organizations for our financial and security needs, we also recognize the need for even a higher level of dependence on people who work there or use its services. We feel this high sense of dependency because we need their cooperation to get our jobs done and to mitigate their malice. These complex relations create mutual dependencies with some kind of reserved trust. Thus, we must learn the art of managing these mutual trusts and dependencies for almost all the work we do. We must establish various trust levels with different people and interact with them based on certain guidelines, rules, impressions, and schemes that we envision and hope to enforce successfully. All these extra relationships and dependencies, and our games to maintain them, cause a huge amount of stress. Yet they are the necessities of working for an organization. The sooner we learn these tough lessons, the less stress we cause for ourselves and others.

Every employee has many colleagues to work with, bosses to report to, and a staff to supervise, each with his/her own needs and expectations. We attempt to grasp these needs and respond to them as constructively as we can, while giving our own needs a higher priority all along. Besides the endless hassle of reconciling these (inter)personal needs combined with individuals' peculiar idiosyncrasies, the pervasive climate and politics of organization impose ongoing pressures and constraints on all employees, thus complicate organization relations even further. Work conditions and atmosphere deflate employees' moods and morale within this hectic environment, too, thus they in turn get on each other's nerves. Depending on their organizational status, responsibilities, authorities, and personalities, they develop unique, harsh views of these relationships and still try hard to face all these incongruities somehow. The big boss, totally devoted to the organization life and objectives, has a unique perception and hopes to develop a special culture and a set of relationships with staff. Conversely, a young person usually joins the organization with pride, innocence, a desire for independence, and very little knowledge of prevalent organization politics and atmosphere.

Organization relations are ominous, not only in the way they affect our tempers, but also how we infect many other people's moods both inside and outside the organization, thus heighten the stress level in society, too. We become responsible for the anxiety of people reporting to us and tolerating our egotistical demands and pressures for weeks and years. We infect our families' lives with our stress, impatience, and desperation. In addition, we are accountable to our ignored 'self' for destroying our precious lives in organizations, as we keep undermining our potentialities and life objectives. We torture our spirits by bearing organization and our bosses' dire demands. Organization relationships are ominous, since the deprivations and agonies they cause make the value of rewards we get, including job security and the chance to boost our Egos, questionable if our health suffers in the process and our relationships with 'self' and family are ruined, too. Yet, we feel obliged to continue with this charade our entire lives.

In general, we encounter resistance in three fronts as part of organization relationships: Our bosses like to suppress us; our colleagues fight to surpass us; and our subordinates always strive to second-guess us.

The snag with our bosses relates to their expectations from us to produce more and pamper their Egos way above our capacity. That is a major challenge for our Egos per se! The problem with our colleagues stems from rivalry and purposeful hurdles they create for one another regularly in different ways. They are all striving to show off their talents and loyalty to the boss and prove their competence and creativity. Usually employees strive to prove themselves by undermining other individuals' contributions and ideas. They resist cooperation and block the flow of information, and actually stir ongoing frictions and conflicts just to sabotage their colleagues' chances of winning favouritism with the boss. Ironically, all these crooked gimmicks feel quite essential and natural to us for surviving in an organization and perhaps moving up the ladder.

Then, our subordinates usually have unrealistic expectations and many unsatisfied needs that they hope we or an organization can fulfil. When their demands cannot be met, they only find us responsible and hostile to them. They blame us for organization shortfalls and pressures. Moreover, if they lose their motivation and efficiency, we face another set of problems. They also like to undermine our authority and expertise for many reasons, but mainly to prove themselves around the department and in the organization. We face conflicts since we usually cannot respond to our subordinates' needs and pressures; but we get into trouble also if we cannot motivate our staff or monitor their performance daily without getting into another round of confrontations and work blockage. When we do a poor job, as a manager, e.g., by being softer on our staff, we do not get the best performance from our subordinates, and our bosses blame us for it, too. Still, if we put more demands on staff to work harder, their grievances to higher management reflect negatively upon us again. Therefore, even when we are a fair manager in an organization, we face too many irresolvable, stressful problems. All along, our subordinates keep second-guessing our technical knowledge and management skill in order to push their own crooked agendas or as an excuse for their low performance and motivation.

In all, the reality of 'organization relations' is that employees should, a) adapt quickly to a variety of individuals' tempers and demands, as well as organization objectives, often at the cost of never finding or following their own personal objectives, b) face debilitating pressures that taint their morale and moods, and c) be prepared to lose their mental freedom and a chance to explore their innate potentialities. These and many other tough dilemmas arise from organization relations and affect our psyches, personal lives, and careers deeply. Yet, every employee has some options to mitigate those pressures.

A few deficiencies discussed here portray the inescapable, immense role of organizations within the structure of human life. The harsh realities of organization life are clear to most of us, but we doubt its scope and effect on our wellbeing, while humans' welfare and survival is becoming subject to the growing role of organizations in societies. We also forget that we deserve some blame ourselves for so much of this chaos, too, due to our poor nature and quirks besides our role in heightening the power of organizations and spreading our Egos within them.

Specifically, we should evaluate our roles and responsibilities and learn how our hypocritical needs and Egos contribute to the demise of organizations and societies. At the same time, we must study the effect of our submission to the rules and demands of organizations on our psychological and physical health.

Options for Organization Relations

We have three options with respect to organization work: We can avoid it, cope with it, or get absorbed in it. From the tone of this book, the ideal would be to avoid it if at all possible, or at least make plans for faster retirement and freedom. The amount of sufferings that we inflict upon ourselves and others by working for an organization is simply too much to ignore lightly. In the big scheme of personal life purposes, especially, the rewards of working for an organization are too little to justify our lifelong 'self' sacrifices. On the other hand, national and world economies depend on organizations and organized efforts. Moreover, we feel responsible to contribute to society and humanity by participating in organization activities and work. Most importantly, of course, there would never be enough non-organizational jobs around if many of us decided to earn our living rather independently away from organization hassles.

In fact, the set dependence between organizations and humans is causing a major social dilemma, nowadays, as most of us need organization work, and organizations need us, too, until they no longer need enough of us in the near future due to automation and artificial intelligence replacing humans. *Then what?*

Some wiser, stoic individuals may find a path to live outside this imposed life structure with simpler needs and values. Sadly, however, most of us must depend on organizations because we cannot locate or design non-organizational works for ourselves. On the other hand, we can still minimize our frictions and stress by learning more about the nature of organizations with the aim of choosing a civil relationship with everybody and our spirits.

A big difference exists between 'having' and 'wanting' to work for an organization. This is a major distinction between the options of coping with organization work and being absorbed in it. Knowing our options and choices, as limited as they may be, we can build our organization life with a higher consciousness, deep awareness, high patience, and low expectations. We know organization is nevertheless helping us fulfil some of our basic urges and resolve our insecurities somewhat. It is also a better option than sitting at home and following a sluggish life. Despite its hazards, which we should remain cognizant of, organization gives us the opportunity to make a living and learn a few things about life, *especially human nature*, and to acquire experiences that only organization settings avail. Even our harsh interactions with our bosses and colleagues are useful and educational if they are used peacefully for self-awareness and social consciousness.

While we 'have to work' for an organization, our best option is to try to cope with its work contents and conditions rather than allowing ourselves get absorbed or stressed out. By coping, we prepare ourselves and our attitudes to view things in a productive perspective despite all the inevitable, unfair pressures. We adjust our expectations, thus tolerate the critiques and cheap shots from our bosses and colleagues much better. Simply, we know why people do or say foolish things. We realize that all these games and hypocrisies are unavoidable and part of the deal. We accept that people's Egos and Models dominate their behaviours and management styles and render them somehow helpless in terms of their debilitating characters. The main goal of discussions in Part II about organizations has been to help us with this 'coping' mechanism, which is elaborated specifically in the next section.

As noted before, the sense of security we expect to get from organization work is tentative at best. However, unless we have built a self-reliant personality and independent career, it would be difficult to resist the limited security that organization seems to offer. Some feeling of security is better than none, after all. Even a shallow perception of security is better than the pressures of insecurity, despite the pains and damages of organization work. On the other hand, our doubts about the stability and reliability of this security might cause some inner conflicts, self-doubts, and self-pity in the end. It is hard to solve all these dilemmas when we need financial and emotional security. Yet, knowing about all these aspects of organization and personal issues related to work can help us make a better decision for our particular case and for building our coping strategy. It all depends on our personalities and the level of our insecurities. If we are not psychologically equipped to face some feelings of insecurity, we are driven to seek security outside ourselves, which often leads to organization work. Conversely, personal independence has a high priority for self-reliant people with low sense of insecurity, whether they choose to work for an organization or not. For this lucky group, keeping their mental freedom provides an offsetting victory and enough rewards to curb the inevitable, occasional feelings of insecurity or the burdens of working for an organization.

While we remain at the mercy of organizations to satisfy our financial and other needs, we may ultimately keep the option of discovering our own independent work open and explore other opportunities all along. Some may pursue side activities more in line with their life objectives and plans to become independent from organization work eventually. Only few of us may succeed, yet our efforts and thoughts about freedom from organizations are crucial psychologically all by themselves. This proactive attitude helps our self-awareness, lowers our anxiety and depression, and offers a constructive approach to gain our independence one day. All along, we keep reminding ourselves that we are only coping with organization work without letting ourselves being absorbed or stressed out. We always remember the bigger picture about the essence of our being, adopt a simpler lifestyle, elude extravagance, and cope actively with organization demands.

Coping in Organizations

By coping, we ensure our efforts and contributions are adequate in line with our responsibilities. We keep the best interests of the organization in mind and give our full attention and cooperation to its activities and goals. We simply stop playing our model and ego personalities to their extremes like those employees absorbed in organization work. We do a decent job without the need to convince everybody how fair we are, how hard we work, how intelligent we are, etc. We do not compliment others just for the sake of playing organization politics, but do not compete unfairly or excessively, either. We avoid immorality against organization without letting our morale be ruined by other employee's egoism and organization demands. We become the master of the work that organization wants us to do in the most professional manner. If we think of better ways of doing some tasks, we bring it to our superior's attention without getting attached to our ideas. Still, we are prepared to see our ideas dumped, politely postponed, or sent through the black hole of bureaucratic channels, if not appearing later suddenly as our boss's own clever idea.

The principles of coping are naturally not easy to grasp before we learn a great deal about our Ego and ways of controlling it. In a sense, coping is equivalent to giving up egoism and false pride largely. Assuming we understand, and adopt, coping principles, they are still very hard to implement. Even when our egotistical temptations (which feel at home within organization settings) seem partly tamed, we must still cope with the constant pressures that organization places on us, directly and indirectly, to become and remain part of its culture, and perhaps even try to become a member of the pack by showing our blind loyalty and sucking-up capability. Actually, our coping attitude might be misunderstood, too, at least initially, and result in serious repercussions. We may break under incessant pressures and give up our commitment to build our sense of semi-independence. Besides our inner strengths that can help us through this harsh, humiliating process, our only consolation is that management may eventually comprehend that our coping intentions are innocent and harmless, if not actually useful for the company's objectives. Hence, they might let us be and do our things somewhat, though they are perhaps not thrilled about the personalized culture that we are now introducing.

It is amazing how, and how much, our managerial skills grow inadvertently because of our coping attitude. As we stop playing organization politics and games, we find it easier to be frank and honest with everybody, especially those who report to us, with tact and a cordial smile. Our staffs sense our goodwill quickly, too, and increase their cooperation and efforts. They notice we are not going to steal their ideas or suppress their suggestions because of our egoism and personal needs. They trust us, as they notice we are not a management puppet or keen to undermine their contributions. They notice that we are helpful to them, more like a mentor than a supervisor. Of course, we cannot ignore the fact that we are still responsible as an assertive manager when it is required. Our subordinates also learn that, while it is easier to get along with their (coping) boss, our demands might indeed be more serious than the case might be for a selfish boss who puts his own interests even ahead of organization effectiveness and efficiency. Everybody may have to work harder and care more, because the coping boss is always conscious and protective of organization interests. Thus, any misunderstanding of our coping attitude and relaxed personality is corrected quickly by assertive reactions. In all, coping does not mean becoming passive and careless, but rather more relaxed and objective. It does not mean less work pressures and productivity, but rather less tension and ambition with no interest to strive for superficial organizational status, or pursuing goals of speedy promotions at any costs.

Another positive outcome of coping is the substantial increase in a person's confidence level. Authentic confidence results from 'self' enhancement, which is an objective of 'coping.' When we overcome our egotistical needs and stop playing our Model too often for the sake of organization status and acceptance, we do not care much about the consequences of non-conformity or our non-compliance. The coping person is not always unorthodox deliberately, though it usually looks that way to the organization. Nonetheless, with coping, some sense of self-reliance erupts in person and results in a big increase in the level of self-confidence. Oddly enough, because of this confidence, the organization starts viewing him/her in a new light and appreciates his/her honest efforts. Organization sees confidence as a symptom of egoism (though not necessarily true), which it often values and perhaps even rewards. However, real rewards would not occur before a person's complete loyalty and submission is noted and cleverly tested. This is a major lesson that we learn about organization. That is, personal image is more visible and valued by organization than one's real contributions. Again, that is why Model is such a prevalent personality aspect in organizations almost parallel to Ego. Showing arrogance (fake confidence) is much more potent than real confidence and actual performance.

The opposite is also true. That is, if we do not know how to maintain and show our confidence, organization has all the power and intentions to take away all the pride and confidence we bring to an organization. With the loss of our independence, we begin to give in more and more to organization's ways and Egos. Harsh, purposeful intimidations persist when organization has no special interest in us and when it notices our lack of confidence. And, of course, when we feel insecure about our jobs, the impact of organization intimidations or indifference could further harm our frail confidence and self-image. Thus, the more organization senses our insecurity and lack of confidence, the more it sees and seizes the opportunity to exercise its authority and its intentions to exploit and humiliate us. Exactly when we need psychological support, it deliberately deprives us from it and instead intensifies the pressures. Thus, the confidence that our developed coping mechanism creates would be precious for securing our future in organizations without being submissive or stressing out ourselves for fitting in. Of course, we must not mistake the idea of 'calm confidence' with 'showy arrogance.' Coping never has any sign of arrogance in it.

Often our colleagues stop taking us seriously when they sense our coping attitude, instead of full compliance—exactly like the games kids play in kindergarten. When our playmates or partners feel that we are not taking the game seriously, they ask us to get serious or leave. This is exactly the way organization games are played as well. If our colleagues, in particular, do not witness our anguish and hardship, they do not consider our efforts adequate and serious enough. They get offended because we cannot hide our coping attitude. And they also get offended, because they envy our *seeming* subtle arrogance and feel ashamed of their full absorption in the organization. They feel sad and mad when their Model driven games do not impress us. As a coping employee, however, we know how to disregard management's and staff's offences without getting frustrated or showing our displeasure. Nor do their sarcastic remarks and oppositions overly humiliate or irritate us. We would not put extra work into a project to prove our points, either. Nor would our Model make too much effort to please everybody for the sake of manipulating them. It manifests merely to show our sense of cooperation and respect that we share to get the jobs done. With coping, we keep a safe distance from organization objectives and work, but perform our jobs to the best of our abilities in line with those objectives. We view work as a contract to accomplish something for the special plans of organization, although they are not necessarily in line with our tastes or personal life objectives. Although this attitude may look, or even feel, like a passive approach to work, our intention is only to relax as much as possible and do a good job for organization, too, while satisfying our own sense of pride for the honest work we are doing for the organization and our staff.

Naturally, mastering all the coping mechanisms noted in this section requires extraordinary talent, patience, and commitment. We learn excellent managerial skills that we cannot acquire any other way, even by going to best universities. These skills are not easy attributes and conditions that all of us can learn and perform successfully, at least not before a long period of learning and practising. That is why coping mechanism has been suggested here as an exceptional, but still feasible, option for enlightened and smart people. Coping requires lots of extra work to defuse the negative reactions of our colleagues and management on most occasions. We should push ourselves to be patient, tactful, assertive, flexible, *maybe even kind,* and so many other things on top of performing the best job we can offer to an organization. But at the end, all this extra work pays off, at least in terms of lower stress and a chance to grow our 'self,' instead of playing silly games and politics to flourish.

Options of Getting Absorbed

On the other hand, when we get absorbed in organization work, work becomes our identity. We take full ownership of it, as if it were the matter of life and death. We become possessive of work and organization objectives. We might even resist organization norms and policies, as we imagine our ways of doing things can help the organization better, even if they are sometimes against the organization culture, including its rigid rules for loyalty and compliance. We get too serious about our responsibilities with the same high intensity and passion we handle personal issues. In fact, a person might get attached at the cost of jeopardizing even his/her personal and family needs. Sometimes, even management might tolerate or support such devotion and temporary deviations from organization rules, as a reward for such proven absorption, if the merits of such personal attachment become tangible. Then again, resisting and rejecting organization culture are not allowed to become a habit.

Absorption in organization work happens in two ways: For the lack of better terminologies, we may distinguish them as 'egotistical' versus 'feeble' absorption.

'Egotistical absorption' in organization is the product of our supreme Ego tendencies to strive for power and recognition at all cost. Organization incentives boost our Egos and stamina to climb up the organization hierarchy for higher status, get our superiors' approval, become a member of the organization pack, and maybe even replace our boss, without him/her suspecting our sneaky intentions. Very soon, we get absorbed in our selfish motivations and intentions, thus we devote ourselves to work and assume a large domain of responsibilities even beyond those specified in our job description. Organization becomes the focus of our lives, because we believe it can satisfy our needs for status, power, and identity. In those situations, one's life objectives melt into the organization objectives. In fact, workaholics and people obsessed with organization work and objectives are products of their lack of dominant personal objectives. They must rely on organization to provide their source of life objectives and achievements. Often organization recognizes and rewards their devotion and loyalty, which reinforces more absorption and dependence. After all, what else can an organization expect from a worker who adopts its objectives as his own (personal life objectives) wholeheartedly, and then puts his whole health and time on line to satisfy them. True, the high rewards these workers get are supposedly well worth their loyalty and devotion. Yet, everybody should decide personally how valuable money or other kinds of rewards can really be when the basic experiences of life—that are achievable, divine, and enjoyable—are sacrificed and ignored.

This kind of 'egotistical absorption' causes many problems for organizations, too. Organization routines and relationships are contaminated due to the severe emotional attachment of these absorbed managers and their rigid way of thinking and acting. Most annoying and harmful, they lose their objectivity, as they get obsessed with organization targets and their peculiar strategies. They cultivate the nucleus of organization philosophy and culture according to their narrow knowledge and mentality. They set the rules of compliance and loyalty. They spread seeds of mistrust, suspicion, conspiracy, and egotism. Staff's levels of contributions and achievements are gauged in term of personal standards that this elite group imposes based on its biases, principles, and, worst of all, its limited vision of life values outside the organization sphere. They stay in the office very late in the evening and soon everybody learns that they must stay and pretend to be working, too, or else risk losing points with the boss. A fierce competition is going on in many organizations, nowadays, in terms of who stays at work after hours the longest. So many people are just pretending to be working so late beyond regular hours merely to play the organization game. The stress and loss of personal time for staff, for no tangible results or reason, is so pathetic, while the level of inefficiencies in organizations and society grows directly due to these pretentious attitudes and organization games.

Suggesting that 'egotistical absorption' should or could be abolished would be naive. We can hardly convince others and ourselves to adjust our Egos, appreciate the real values of life, and find our own life objectives outside organizations to satisfy our personal needs for achievement and fulfilment. Most of us are ready and willing to be fully absorbed in an organization to satisfy our Egos and ambitions the best we can. This is the most desired level of personal involvement in an organization. Besides, a good majority of us do not have, or cannot develop, personal life objectives or philosophy, thus welcome the opportunity to adopt organization objectives as our own. In fact, most of us try to reach the highest status in organizations, although only a few succeed due to various obstacles, including our limited or bruised Egos, our Models' frailty to dominate or manipulate others, our inabilities to demonstrate enough loyalty to organization, etc.

Organization problems and relations affect us deeply, not only because they last and affect our entire lives and cause sufferings, and not only because we seem so helpless to do anything about this entrapment, but also because it is our own egotistical needs and ignorance that have created this whole mess. It is not the next person or our neighbour who must adjust his attitude and Ego to reduce humans' misery. Only our own shallow lifestyles, reliance on organizations, hang-ups, and Egos have brought us to such a dismal state of helplessness. Meanwhile, the enormity of modern humans' egotistical absorption in organizations in line with vile socioeconomic mechanisms has brought humanity to its knees.

'Feeble absorption,' on the other hand, reflects a sad state of ultimate helplessness. We neither are accepted in the organization pack due to our Model and Ego shortfalls, nor have learned how to cope with organization life, while also unable to break away from it completely. In this pathetic state, we do not know the art of coping to maintain at least some pride and relative control in the organization. We simply yield to organization demands and still try hopelessly to get its approval and acceptance. We have been disappointed repeatedly by organization's response to our loyalties and show of compliance, and we have not been allowed to pass certain levels of organization hierarchy. As noted before, this happens for many reasons. We may not grasp or cannot play organization games or politics expertly, or we do not have the right charisma and mix of model-ego personality. Thus, nothing we do would help our case. We are solely sacrificing more pride and energy. Eventually, we may give up struggling for approval, but are now completely dependent on organization for everything we have in our lives, including our sense of security, financial needs, a family, and a source of amusement and purpose in life. If our organization life were taken away from us, we would have a hard time to adjust and survive.

In 'feeble absorption,' we have a low self-image and ability to enforce even a moderate sense of independence. We have simply given up not only our hopes for organization advancement, but also our sense of self-worth and ability to analyse or value our life. In 'feeble absorption,' we do not show any sign of resistance to the source of our problems. Instead, we embrace organization demands even harder out of our sense of insecurity and need for dependence. We are purely absorbed and diminished. In this sad state, we probably cannot even grasp the philosophy of coping that can help bring our self-image and independence back to an acceptable level. It would be too late most often after a person is feebly absorbed, anyway.

It is interesting to know that we may be in either 'egotistical' or 'feeble' absorption state temporarily during various stages of our organization life. In the early years, we could be in any of these two, and perhaps even a 'coping,' state and then gradually move to a final, steady state that can be characterized by either of these two types of absorptions. Due to irregular disappointments or unexpected encouragements and promotions, we could move to many directions. However, they are temporary. We soon reach the kind of absorption that our ego-model personalities support.

Organization Lessons Ignored

Most of us have noticed and felt organizations' typical problems and lived with their related pains and anxiety. Still, we doubt our impressions of the inherent hypocrisy that taints all organizations like a plague. Nobody, not even governments, seems interested or able to do anything about the situation, either. We just undermine or justify organization evils, since we need a job and a setting to boost our Egos. We feel humiliated when organizations suppress our drives for individualism and crush our Egos, especially if it appears to be surpassing the boss's acceptable tolerance level. Then, suddenly, we might feel good about organization when our bosses or colleagues pamper our Ego for their own purposes. The perpetual cycles of enjoying and resenting our jobs coincide with the constant rotations of our Egos being suppressed or boosted. Nonetheless, while in the surface we have our good and bad days in an organization due to the state of our Egos, our psyches are hammered under continuous pressures and all the stress from the cyclical humiliations, doubts about organization intentions, our role in the midst of it all, etc.

Like any other kind of emotional relationship, we have three options in an organization, too: cope with it, get absorbed in it, or abandon it. Any of these options has its purpose and means, each with its own limitations and potentials, as noted before. However, based on our decision, the consequences of our lifetime efforts to manage and endure this relationship differ, while our spirits and psyches are affected accordingly as well.

Since organization is run predominantly through Ego and Model, seldom does a Self-driven person work in an organization for long or remain pure. Surely, some Self (compassion mostly) emerges in the attitudes and performance of employees now and then. Yet, mostly Ego and Model combine to create the best means of exploiting others. This type of exploitive mentality best depicts the characteristics of an organization. It gives us a chance to develop and impose our Egos with the aid of the manipulative power of our Models. Our membership in organizations allows and guarantees this right for all, as long as we demonstrate our loyalty and pamper our bosses' Egos properly, routinely. This alleged privilege of organization work abolishes our chance of applying compassion and fairness, as a sign of Self, for running organization affairs. The more organization allows us to feed our own Egos, the more we lose our Self and spirits. Any innocent newcomer to the organization sees all these facts and learns so many crooked gimmicks quickly to adapt him/herself in order to flourish. Meanwhile, s/he gradually builds up the same mentality for running all other facets of his/her life, too. When s/he starts working for an organization, s/he quickly learns that control and compliance are the basic principles of survival, but also the gate to the ego-land. The kingdom of egoism is awaiting him/her with an abundance of absurdities and ignorance of the Self.

We learn many gloomy facts about organization and lose our morale by working in one for a few years. However, mostly our cynicism increases about the purpose of all those futile activities, rivalries, and humiliations. We wonder why people behave so oppressively and offensively towards one another. What is the point of so much hostility behind those superficially calm, happy faces? For some of us, it could be quite shocking if we have not heard about the realities of organization and suddenly face it head on. We struggle forever with our doubts about human nature and the way we interact. We strive to grasp and cope with so much wickedness in organizations. We move from one organization to the next in search of humanity, less humiliation, and bearable work conditions. We may never stop doubting an organization's absurdities or its ability to secure a source of employment for us. Yet, we eventually establish some kind of relationship with it and strive hard all our lives to keep our jobs and justify our narrow purposes for this relationship. We try to establish a relationship with an organization due to our job responsibilities as well as our dependency on it. However, this relationship is not limited to what we produce and how good the products are. Instead, this relationship must be judged in terms of psychological advantages and aggravations inherent in organization work.

Imminent Organization Revolution

Nevertheless, we feel obliged to work for reasons enumerated in Chapter Three, but mainly for making a living. Meanwhile, however, many people are getting trapped in their jobs just for satiating their endless thirsts for power, self-gratification, or wealth. Still, we could at least gauge our criteria about these kinds of achievements versus our natural needs for identity and spiritualism, instead of only following the crowd, growing a phony personality, and perishing in society. We might adjust our mindsets to explore our being now and then, while also fulfilling our primary needs for working.

Surely, people who denounce organization work and culture might appear hostile, rigid, and incapable of social adaptation. Still, infamy is the price they should pay for their convictions on top of their struggles for earning a living. This group is making a major life decision to resist organization temptations for money and status, and to repress their egoistic drives that can be best pampered in organizations, all for some seemingly worthy causes (personal and global) they believe in. They abandon their direct relations with organizations (public and private) in an attempt to strengthen their sense of independence and responsibility against the cruelties that organization life renders the whole society.

We could *naïvely* imagine that current organization structure and characteristics might change if most of us grasp and resist its crooked culture a bit. From a global resistance, thru constructive coping and other methods noted above, a fundamental revolution might eventually happen in the structure of future organizations. On the other hand, the pressures of fast deteriorating economic productivity and rising work inefficiencies might eventually force major changes in organizations' format, anyway. Heck, the entire economic structure around the globe appears too vulnerable and bound to collapse or change somehow soon, let alone the format of organizations supposedly serving those economies.

Eventually, the nature of organizations might improve slowly somewhat in response to universal awareness within and outside organizations. Both groups—the ones denouncing organizations' current culture totally, and those facing them positively, mostly thru coping—share the responsibility of changing organizations and ending the demised governance of egotism and inequality. In reality, we *might* just be able to modify the organization culture, but not its objectives or role in the economy before finding a way out of the perils of capitalism. Yet, even this basic mission would be much tougher than we can imagine. In fact, it feels impossible to revamp the organization culture without overhauling its nature altogether, including its 'profit maximizing' objectives, form, and philosophy. It depends on how creatively and cooperatively we can go about it. On the other hand, with human needs and nature being formed in such poorly peculiar ways, the prospects do not appear too promising in terms redefining the role and nature of organizations without first facing up to the humanity's looming state altogether! Changing humans' current mentalities by some magical means would be our primary objective in the next few decades before losing humanity altogether.

PART III
Companionship and Marriage

CHAPTER SEVEN
Love and Loneliness Dilemmas

'Human relations' is even trickier and more important in families than it is in organizations. In fact, belongingness and love have the strongest mental impact on people's lives both positively and negatively. Although they are medium range needs on Maslow's personal needs tree, they are emerging as psychologically urgent 'attachment needs,' nowadays. These needs preoccupy our minds the most all our lives, since our needs for food and security are somewhat attainable and automatic in modern societies. In that sense, 'search for a companion' manifests as a basic human need, since we crave it so intensely and passionately and yet often fail to satisfy it properly, if at all. Finding the right companion makes the biggest impact on our psyches, as it instigates our emotions and outlooks deeply. Companionship provides happiness when it is successful, but stirs extreme disappointment and pain when it causes arguments or separation. Sadly, the latter case is becoming more prevalent.

Family relationships' health is in turn an important factor for maintaining the socioeconomic welfare of any nation. In modern countries, in particular, the deteriorating social condition makes the study of relationships extremely urgent and sensitive, mostly as a *basic* personal need, as well as a complex socioeconomic crisis. This author's comprehensive book, *The Nature of Love and Relationships,* provides a full picture of this critical topic. The discussions in this chapter are brief and just for highlighting love and relationships as vastly significant decisions of humans in the current era.

Love and loneliness cause major life dilemmas for most of us, because we seem helpless in choosing a viable option for living and loving. We neither know how to relate effectively, nor are trained to live rather independently. Instead, we are fed with all sorts of fantasies about love and filled with the fear of loneliness. As noted in Part II of this book, our deep dependency on society and organizations for subsistence and services already competes with our needs for self-realization and independence. Then, love and companionship needs stir an even higher level of personal dependence and desperation for us deprived humans. In the end, a variety of our conflicting needs create many personal dilemmas for us all our lives.

Right after earning our partial sense of independence from our parents, we find ourselves in need of loving and being loved. Sexual drives intensify and complicate the matter even further. Therefore, before we really get a chance to test and enjoy our independence, we get drawn into deeper sources of dependence, like love and companionship. We feel our need for dependence even before we actually meet somebody or build a relationship. The mere sense of loneliness and need for a companion weakens our whole image of being and freedom. After we meet somebody and actually start a relationship, the level of dependence increases even more. While trying to cope with, and nurture, our feelings of love and dependence, our inherent need for individualism, as an independent, assertive person, keeps imposing another set of deep inner conflicts. Our struggles to distinguish, consciously or subconsciously, our love needs from sexual drives become an added source of confusion and doubts.

Overall, our obsession for independence and our inevitable submission to our urges for love and sex turn into big dilemmas

Part III: Companionship and Marriage

throughout our lives. We strive all along to solve these dilemmas by fixing (and balancing) our feelings somehow, helplessly and uselessly. While we feel independent and in control during some periods, soon our need for love strikes us along with the need for dependence that comes with it. For either love or sex, or merely eluding loneliness, we must rely on somebody else who is willing to share similar feelings or experiences with us. Our relationships need mutual dependence and understanding in order to stabilize. Without some degree of commitment and integrity, relationships do not last or take the required form to fulfil both partners' needs for a companion. These requirements create a major paradox in our personal lives, but also across the society.

Our ceaseless failures to satisfy our need for dependence or independence cause psychological shocks, and cause depression. For one thing, we start to doubt our identities and 'who we are' without a companion. Yet, we also distrust companionship and our need for love. We doubt the effectiveness of our approaches to find and manage those needs. We start to doubt our abilities to fathom our preferences and options and our knacks for living independently. We get entangled between our emotions and logic fighting forever.

On the one hand, our chronic doubts could be a blessing for avoiding the risks of hasty decisions that often our raw logic or emotions impose upon us, such as a sloppy marriage or divorce. On the other hand, our stressful doubts during the endless cycles of dependence-independence are not easy to handle, either, as we feel helplessness in decision-making. These conflicting personal feelings are painful and seem irresolvable, while we wrestle with relationships' hassles in society and wonder about couples' dire failures to relate, nowadays, in spite of their deep psychological needs for a reliable companion.

All along, our fear of loneliness competing with our deep urges for individualism and independence cause lots of pains and depression—as another outcome of our loneliness dilemma.

Marriage and companionship are major sources of lingering doubts in life, because both options of living alone and with someone else cause us pain and stress, nowadays. Often, loving someone makes us feel even lonelier when we cannot relate to him/her effectively and also feel unappreciated and helpless. This never-ending source of doubt and stress is a reason why marriage has become a major life decision. Our warranted doubts about relationships and the pains of our conflicting urges for dependence and independence, reflect the deteriorating state of relationships and the rising complexity of our basic needs for companionship and love. The vast scope of marital issues is best evident from the ongoing frictions and problems in our own or other families as well as the accelerating percentage of marriage failures. In all, the extreme levels of deficiencies and deprivations caused by love and loneliness in modern societies make the subject of marital relationships very sensitive and vital for individuals and societies. We are facing a major crisis and nobody seems to know how to go about tackling it, either. In fact, nobody seems to really care about the **roots** of this social pandemic, anyway!

Motives behind Relationships

Our *needs* for sex, love, and compassion constitute the natural motives behind relationships. Furthermore, cultures and ethics demand that we engage in a formal ritual to make relationships binding and dependable. The purpose of these rules is to protect individuals, enhance family values, and strengthen the nucleus of social structure. All along, we have learned to envision a stable relationship (preferably a formal marriage) with a person we have spent a lot of time to find and tame. On top of these natural and cultural motivations, however, nowadays partners have grown very high expectations from relationships in line with their rising personal needs and dreams. These demanding needs, especially partners' obsession for love and attention, have grown drastically in recent decades, thus making the task of relating in relationships difficult. People are desperate to find happiness, which they think erupts mainly through love and relationships. However, this is a weird expectation—to make our partners responsible for bringing us that illusive happiness that we seem incapable of finding on our own. We just ignore the fact that since nobody can find that elusive happiness, expecting it from one another in a relationship is pure silly.

Accordingly, the relationship environment has also become too complex and instable in line with people's rising pomposity, greed, and unreliability. While they seek deep love and lasting relationships, their sense of commitment to cultural and family values have diminished. No new guidelines exist, either, to offer at least some basic rules of relating in relationships and to keep partners' egos manageable. Accordingly, people get into their relationships with crooked motivations and idiotic expectations. While they have become oversensitive and obsessed with finding love, they have little compassion and patience themselves. Under this confusing situation, people settle for a mate for all the wrong reasons without adequate knowledge of relationship needs or even a true sense of love, although they naively consider 'love' the main success factor for building their relationships. Then, they also leave their relationships with equally selfish motivations and hasty decisions in pursuit of better companions and more sexuality. People often seem to get married with their calculating minds and agendas, while misperceiving or dismissing the real purposes of relationships.

Overall, it has become too difficult to assess partners' (usually crooked) personal motives for starting a relationship beyond the natural needs of humans (for a companion). Therefore, a keen assessment of both partners' motives is useful before making a decision or committing ourselves to a binding relationship. Of course, all these doubts, decisions, prudence, and procrastinations have severe consequences on the quality of our lives, positively or negatively—mostly negatively in the new era. Yet, we cannot, nor is it wise, to elude them.

Surely, life is more beautiful and tolerable when the outcome of our decision about a companion is positive and we have a peaceful, pleasant life with a person whom we deeply care for and understand. A compatible, tender partner brings the most gratifying experience for a normal person with good intelligence. Conversely, if our decision turns out bad, which seems to be most likely, nowadays, the repercussions are often too extensive and destructive. Decisions about marriage normally result in one of these extremes, although some couples learn to live peacefully together despite their conflicts and differences. These facts seem to be obvious and commonsense. Yet, for whatever reasons, most of us fail in our decisions. More than fifty percent of marriages in North America lead to divorce. Then, another great majority of couples live separately or keep living in substandard relationships all their lives with no guts to get out of them.

If we think we are so smart when we are making our marriage decisions, then why are most of us failing? It seems that we are wrong in our decisions because:

i) We are unaware of the purposes of marriage outside our sense of attraction to another person, superficial lifestyles, and our idiotic, high expectations.
ii) We do not analyse our own or partner's motives adequately, or ignore them for emotional or other reasons.
iii) We do not know enough about relationships' unique needs and the individual we are planning to marry.
iv) We are not familiar with the harsh realities of married life beyond our limited observations of our parents and perhaps some friends or relatives.
v) In fact, we do not take our parents' advice seriously, either, because we naively believe we are immune to their types of mistakes and problems.

In all, we do not know what we are getting into. Even worse, no longer any reliable principles and guidelines exist for couples to use for planning and maintaining their marriages. Meanwhile, people's extreme Egos and misperceptions keep increasing their expectations from relationships.

Considering the magnitude of marriage decision, we have not learned how to define and study relationships' relevant success factors. We do not spend nearly enough time to learn and apply proper criteria to gauge marriage variables and situations. Heck, we do not even have any primary guidelines and models these days, anyway, to use for doing these analyses. Of course, we take a lot of time supposedly thinking and evaluating our options and decisions. However, our hesitations and doubts about marriage or selecting a companion do not necessarily mean that we are aware of or studying the matter logically. We are not informed about the right factors to consider, anyway. Especially during the courting period, we are overwhelmed with dreams and emotions that are more distracting than helpful for an objective assessment. We are usually swayed by our infatuation and sexual needs; we believe we should compromise; or we undermine or ignore our priorities, purposes, and decision's prospects *for now*. We do not realize the importance of this decision, as we cannot sense the repercussions of bad marriages, like an epidemic, nowadays. Often our motive for marriage is just a change in our boring lives. Sometimes, a partner views marriage merely a means of financial security. In another case, a person lowers his/her standards of an acceptable spouse, since s/he is getting old and perhaps her 'biological clock is ticking' too fast. Thus, we jump into a marriage carelessly, hoping that it would work out fine. Marriage is certainly a big change, but as statistics indicate, it is usually a change for worse.

We (especially women) often seem to spend more time, logic, and energy on simpler decisions, such as buying a pair of shoes, compared to marital decisions. We let our emotions, loneliness, and love affect our marital decisions disproportionate to the high risks of relationships in the new era. Relatively, we fuss much more about buying a pair of shoes, nowadays, because we are familiar with the right factors for this decision. We try to stay rational, instead of emotional, to gauge its quality, our need for it, where we are going to wear it to, its price, etc. We wish to justify our decision logically (because we must pay for it) instead of emotionally per se (simply because we like it). Yet, considering the lifetime risks of marriage, we do not know, or study, all the right factors and our motives properly. *Do we think marriage and divorce are free?!* When it comes to love and sex or the mirage of marriage, we often lose our logic and foresight prematurely. We feel too lonely to worry about the sad state of relationships.

By the way, humans' long list of obsessions for many things, including shoes, love, or happiness, show their innate irrationality and carelessness regarding their real needs and plans, instead of studying and fulfilling them. Driven merely by our obsessions for love and happiness, financial rewards, or false emotions, we fail particularly to measure the needs and complexity of relationships enough in advance. We are unrealistic regarding life, as we are hypnotized in a world of illusions.

Thus, we need two lists of: 1) Irrelevant factors and motives that preoccupy partners and damage their relationship decisions, and 2) Relevant factors corresponding with the sensible purposes of relationships. For a stronger commitment, such as marriage, we must be even less flexible and sloppy in terms of choosing the relevant success factors than in the case of a simple cohabitation.

Irrelevant Purposes of Marriage

The most common misperceived reasons nowadays for marriage or a serious relationship are:

Love Need: We crave this strong, beautiful need permanently, but often at the expense of a lifetime misery and disappointment. We are misled by mushy movies that show how love makes our lives eternally beautiful and happy. We take those corny stories too seriously!

'Love need' occurs in three ways. First, we crave being loved, like a psychological deficiency. Second, we imagine and believe we adore a particular person and cannot live without him/her. Third, we build an image of love superficially in response to the sentiments that we receive or believe a person is offering us, which we usually accept out of loneliness, desperation, or our innate urge to love or be loved—thus we replicate the feeling of love. None of these love criteria is directly relevant for building a serious relationship.

Security and Dependence: This factor misses the basic principle of self-reliance and self-image that we value so much, nowadays. Starting a relationship in a weak position would not help it in the long run. Partners' lingering insecurities taint their relationship, nonetheless. The spouse who needs special attention and a sense of security would most likely be disappointed after marriage to find out that his/her spouse does not care or cannot provide the extreme attention expected of him/her. The spouse pressed for paying special attention is eventually fed up with his/her partner's abnormal demands, oversensitivity, spite, and erratic withdrawals from the relationship. The frictions grow at least two folds if both partners are insecure.

Financial Gain: It is needless to point out the immorality and irrationality of planning personal gains as a purpose of marriage or companionship. However, many partners bring their selfish, calculating nature to relationships, nowadays.

Convenience: One or both partners might consider marriage a means of convenience, financially or emotionally. Sometimes they do it for changing their monotonous life routines. Family and cultural pressures to build a family often lead to these types of marriages, too. Marriage is used as a scapegoat, while partners remain oblivious of its enormous potential for causing major headaches, frustration, and inconveniences of its own, instead of solving their initial personal problems and inconveniences, which partners had hoped to solve thru marriage. This mentality reflects couples' naiveté about relationships' special needs and capacity.

Relevant Purposes of Marriage

Three relevant purposes exist for marriage outside the instinctual needs to mate and have a family. They must exist simultaneously for making a positive decision about a particular marriage. These *compound* purposes (motives) maximize the interests and welfare of two intelligent individuals who view marriage as an institution or partnership. These *marriage success factors* are introduced below and then elaborated in the next chapter. §

Increase Life Enjoyment: Marriage provides the opportunity to explore life better jointly. Obviously, sex, love, and compassion prevails and provides relief and enjoyment, especially during the early stages of our lives when we need all those good things the most. However, sharing experiences in general and doing certain activities also intensifies partners' enjoyment of life extensively. Life's inherent values become more vivid and meaningful when they are appreciated jointly, while partners express their feelings and interpretations of events. The mere opportunity of talking or whining about life and social issues gives couples a warm sense of relief if not joy. Married people have a longer life expectancy, mostly because they can share their joys and anguish. They get an opportunity to share their hurts, mitigate the effects of external pressures on them, and get back into happy mood cycles faster.

Support and Cooperation: Marriage should provide a suitable environment for cooperation and teamwork to solve problems, while partners strive for higher personal achievements. Partners' joint participation in household and family affairs brings better

---

§ This author's book, *Marriage and Divorce Hardships*, discusses marriage purposes in much more details.

results and a higher synergy with less energy wasted by each partner. More importantly, partners are expected to support each other functionally and psychologically in order to grow, think clearer, and stimulate a variety of communications that would be creative and thought provoking.

Sensible Commitment: 'Companionship' is the main purpose of marriage. Yet, while 'companionship' conveys a natural sense of romance, the notion of 'marriage' sounds more like a contractual obligation of partners for a joint venture. That is, marriage often feels less romantic than what we imagine about companionship per se. This subtle expectation of romance fading with marriage is a realistic vision, of course, based on what we subconsciously know and observe in most marriages. Our negative experiences and broad evidences in society have created an inherent cynicism about marriage. Men, in particular, appear less keen for marriage maybe due to their lesser maternal urge than women, higher urge for independence, and higher cynicism about married life and its inevitable responsibilities and anguish.

It seems as if we expect the innate purpose of companionship lose its steam eventually in spite of partners' unparalleled initial love and romanticism. Accordingly, marriage seems more like a scheme to keep partners together under situations not tolerated in a non-committal companionship. Although we are not naive to assume that problems of alienation can be resolved by making separation difficult through marriage arrangement, we believe that some simple formalities (like the ones we now have) can protect us from situations where we make hasty and regrettable decisions when our agitated Egos explode. Through marriage, we are forced to learn and apply some commonsense in making our relationships work instead of searching for an ideal mate forever. We feel a higher obligation to make our marriage work. After all, ideal couples can be found only in fairy tales. However, couples are unaware of, or ignore, even this basic purpose of marriage, nowadays, i.e., a sensible commitment and the immense level of knowledge and compassion required to make it work.

In marriage, we may eventually learn that stubbornness and false pride only lead to alienation and separation. We should also learn to expect the chance of losing some intensity of the passion exchanged by partners earlier, but hope to acquire the wisdom of comradeship to accept, and adjust to, our partners' imperfections. These same imperfections would have separated partners if they were not married, and had not learned the means of curbing their obstinacy and false pride.

Accordingly, a particular purpose in marriage distinguishes it from a simple companionship in terms of *making* the relationship work as long as logically possible. We may refer to this wisdom as a 'sensible commitment.' Yet, most of us are either unfamiliar with this purpose of marriage (a success factor) or do not work on it consciously as a major requirement of marriage.

At the same time, contrary to many partners' naïve dreams and expectations from their marriages for full commitment, 'sensible commitment' refers to partners' abilities to relate in many respects *in order to develop* a natural sense of commitment to withstand hardships and conflicts. Before getting married, partners should grasp the need for a sensible commitment as a major 'relationship need.' Yet, this sensible commitment must also grow naturally in line with partners' rising skills to relate peacefully and cordially, instead of only expecting a blind commitment egotistically. Our contemporary view of marriage is an incomplete picture, which we have learned from our parents and movies. We have never had a chance to grasp the real purposes (and shortcomings) of marriage before we get into one. Once we are in it, we do not know how to assess and respond to complex situations prevalent in modern relationships, either. We either suffer through it too much for too long helplessly or run away from it prematurely, depending upon our emotional and arbitrary criteria for tolerance.

Analyzing Marriage

Peter Drucker, the prominent teacher and writer, who introduced the concept of 'Management by Objective,' often made a succinct comment to his students about the characteristics of a good paper. He told us that, "A good paper has an 'Introduction' that could be a good 'Conclusion' and vice versa." This interesting principle works best with the concept of marriage, too. That is, we should think and discuss divorce (risks) at the time of marriage, and think and discuss marriage (intentions) when contemplating divorce. We can use this proactive principle in gauging our marriage and divorce decisions. This idea's purpose and means of practising it will be elaborated shortly, but how practical discussing divorce at the time of marriage, or vice versa, feels?

Naturally, it sounds depressing and dubious to discuss divorce when we are in love and only imagine our wedding plans and all its related joyful events. We are hesitant to ponder or raise this insensitive issue, as we do not wish to spoil the romantic mood. We do not dare to disturb even our own feelings of love and joy, let alone discussing such pessimistic topic with our prospective partner. Some rich people might insist on a prenuptial agreement, but nobody, especially common folks, discusses the possibility of divorce, in particular. It surely feels unromantic and our beloveds would react and resist listening to our seemingly insensitive and calculating thoughts about divorce likelihood, and then sharing his/her sensible views, too! Yet, those reactions and resistances are all also part of the evaluation process. We might be labelled cold and paranoiac. However, allowing these thoughts stop us from doing a proper evaluation would be our first mistake in marital life. If our views agitate our partners, the situation would present a good opportunity to gauge (and predict) his/her way of reacting during difficult times and use the information for our decision. It is wise to arouse, now, those hidden emotions that would surely erupt later in marriage. Actually, it is necessary to initiate a process to unravel our partners' thoughts about sensitive matters and examining their knack to negotiate and compromise. All these issues would come out for discussion and dire dispute sooner or later, so why not sooner? The romantic mood we are trying so hard not to spoil subsides rather fast after marriage, anyway. You can bet all your material and mental assets on that! The problem is that these ideas have been even less considered in modern societies with the advent of people's obsession with love and romance. Thus, inventing a smooth premarital negotiation process, including the most contentious issues among couples in modern societies, would help marriages a lot. Surely, all these ideas sound so bizarre and unrealistic, but they would feel natural and necessary if people realize their benefits, as listed later.

Most of us hide foolishly behind our emotions and resist the truth we know or hear about marital life. However, avoiding the facts would neither help us now with our decision about such a serious commitment, nor change our marital outcome once the sad relationship realities and emotions erupt like a volcanic mess. Therefore, we are definitely better off to test the waters now—without provoking our partner with our approach, of course. For example, if we think that having a prenuptial agreement is useful, we should not hesitate to discuss it with our partner in fears of spoiling the mood. Of course, if we are **realistically** certain that such an agreement is not practical or needed, discussing it as a hypothetical situation might not help too much, although it would not hurt, either, at least for testing the partners' knacks for calm negotiations. In all, we must disallow our timidity or interpretation of 'practical and necessary' force us choose an optimistic position about our marriage's future. On the contrary, always work from the worst-case scenario position *very tactfully*.

Premarital Negotiations

Then again, what does discussing divorce at the time of marriage mean? In line with 'Forward Thinking' topic in Volume I, the goal of thinking and discussing divorce in advance is to ponder the scenario in which divorce becomes inevitable. After all, this is a very likely scenario in modern societies. Thus, as a starting point, we must read books about divorce and learn about the headaches of irreconcilable marriages, wherein stressed couples face tough situations. We must learn about the hassles and pains of divorce or being trapped in a shoddy or unproductive relationship. Many marriages end up in a painful stalemate, since partners have no courage or resources to pursue other options or start all over after a divorce. Again, these ideas, even for taking the time to read a book about the hassles of divorce, sound so idealistic and beyond any normal person patience, let alone a passionate couple eager to prove their devotions along with utmost trust in each other's words and sincerity! Still, being at least familiar with this option about premarital negotiations is useful all in itself.

Anyhow, by pondering divorce, we do two things:

First, we contemplate the most common impact of divorce on people emotionally, psychologically, physically, and financially in general. Many books and articles about divorce and its effects on individuals and their children are available. This background can help a lot. The amount of time we invest on this education would be highly justifiable and valuable. The more time we spend on grasping the hassles of a bad marriage and divorce, the more time, nerves, and money we save later.

Second, we try to predict the potential causes of divorce and weigh its consequences according to our particular situation and personality. Divorce is discussed in detail in Part IV. Especially, the newlyweds or those who are considering marriage are highly encouraged to read all the chapters in Part IV carefully. They may learn to imagine most probable scenarios and their positions and reactions under those likely scenarios, and then multiply those imaginary senses of failure and despair by ten folds.

Certainly, our positions and feelings at the time of divorce vary based on many factors, particularly our age and the years of being married. Anticipating our feelings in such a position, in a distant future, is hard, but not impossible, especially if we read some books about divorce. For example, we can learn that the sense of loss and desperation after divorce are many folds more severe than the feelings of loneliness or losing a mere companion per se, which we all are familiar with already. In spite of equal love in both 'marriage' and 'companionships,' the pains of failed commitments and demands after divorce are much nastier relative to a mere separation in a basic companionship even if sharing our kids does not become an extra source of pain. We can learn that the sense of loneliness and failure after a marriage breakdown is much harsher and more painful than the loneliness we feel during bachelorhood when we are young and have not basked in many years of marital dependency and conveniences. After getting a basic impression of the harsh effects of divorce, try to multiply it ten folds to possibly gain a more realistic sense.

By the way, the feelings of loneliness intensify exponentially according to our age, too. If we find loneliness intolerable now that we are young and full of urges for independence, we might be able to imagine the shock and anguish of separation after a long marital experience. During marriage, we lose our sense of independence gradually, as we get attached to our family and a new lifestyle. We get softer and more vulnerable to the feeling and state of loneliness after many years of joint life. In a sense, it would be preferable to remain single and hold on to our sense of self-reliance than marrying, becoming vulnerable, and then being left alone and confused. Reading books about 'how to cope with divorce' and Part IV of this book would show the huge troubles and confusion that divorce causes. The pain of loneliness is only one of many repercussions of divorce. We also feel cheated and deprived of a fruitful life. We feel like a big loser—unappreciated, misunderstood, abused, and so much more. Most of us curb the feelings of loss and loneliness a bit eventually, after a few months or years, if we gain our sense of independence. Still, some deep scars in our psyches would hurt us for the rest of our lives.

The task of evaluating divorce scenarios is not easy, but more importantly it is not intended to cause apprehension and paranoia about marriage. We only want to make our marriage decision as educated as possible. And the fact is that no knowledge is more relevant about marriage than the information about divorce. Next to a review of hypothetical divorce facts and scenarios, a review of partners' positions and characters at the present time is also useful. This assessment includes a thorough review of partners' assets and liabilities brought into this partnership, financially, emotionally, psychologically, and physically. This is the time to measure partners' capacity, mostly in terms of their inherent compassion and intelligence, to share a joint life and relate.

Thinking divorce at the time of marriage is only meant to be an educational process to prepare both partners for a productive relationship based on a viable relationship model, or stop them from making a big mistake (i.e., marriage) that they would regret. No amount of time spent on this educational process is ever a waste—until partners are quite sure one way or another. Then, they could **write** a simple agreement to demonstrate their initial wisdom and efforts to make the right decision, but also remember all these conversations and promises. Many of these issues and agreements help in preparing and signing a marriage contract.

The notion of 'thinking divorce at the time of marriage' would become also handy for choosing a proper relationship model. Partners should grasp the implications of relating within that type of environment (a particular relationship model)[**] and study the factors that are essential for maintaining a relationship. Partners' discussions prepare them for negotiating the topics that become contentious when the possibility of divorce comes to fore in the future. When divorce feels inevitable, recalling their initial conversations and contract would prove most useful. This would offer the best time to 'think of marriage at the time of divorce,' as explained in Chapter Ten.

[**] Relationship models are explained in this author's book, *Relationship Needs, Framework, and Models*. Relationship models should be designed more precisely in the near future, though, in line with finer research.

Developing a Partnership Agreement

We all live with strong senses of romanticism and hope. Yet, it is prudent to view marriage a risky business partnership, nowadays, besides a romantic adventure. Naturally, this sounds like a silly, cynical proposal to even ponder, let alone push on our beloved coldly. However, the sad truth is that the real life and marriage environment cannot be any further different from the image that most couples build from love stories and movies, nowadays. All the evidences from family relationships and divorce statistics show that marital life in modern societies turns into a contentious partnership, anyway, with couples fighting hard for their rights and equities. Spouses are adamant and alert regarding even their household activities being always distributed equally and fairly between them, let alone their financial issues. Therefore, with this mentality and reality in sight, maybe soon the society learns how to handle marriage practically like a *romantic business,* too!

Ironically, marriages now look like business partnerships that has been put together hastily without partners knowing much about the business they were getting into, their capitals and assets, and their shares of total equity, just in case the business dissolves, etc. Of course, all other purposes of marriage are also crucial and will be discussed soon, too. Yet, we should begin our evaluation process with business factors, since, in the end, money always becomes a contentious issue, especially when partners get hostile near the divorce stage. Teaching these harsh realities of the 21st century at high schools is important, so that the youths' mindsets are readily prepared for these new social facts.

In the absence of a better system, judicial systems follow the 50/50 asset distribution rule for most cases. Surely, this cannot be an equitable formula, since partners' income and initial assets can never be always equal. Many other sensitive financial issues, such as family budget, savings, investment decisions, and financial controls play prominent roles in family affairs, nowadays, and create painful frictions, since they are not discussed and decided on at the outset. Then, after marriage, the more domineering and demanding partner begins subtle tactics, or maybe even nasty manoeuvres, to take charge of the affairs, with the other partner losing his/her voice in most matters. All these contentious issues become the sources of arguments, conflicts, retaliations, and all kinds of nastiness that soon taint most relationships.

Most likely standard marriage contracts will become available to the public soon, so that couples can only fill out some clauses and sign it. All the topics requiring a discussion are also noted in an accompanying pamphlet to guide partners thru their premarital negotiation and mental preparation before making their decision. The process would feel simple and rather natural with no need for partners to think of the details themselves, but only follow the format and guidelines offered in the upcoming standard contracts and accompanying pamphlets.

Two people can cohabit for as long as necessary to figure out these details and study each other's temperament, patience, etc. Learning about each other's knack for teamwork and negotiation is a crucial strategy for establishing the depth of items that require discussing in advance. Then, if they wish, they can write the agreement and make their cohabitation official, if they really think their marriage has some tangible benefits for a long haul.

A big goal of 'marriage evaluation process' prior to wedding is to unravel major personality differences and high potentials for future clashes. This process is especially useful for alerting young partners about the highly likely marriage problems and getting themselves ready for both facing and preventing them rationally. It helps them learn about the tough (but crucial) requirements of marriage, especially its financial and teamwork requirements. Predictable, contentious issues in modern marriages that couples are often ignorant about should be listed in standard contracts, so that they get an opportunity to ponder and learn. Even if a partner reneges on his/her written commitment or agreement, we still know that we had done our homework in communicating our fair expectations at the outset. If a marital relationship suffers, it would be due to new ideas and demands that a partner suddenly tries to impose on his/her partner. Normally, partners should not agree with each other's new proposals and demands, unless they look reasonable, in which case their agreement could be modified properly and formally if it is a serious matter. Still, partners must make sure they are not manipulated, which is sometimes hard to know, while causing additional marital conflicts and alienation, too.

These scrupulous steps are in fact in line with the fourteen 'Relationships Success Factors' discussed in the next chapter and listed in Table 8.1 on Page 144, especially the last item: Expressing personal expectations.

Personal independence in marriage is jeopardized due to not only emotional issues, but also loss of basic control on financial and personal preferences. Arguments start about who should be responsible for what, whether all their income should go to a joint account, how, and who has the final say about expenditures versus savings, the kinds of investments, etc. All these matters require teamwork, mutual understanding, goodwill, faith, and most of all great communication skills. Negotiating and assertiveness before marriage can mitigate a *reasonable portion* of the arguments and aggressiveness that normally erupt after marriage. Especially, partners getting an opportunity to evaluate each other's knack for negotiations without getting nasty or testy would prove precious.

Then, partners must remember and honour their agreements, while they stay calm, assertive, objective, and willing to negotiate after marriage, too. One partner should not allow emotions and subtle tactics of the other partner influence him/her to forget his/her established rights before marriage. Loss of independence and financial controls often happens gradually when one partner finds the chance to abuse his/her partner's soft spots and take charge eventually. When the controlled partner feels these manoeuvres, s/he can either cope and suffer, or get into horrendous waves of fights and struggles, and then, most likely, go for separation.

Besides minimizing partners' power clashes, the main goal of partners' initial discussions and consent about a fair and friendly financial scheme is to secure their relative financial independence in general. Mixing their income, investments, bank accounts, etc. is not appropriate for the new era. In fact, the main features of this agreement should be ideally put in writing and signed by partners merely for remembering their commitments. Even better, serious and complex issues should be put in binding (standard) contracts to protect partners against future claims and demands.

The scheme is not meant to reflect tight controls and measures for everything. The big idea is to maintain personal independence and controls over one's financial decisions even after marriage. Partners would certainly be generous towards each other without feeling obliged to account for what they do with their savings beyond what is necessary and agreed to for joint family expenses and capital purchases like a home, car, etc. The scheme should definitely be fair, flexible and friendly and treated as a financial plan for mutual understanding and consent. Obviously, when one partner does not work or have enough income for any reason, the other partner makes a higher financial contribution towards family expenses. However, partners should have their own savings and investments in general, while they could also have joint savings and investments if they both desire, but not as a marital mandate or dictated by one partner.

Discussing and possibly documenting each partner's share of duties and family roles, especially when children are born would not be a bad idea, either. These preliminary arrangements are not meant to be too strict like a treaty or constitution. Rather, they will be adjustable later by negotiation and goodwill. All we need to establish before marriage is a sense of mutual understanding and responsibility, comradeship, financial structure, flexibility, and good intentions. Above all, this process would help partners' grasp of each other's needs (now and in the future). It shows their negotiating skills and it lays out the foundation for a teamwork atmosphere that should prevail in a healthy marriage. Hopefully!

Conversely, if prospective marriage partners do not see the need for these friendly negotiations, or discover big disparities in their needs, they have saved themselves the big hassle of marrying and arguing forever or opting for divorce. Ideally, they stop getting into a marriage that seems doomed already.

Then again, we cannot defeat humans' evil nature mixed with lots of mushy sentiments and rising lunacy! Thus, we should still be ready for the usual marital problems that often arise. The only thing any kind of premarital negotiation and agreement can do is: <u>To reduce the chances of early frictions after marriage, prevent big misunderstandings between partners, display partners' knacks for discussion and teamwork, and start with a more realistic sense about marriage. We should even expect many partners dishonour their agreements and claim they were fooled into signing them, even if a third party had explained and witnessed partners' words and intentions to them.</u>

On the one hand, the idea of premarital negotiation or contract feels absurd! On the other hand, the notion of 'thinking divorce at the time marriage,' as a tool for anticipating and preparing for marital conflicts, makes so much more sense now after reflecting upon the intentions of this book's radical points, including even the loud idea of premarital negotiation and a written agreement!

Surely, without some level of faith and mutual trust between partners, they can write a ten-thousand-page agreement and still see it violated after the marriage. Hoping that partners would stay rational, fair, and patient is naive and a good reason to doubt the value of the logical approaches suggested in this book. Still, for the same reasons, pondering all these precautionary measures before marriage seem to be our only chance for reducing our most likely future headaches. Meanwhile, all we can hope for is that someday soon we realize the need to be a bit more logical and practical about our marriages, mostly for own good.

A major marital problem develops when one partner notices a sudden change of position in the other partner. Especially, when partners do not talk about family budget, work, income, and other arrangements before marriage, the partner who has withheld his/her demands suddenly finds the courage and urge to parade his/her emotions and needs. This would not only come across as a change of personality, but also a sign of rebellion to the other partner. If partners have an opportunity to express their demands (which could in fact reflect their legitimate needs) at the time of creating their marriage agreements, the perception of personality change and new demands would less likely erupt and cause a big shock and friction between partners later.

Again, as stressed a few times already, finding the courage to implement the thoughts and steps of preparing an agreement with our partner is a major task these days. Yet, this would become a natural and common practice in the near future, simply because it would both prevent those potentially doomed and risky marriages and reduce the common frictions that often emerge soon after marriage. At least a sizeable group of practical partners might start to prefer this approach to the merely romantic, sloppy means of marriage, nowadays, which usually leads to big headaches.

The whole point is that a little bit of time and controversy at the beginning, before marriage, would not only save tons of time and hassle during separations, but also strengthen the marriage. A judicial system should find ways to recognize and facilitate the process of preparation and legal documentation of a preliminary agreement for all marriages. They might do so if they realize that all the time and efforts partners might spend on negotiating and preparing an agreement is fully justified. It saves a lot of time, money, divorces, and agony later for people and judicial systems. Especially, all the extra work before marriage when we are young is more bearable than doing ten times more work and enduring the pains of divorce when we are older and have less energy and patience. Partners should really take their times now that they are allegedly in love, calm, energetic, and collected, instead of pulling their own and each other's hairs during the stressful period of divorce as two mad, ferocious enemies.

Surely, viewing marriage as a *romantic business partnership* would appear ridiculous, insensitive, and impractical to us. When we feel love towards someone, swiftly our eyes, ears, and brains go on vacation and refuse to consider the simplest suggestions or words of wisdom, let alone bothering with business transactions that hinder the prospect of winning someone's heart. All those romantic feelings of love that we read in poetry books are true and apply to all of us to some degree. They fool all of us. When we believe we love somebody, we can give everything we have and sacrifice even ourselves just for having his/her love or even the mere honour of his/her company. Nothing else matters to us at that moment except being part of his/her life now, forget what may happen in a few years. When we are in love, we undermine all the essential factors for a workable relationship and assume everything would work out nicely at the end. We naively believe love would solve all the problems, even if 'love' were one-sided. But in reality, the opposite is true: Peculiar relationship problems and widespread personal idiosyncrasies kill even true mutual love very quickly. All those love stories in books and movies, as well as our own feelings of infatuation, are incredibly misleading and untrue. This book's ideas are based on not merely scientific facts and statistics, but also this author's several experiences in marital and love affairs and their agonizing outcomes. Still, none of these cautions would probably convince the youths to look at their love affairs more practically in line with the realities in the new era!

Sadly (or luckily), no remedy for love and its traps exits. As long as we hear and read about marriage and divorce facts, the victory of logic over emotions or vice versa would be a matter of personal character. The option of cohabiting before marriage is helpful in restraining the overwhelming sense of infatuation, so that logic may find a chance for evaluating the hard, hidden facts of marital relationships, nowadays. Yet, even cohabiting may not help much for many reasons. Partners may become dependent and addicted to each other's love and task-sharing conveniences before they get a chance to express their needs and find a suitable relationship model for them. More importantly, though, people's true characters often emerge only after marriage. People change a lot too, so unexpectedly, especially when some new adventures or financial incentives lure them. Unfortunately, modern societies are vastly conducive to corrupting people and their marriages.

Aside from the issue of love—even when we believe we are immune to the blinding effects of love, and when we believe we are a logical person—we can still get trapped in a relationship for some other irrational thoughts or beliefs. In particular, we usually trust our logic too much and think, "Why should I go through the hassle of evaluating divorce scenarios and viewing marriage as a business *when I really know and trust my partner* already?"

Knowing Our Partner

This trilogy stresses on the task of 'knowing ourselves' to enrich our lives and avoid life's traps. Our ability to grasp our needs and our 'self' could help our relationships, too. Yet, knowing 'who we are,' even if we acknowledge a need for it, is a lifetime venture that demands a lot of sincere efforts, perseverance, modesty, and motivation.

We believe to be the best judges of our thoughts, actions, and emotions, yet are too biased about both our qualities and quirks, and thus remain forever ignorant about 'who we really are.' We do not even know how to explore our unconscious mind to sense the truth about our essence—the 'self,' which holds the secret of 'who we are.' We touch and feel certain traces of 'self' from time to time when novel dimensions of our existence unfold in front of our eyes unexpectedly, often through some profound thoughts or a deep sensation, perhaps love for another person. Yet, we do not appreciate the gist and significance of those experiences.

We might discover certain things about our personality and 'self' slowly if we are patient and persistent. Often, our discovery is enlightening or shocking to us. Yet, knowing who we are is a difficult and lengthy process, despite our supposedly analytical brains, objectivity, deep convictions and thoughts, and all the controls we believe to have over our minds, emotions, judgments, and attitudes. Therefore, finding who we really are remains only an abstract idea for most of us.

Now, if knowing 'who we are' is next to impossible, despite our relative control over 'self,' just imagine how difficult it would be for any of us to know 'who they are.' How naive we should be to think that we know our partner adequately. This is practically impossible, since even our partner would not know 'who s/he is,' let alone an outsider who surely has no access even to her/his conscious or subconscious.

The task of guessing who others are gets more complicated in close relations due to extra assumptions we make about them. For example, not only we think we know who we are and who they are, but also **we assume they (our prospective partners) know 'who they are.'** We assume that the way our partner is presenting her/himself to us is based on his/her knowledge of who s/he is, or s/he is honest about his/her presentations of his/her character, at least to the extent s/her knows. In reality, however, our partner is not only unaware of who s/he is, but most likely confused about his/her identity like the rest of us. S/he actually hides his/her evil thoughts and plans to fool us, while showing off a fake, appealing personality, too. We assume his/her reactions and judgments are rather studied and coordinated based on some logical and valid knowledge of who s/he is, when in reality s/he is drawing on any of his/her three aspects of personality to deal with us at any time often with little conscious or conscience.

There are still other erroneous assumptions on our part. Not only we think we know who we are and who they are, and not only we assume that they know who they are and they remain faithful to who they are in dealing with us, **we also assume they know 'who we are.'** How many times have we complained and felt disappointed when we had thought that our partner had not appreciated who we were (after all this time)? Yet, we continue with our poor logic to assume that s/he should have known us and our expectations, because we have tried to explain everything to him/her so many times (god knows through which aspect of our confused personality). The simple fact is that even if our partner were smart and motivated enough to try to know 'who we are,' s/he would not be able to really find out who we are for the same reasons we would never know who they are. It is naive to expect people understand us. Others understand us according to their perceptions, which is always a very limited viewpoint. This matter gets even more complicated when all of us try to display phony personalities in order to fit in society or get recognition. We attempt to hide our naiveté and instead become haughty to assert ourselves and prove our identities.

Our zeal to fathom 'who we are' and 'who they are' expands at a few more levels. For example, we can ponder the case in which we assume our partner also believes that we know 'who we are,' etc. Or, we may think that what we do not know about our partner's family background, genes, and rearing experiences do not affect the outcome of a relationship. However, in most situations they do. Parents and close relatives sometimes interfere and influence our married lives directly and indirectly as well. Therefore, even our partners get more confused about 'who they are or should be,' especially for their relationships with us.

Anyhow, our natural obsession to figure out people (knowing who they are) is an endless, exhausting, frustrating effort in vain. It is only an innate, routine human tendency, maybe a biological design, for handling people. And the closer people are to us, and the more we must deal with them, the more we feel pressed to know them the best for facing them most appropriately. We do it all mainly like a defence mechanism, but also for other purposes.

One main hurdle for knowing ourselves and our partners is that we apply different aspects of our personality to communicate with, and manipulate, one another. Very seldom do we apply our 'self' in our encounters to remain sincere. If we did, we would have a much better chance to understand and know one another. Instead, we apply our Egos and Models widely to hide our secrets and intentions mainly for satiating our egoistic needs. Using these aspects of our personalities so prominently stops us from knowing who we are and who they are. It taints the content and meaning of relationships as well. We pretend to be a nice person to attract someone we think we love or want to lure. We hide our immense egoism and selfish desires until the initial love fever subsides. We also learn about humans' vulnerability and use this knowledge to manipulate one another as much as we can. For example, we try to fool our partner with our phony compliments for soothing his/her Ego or insecurities. The weird thing about human nature is that we all welcome these compliments even when we know they are insincere.

Often, we block information channels subconsciously. For example, when we are in love, we keep justifying our partners' intentions. Our 'love need' is merely too strong to give logic a chance. We simply do not want to lose our companion even if we must deceive ourselves by closing our minds to the obvious signs of egoism and bad character radiating readily from people we love. We keep giving a benefit of a doubt to them, but also build a barrel of doubts about who we and they are. Those doubts do not get resolved as long as we keep justifying our own or their bizarre actions and intentions. This accumulation of doubts about ourselves and our partners hurt our relationships and psyches. We fight with our rising inner conflicts while we cannot think straight or accept the risk of losing the person we love.

Without getting into more details for our narrow purpose in this book, it suffices to remember that partners' assumptions about knowing each other is hardly correct, even if they have been in love and had a long relationship. Those assumptions are surely naïve and become direct causes of stress and big disappointments. It is even more amazing that we intentionally ignore even the clear signs of personality issues and crooked motives of a person when we seemingly fall in love with him/her or feel lonely. Love and loneliness dilemmas are quite complex, while they make us do all sorts of weird and sometimes wild things in our lives.

CHAPTER EIGHT
Measures of Partners' Compatibility
Relationships Success Factors

A couple's compatibility depends on their personalities to fulfil the three 'marriage purposes' discussed in the previous chapter, i.e., their abilities to support each other, raise their life enjoyment, and make sensible commitment. These three compatibility factors are discussed later in this chapter. Yet, partners' three personality aspects (Ego, Model, Self) clash and infect their compatibility, too, thus this topic is addressed briefly first.

Compatibility in 'Personality Aspects'

Refined studies might help predict partners' ability to relate with minimal conflicts based on their personality aspects' levels (Ego, Model, Self). Obviously, if partners have strong Self orientation, they have the highest chance of compatibility and relating. Yet, Ego and Model often infect relationships in so many odd ways, nowadays. Compatible partners are becoming rarer due to the growing depravity of personalities and social systems, as well as people's rising expectations from relationships in the new era, while both Ego and Model ratios are also accelerating.

Ego reflects mostly a demanding personality and Model is too needy and superficial. With moderate levels of Model and Ego, people can usually get along somewhat. However, the excessive Model and Ego makes most relationship intolerable. In particular, these conditions make the chances of teamwork very remote and prevent a healthy and productive relationship environment. Of course, people often stay away from such excessive personalities, although detecting these flaws in others and ourselves is hard. Therefore, another challenge is to determine which personality dominations of partners can possibly match, if at all. Can people with rather high Ego or Model ever find a suitable relationship, and how bad our world will be in a decade, considering such a fast-rising level of Ego and Model in modern societies?

We might not be able to find a definite remedy for this dire social downfall before doing some detailed research, yet Ego and Model dominance in society is becoming too alarming to ignore. Still, we may at least study the chance of raising the compatibility of couples with marginal personalities in terms of Ego and Model within various types of 'relationship models' suitable for them.[††]

Major problems arise when we naively force ourselves into a doomed relationship. For example, we may have a domineering Ego or Model, but do not know, care, or do anything about it. We hide our flaws long enough until we win the love of someone we like to marry and then release our real personality very casually. In this case, we hurt ourselves as much as our partners by getting into a likely doomed marriage. We may or may not ever find the motivation and chance to overcome our personality deficiencies. Yet, marrying somebody while either or both partners have high Ego and Model tendencies only leads to long-term suffering of both partners. Unless we learn to become a more rational and perhaps humbler person, not getting into serious relationships is the best choice for everybody, especially considering the likely damage on innocent children who end up facing their parents' animosity and fights. Yet, this is such a naïve advice and a high expectation to place on selfish people with huge Egos.

[††] See footnote on page 129 about 'Relationship Models.'

Naturally, the main hurdle is that gauging our own or other people's personality aspects is difficult, since people fake their personalities readily, especially during the initial stages of their relationships. Still, everybody can assess reasonably well how a person stands in terms of Ego, Model, and Self. Especially, if we are clever, we can do some quick tests to measure the intensity of another person's Ego or Model. Accordingly, if Model and Ego look rather high already, partners should become extra cautious. In fact, they must now measure not only each other's Egos and Models' intensities more precisely, but also their tolerance levels required for a most likely too risky relationship. We might even choose to seek the opinion of an impartial third person about this matter. The mental guard that prospective marriage partners have towards each other is rather turned off or defused when they are with other people. Thus, an outsider can see hints of personality aspects that two partners hide, or cannot detect about, each other.

Often, people's personality characteristics, especially Ego, are not apparent even to themselves. However, they reside deep in our unconscious awaiting a chance to surface with a bang. For example, it is possible that a partner's extreme sense of anger and aggression has been repressed within him/her for years, perhaps due to domineering and abusive parents. At some stage of his/her life, these feelings may finally erupt in either an explosive or a gradual manner to reach a perturbing extreme. Often, childhood traumas erupt in destructive forms and most likely stay with the person for the rest of his/her life if they are not cured seriously. These deep defects, e.g., passive/aggressive personalities, are hard to detect, though, as people misrepresent themselves intentionally or inadvertently in hopes of confusing or attracting others.

A related crucial factor that prospective partners must gauge is their compatibility in terms of their approach about making and spending money. Most Ego and Model driven personalities have peculiar financial preferences and usually higher risk orientation, too. Therefore, gauging each other's knack for financial stability (financial sense) is useful, especially for conservative and simple people, to ensure they are compatible in that regard. Otherwise, avoiding that union might be a wise decision.

Aside from the prominent role of people's personality aspects for their compatibility, as discussed briefly above, couples should have, particularly, the right personalities and mindsets for:

1. Increasing Life Enjoyments
2. Support and Cooperation
3. Building a Sensible Commitment

This chapter will discuss the fourteen compatibility measures (Relationships Success Factors) listed in Table 8.1. While working on these 14 success factors, couples should also work on the 6 'Alienation Preparedness Factors' discussed in Chapter Eleven.

Table 8.1: Compatibility Measures
(Relationships Success Factors)

1. Compatibility to increase life enjoyments
- General attraction
- Communication and negotiation abilities
- Activities and thoughts to share

2. Compatibility for support and cooperation
- Teamwork
- Support to pursue personal goals
- Functional and psychological support
- Joint problem solving capabilities
- Knack for financial stability (financial sense)

3. Compatibility for a sensible commitment
- Patience and Flexibility
- Forgiveness
- Dealing with anger
- Compassion
- Awareness of commitment
- Expressing personal expectations

1. *Compatibility to Increase Life Enjoyments*

An implied expectation in relationships is to create mental and physical synergy in all respects for reducing life's burdens, which then leads to higher life enjoyments above the levels that partners can achieve personally. If partners are incapable to achieve this added mutual joy, the purpose of marriage becomes doubtful; partners start to doubt the value of staying in a lousy relationship. Thus, a few essential factors that raise partners' life enjoyments are discussed below.

General Attraction
Obviously, general attraction brings two individuals together quickly and provides a great foundation for building all the other aspects of a joint life. It simply reflects our needs for sex, love, compassion, and companionship, without the extreme notion of being in love or desperate for it. General attraction is the positive feeling of intimacy with our partner, *physically and mentally*. It is an authentic connection between partners, rather than a flimsy infatuation. Yet, this attraction stirs teamwork, while partners also satisfy each other's need for love and sex naturally. It also goads partners to grow their patience, flexibility, and tolerance, whereas without such attraction they would feel trapped or seek separation with every small setback.

Communication and Negotiation Abilities
Partners' compatibility regarding personal values and philosophy of life is important for increasing their life enjoyment, but their ability to communicate their viewpoints effectively is even more crucial for raising their life enjoyments. They should be flexible, articulate, and patient, instead of opinionated, hyperactive, and dogmatic. They should be able to express their feelings and needs calmly without getting into quarrels, or withdrawing fast, because their communication feels futile and frustrating, e.g., when they fail to manipulate their partner perhaps. Actually, a major test of

compatibility is partners' abilities to discuss their concerns calmly and intelligently. Their abilities to negotiate and be assertive are vital for keeping communication channels open and productive. Conversely, oversensitivity and emotional reactions stop partners from looking for their common interests even when they have some. Without communication, exploring their common grounds and possible compatibilities, to increase their life enjoyments, gets difficult. It would feel as if partners were severely incompatible when they both might in fact have enough high personal qualities to share a happy life.

Communication plays a wide range of roles for team playing, relating, sharing experiences, psychological relief, etc. Therefore, it is an important factor for increasing partners' life enjoyments. Fortunately, the quality of communication is rather easy to gauge if we look for the right clues actively.

Most communication problems arise when a partner becomes the sole (or main) communicator prior to marriage. Partner 'B' agrees with, or simply absorbs, whatever 'A' suggests without expressing enough personal opinions. Thus, 'A' believes 'B' is in agreement with him/her and his/her viewpoints, which gratifies A's egoism and sense of control. In reality, though, this is merely a sign of potential problems waiting for future explosions.

Partner B's seeming passivity might be for several reasons. S/he may disagree with everything or most of what 'A' says, but holds back his/her comments just to avoid contradicting 'A' and jeopardizing their relationship. Or s/he might be dominated by 'A' and does not *yet* know how to correct the situation and be assertive. Or, s/he does not have any special ideas to contribute to their communication, thus s/he remains content with this one-way communication, at least for now. Thus, an incomplete, stressful communication process prevails between partners.

Then, after marriage, the timid (or passive/aggressive) partner 'B' makes his/her abrupt entrance eventually with a new tactic as a very active/aggressive partner. S/he makes her voice heard to make up for all the past inhibitions, and because s/he does not know a better method of communicating, so in most cases she appears harsh and rebellious. Even if there were a slim chance that 'B' does not rebel, 'A' would eventually feel the void and the lack of some intellectual communication with his/her partner, especially when his/her efforts to communicate are blocked by passive aggression and retaliation. An Ego driven partner (maybe 'A') dominates their communication and relationship too much. Conversely, a Model (maybe 'B') tries to accommodate his/her partner by agreeing with his/her viewpoints and perhaps even encouraging his/her way of thinking. Eventually, however, both partners feel dissatisfied with their meaningless communication and its results. Especially, Model (maybe 'B') who only listens in the first phase usually rebels or withdraws eventually, leaving 'A' completely in shock and rejected.

Life enjoyments stem from good communication and calm exchange of valuable thoughts. If partners cannot stir each other's thoughts, they eventually look for it elsewhere. Thus, prospective marriage partners must know what communication entails and ensure that theirs is enriching and compatible at their intelligence levels. Partners need good communication skills in order to relate effectively. However, another important role of communication is to increase partners' enjoyment in life.

We can test communication abilities easily. If communication is dominated by one side, if partners always end up fighting and withdrawing, if one or both partners are not able or willing to express themselves and are secretive or ignorant, or if a partner is deliberately only a listener, then most likely there would never be a reliable and healthy communication between partners. Surely, communication is the main cause of relationship failures due to its essential role for cooperation, relating, sharing experiences, and increasing partners' life enjoyments, etc.

A sign of good communication is partners' zeal to share their thoughts equally, get into arguments without ending in fights or withdrawals, find means of compromising from time to time, and know how to negotiate for achieving productive results. There would probably be some occasional fights and short withdrawals between these couples, too, but the frequency is low compared to couples who usually get into trouble every time they attempt to communicate, or nothing comes out of their communication.

Activities and Thoughts to Share

Without compatibility in lifestyle and thoughts, marriage would be an endless cycle of burning rage and freezing apathy—fights and withdrawals. Partners should have common thoughts to share regularly, in particular on personal topics such as hobbies, life values, self-awareness, and philosophy. They should enjoy their discussions per se, rather than doing it randomly merely out of necessity, mostly for solving their growing problems.

While boosting their life enjoyments by sharing their *thoughts*, partners should also share certain activities and seek means of appreciating the aesthetic values of life and Nature. If they do not have compatibility in *things* they like, and like to do, at best they end up doing mostly their own things, while missing the joy of sharing activities and thoughts, as inherent human needs.

Some people have peculiar needs or insecurities that reduce their chance of compatibility with others. For an artist who finds high values in art and Nature, for example, living with a partner who is indifferent about these experiences would feel tough and lonesome, especially if his/her partner does not have enough things to do him/herself, which would then often lead to more nagging. Of course, partners need not appreciate everything equally all the time as long as they have enough thoughts to share and things to do together without partners losing their interests and independence or feeling pressured for attention.

Many couples get into serious quarrels due to their narrow perceptions about inadequate attention, differences in tastes of food, the house they like to buy, outdoor activities, common friends, and other basic things that nobody could have imagined would cause so much friction after marriage. Obviously, partners would never agree on everything. That is exactly the reason an effective communication is necessary to discuss their opinions and differences calmly. With good communication, some of their conflicts due to inadequate attention or general disagreements can be resolved. They learn to make the best of their times together for sharing at least some thoughts and activities, while they give each other ample space for independence.

One way of testing and measuring this special compatibility is to prepare a list of major interests and activities that partners like to do alone or share together, without trying to influence, judge, or ridicule each other's tastes and preferences. Of course, some of these interests should have become obvious during the initial courtship without a need to prepare a list. However, making a list together indicates the seriousness of those activities and interests as part of their life plans and not only during a short period. The list must contain only the items they regularly do and are sincere about, and not merely their dreams. Simple things, like a stroll in Nature, athletic activities, artistic urges, reading and discussing a book, and gardening are some good factors for gauging partners' compatibility. Then, they can sit back and decide how they can satisfy those needs (their own and their partner's), without too much compromising out of pressure or for keeping their partner quiet. And they must surely stop assuming they can change their partner gradually and enjoy sharing the same activities.

Therefore, the first set of compatibility factors (for increasing life enjoyments) consists of, i) General attraction, ii) communication method and content, and iii) major thoughts and activities that partners share. Together, these factors raise their life enjoyments.

2. Compatibility for Support and Cooperation

The second group of compatibility factors contains the elements of support and cooperation in 'family,' which requires partners' goodwill and conscious efforts. Clearly, couples often have the intention of cooperating and supporting each other to achieve common family objectives along with their personal goals. Yet, they hardly know what relationship needs and objectives are and how to go about satisfying them.[‡‡]

Everybody has some vague ideas about marital obligations and duties. However, support and cooperation is much broader than obligations and responsibilities, which have lost their own roles and meanings in marriages, nowadays, anyway. Our needs for individualism and equality have eroded all those good family values, including obligations and responsibilities that prevailed in old cultures. Therefore, partners must now measure, at the outset, their own and their partner's compatibility factors for support and cooperation, e.g., compassion and teamwork capacity, instead of depending on their implied intentions and promises.

Raising children is still the most basic and natural intention (rightly or wrongly!) for building a family. Children are our only creations with such complexity in physical and mental capacity and a soul, too. This exalting creation that we so casually view as our common objective in marriage is developed in response to our instinctual need and intention for cooperation and support. Without a mutually strong sense of compassion, cooperation, and support, even this basic objective remains invalid and cannot bear fruit. Raising healthy kids without spoiling them requires smart parents, yet partners' quarrels even about how much they should indulge their children ruin their kids' psyches and future these days, too. Humans have uniform instinctual needs to exchange compassion, support, and cooperation with someone we trust in order to share and achieve better things in life, yet we have not still figured out how to do it effectively. Partners should be able to look up to each other to play their roles effectively and boost the quality of their marital relationship.

The five major factors related to this category of compatibility are discussed in the following pages.

[‡‡] Relationship needs and objectives are explained in this author's book, *Relationship Needs, Framework, and Models*.

Teamwork
Partners' knack for teamwork is the first criterion (factor) to measure for 'support and cooperation' compatibility. Teamwork deficiency is not merely a symptom of personal negligence, but rather bad universal training, as competition is evident and vastly encouraged in everything we do. Nowadays, the world economy and competition influence our mentalities and attitudes too much. The important lesson we learn at home, at school, and in society is to compete and win in order to prove our identities. Our worth as a person is mostly determined by our superiority over others. In professional sports, physical ability and competitiveness lead to outrageous levels of compensation. Our children want to be like so and so basketball or hockey player in order to be rich. The sense of competition defines the whole purpose and structure of organizations. In our jobs, we get involved with ruthless rules and strategies to defeat our company's competitors, and we get into competition with our colleagues and bosses, too, to acquire higher positions and money. Accordingly, we are sacrificing our compassion for competition. This mentality is not restricted to social and economic settings. Family life has also become equally contaminated by this evil.

Instead of teamwork, marriage partners, nowadays, appear more and more in competition with each other in all respects with similar tactics and mentality they apply for outside competitions. They compete to acquire the power and status in their families, as though it were another heartless entity to capture and control. Overall, competition is lowering the level of trust that teamwork requires. Another big factor that impedes teamwork is people's obsession, nowadays, to stress on their 'individualism,' without knowing its true meaning. They merely perceive and express it in a demented way by becoming more selfish and aggressive.

Marriage partners fight to set their territories and force their viewpoints. They struggle to dominate the situations and each other. They compete for the love and respect of their kids, while strive to push their worldviews on them. They compete by trying to prove they work harder, deserve more, are hurt more, make more money, are right, know more, etc. Accordingly, even their simplest disagreements turn into vile quarrels, retaliations, or desperate submission of one partner. Children soon learn who runs the household, has the ultimate power to set the direction of their lives, and overrule their whims.

Overall, despite widespread propagandas in organizations and society, teamwork has found very little application in our lives. The pretences and talks of teamwork may deceive us to think that perhaps we can finally go beyond individual Egos and harmonize our intentions regardless of our personal interests. Alas, the sense of rivalry, as the core of our social values, has also inflicted our family life and is preventing teamwork. Then again, partners need teamwork daily for supporting each other and for implementing family values and objectives. As long as partners place personal goals ahead of family objectives, there would never be a chance for compatibility in support and cooperation.

Like most other personal deficiencies, partners' obsession for competition and control in family life emerges at various degrees. We can try to gauge the intensity of our partner's competitiveness and domineering attitude rather than expecting to find an absolute team player. We can measure our partner's teamwork capacity from his/her reaction to losing in a game, or when there is a choice between collaboration and competition. We can design situations and games to learn about our partner's egoism turning into rivalry in everything s/he does. Then, we can take the same tests ourselves and determine how good a team player we are!

We fail to create a teamwork attitude and environment also because we are quite dogmatic and like to insist on being *right* about everything, and to prove our partner *wrong*. We like to have the last word about everything and we are certain we know the best for everybody. This attitude becomes more evident after marriage when partners feel less obliged to impress each other by their humble and gentle behaviour. Just to use an anecdote, a couple (J. and M.) often used to joke sarcastically about a global reality, perhaps in a rather exaggerated tone for fun. J. said that prior to their marriage, M. kept saying, "You are right," about everything J. said. But right after marriage, the first comment poor J. had made, M. had said, "You are wrong."

"I've not been right about anything since," J. said with a sigh!

Regardless of the apparent exaggeration and humour of this anecdote, it reflects the gist of dramatic change in relationships after marriage. Partners should discuss their 'common' goals and find out how they are planning to go about them and what those goals really mean behind the surface.

Support of Personal Goals

Teamwork is mainly essential for satisfying relationship needs and objectives, but also for helping partners pursue their personal goals. Partners must demonstrate their interests and abilities to support each other to succeed in life. In fact, it is important that partners know their major personal objectives in life and discuss them together at the outset seriously. The intention is to evaluate each other's true feelings and reactions about their goals, which are usually left out in casual conversations. The main reason is that only few people develop realistic long-term life plans, mainly because they want to remain flexible and make the best of socio-economic opportunities becoming available to them.

Nevertheless, if personal aspirations are discussed a few times, especially if we are already pursuing those objectives, partners' true reaction and likely support can be witnessed and assessed. However, it is also important to have real personal objectives rather than faking ideas (dreams) that we are not serious about. Naturally, partners can always ponder and discuss new ideas and goals after marriage, too, along with their level of seriousness and sincerity about those new personal plans. They should show their interests to get each other's input.

Many family frictions arise because partners forget to discuss their personal objectives sincerely, but mention all kinds of lost dreams due to marriage merely for blaming their partner for their failures. Often, a partner has a vague idea, or maybe even a strong desire, to pursue some special goal and mention it casually. Then, s/he neglects her/his plans because of his/her lack of motivation, perseverance, ability, or any other personal shortfall. Yet, s/he uses marriage as an excuse for his/her own failure. S/he even believes in this injustice him/herself eventually. Often when a partner does not have serious personal goals in life, s/he holds the other party responsible for his/her perceived or real failures. Sometimes, they are so arrogant and stupid to blame each other for their imaginary lost opportunities to find a suitable partner when they had been younger and more attractive!!!

The point is that if partners allow marriage stop them from pursuing their life plans or finding better matches, they must only blame themselves. If we make mistakes or get trapped in bleak situations against our plans, we may blame our fates or personal negligence, but making claims or blaming our partners for our failures reflects merely our poor character and immaturity.

Our partners should not be used as scapegoats if we ignore our personal aspirations before marriage or do not develop the motivation and stamina to pursue them after marriage.

Another cautionary point is that if a partner has lower needs and aspirations in life than the other, s/he might try hard to bring his/her partner's ambitions down to the same level as his/hers, instead of making an effort to catch up with him/her. A partner's lack of life philosophy or aspirations affects both partners' lives adversely. Especially troublesome would be when one partner's life philosophy and aspirations are outside the popular social norms so unlike the other partner's.

Functional and Psychological Support
Partners can usually assess each other's psychological strengths and stability by gauging their patience, compassion, and similar basic factors. A hyperactive, dogmatic, oversensitive partner can never manage even his/her own life, let alone help his/her partner during crisis. Before making the marriage decision, partners must

trust each other's psychological capacity to back their personal needs and goals. They must trust each other's capacities to offer psychological and mental support in general for all kinds of likely marital and social issues. This kind of support relieves partners' normal stress from daily work and life challenges. It also boosts their communication and deepens the scope of their relationship.

Joint Problem Identifying and Solving

Along with partners' ability to communicate, they should also be good in joint problem identifying and solving. This needs mutual grasp of each other's analytical knack and use of logic in gauging and addressing common situations and issues, finding practical solutions, and making rational compromises. Testing this ability is not difficult, either. A hypothetical family problem or any story from the news can be discussed along with personal suggestions about a solution. We then wait for our partner's participation and suggestions for solving the problem at hand. We can assess the process after a few typical discussion sessions.

Knack for Financial Stability (financial sense)

Partners must have a personal knack, plus joint compatibility and responsibility, for maintaining the financial stability of the family with a concrete plan and sense about their financial resources and expenditures. If they cannot work together and support each other to achieve their long-term financial needs, their marriage would be full of frictions and headaches.

The second group of compatibilities that we should seek in our marriage partner consist of, i) teamwork for common objectives, ii) support to pursue personal goals, iii) ability to provide mental and psychological support, iv) joint problem solving capabilities, and v) knack for financial stability. Together these five factors induce an environment for support and cooperation to nurture a friendly and constructive relationship.

3. Compatibility for Building a Sensible Commitment

History and our personal experiences clearly show that all the promises and vows we exchange at the wedding and all the good intentions we have when we join with our partner in matrimony are worthless when all the right factors of compatibility are not seriously thought through and analysed. So irrationally, most of us partake in some useless wedding rituals and fool ourselves with such comical and hypocritical exercises regularly. When a couple is incompatible, life often becomes hell for them. Hence, breaking their promises and commitments becomes most natural and viable for them. Some particular personal traits of partners can make their intentions for commitments rather more realistic, however. Those traits would help them reconcile their problems easier, thus sustain a somewhat healthier marital relationship. The opposite is even truer: Without these compatibility factors, the chance of marriage success is slim. It does not matter how much partners promise or pretend to be making compromises, they would not succeed without some inherent sense of commitment that the following general factors might guarantee to some extent.

Patience and Flexibility
Partners' ability to grasp and tolerate their moderate differences, rather than turning them into clashing issues, is the backbone of all marriages. Without patience and flexibility, we break under the first wave of marital difficulties and decide to escape the stressful situation, instead of trying to find sensible solutions. Yet, most of us do not realize the need for high levels of patience and flexibility, nowadays, not as a personal sacrifice, but a harsh new reality and requirement in relationships. Most marital problems, nowadays, relate to Ego clashes and struggles about who is right and who is stubborn. Often, no major problems exist and partners might even like each other, in spite of their crude personalities and endless frictions. In such situations, false pride and obstinacy goad partners to declare war and go for separation. However,

patience and flexibility (to override false pride and stubbornness) would help partners cool down initially and then come to some personal understanding of mutual problems eventually.

Managing Anger

Anger is a common, natural reaction. However, what we do with it, and how much we are able to control it, is crucial. One's ability to control one's anger is genetic and hardly learnable before some major personal quirks are handled. As a factor of compatibility, we must look for our partner's, as well as our own, ability to deal with anger. Most often anger erupts when either or both partners are highly opinionated, egotistical, and must have the final say in everything all the time. Unless one partner does not mind being dominated by his/her partner, soon resistance and frictions lead to alienation and separation.

Ability to Forgive

Another factor of compatibility is partners' genuine capacity to forgive, instead of being spiteful and reactionary. Naturally, when one partner makes a mistake, spite and retaliation would solve nothing. If mistake is too harsh and hurtful for one partner and cannot really be forgiven even after a period of cool down, then perhaps not much is left to do but to seek separation. However, if the mistake is not intentional or an extreme disappointment for the victimized partner, s/he must have the ability to forgive if they are both willing and able to learn a lesson from their experience. Sometimes, the victimized partner continues to live with his/her partner with the intention or thoughts of retaliation, which would only increase alienation and pain for both partners. Thus, gauging both partners' abilities to forgive and learn from their mistakes after clarifying the causes of their disagreements and frictions is also vital. These types of abilities are not difficult to observe and assess during the initial courtship. Then again, it is obvious that measuring all these factors or overcoming our emotions to avoid a likely troublesome marriage is quite hard and needs wisdom.

Compassion

The level of compassion is indirectly helpful in keeping partners compatible, as it keeps our Ego under some control. In fact, one's ability to forgive, control anger, and exercise tolerance shows one's level of compassion and life outlook in general. A sign of snobbery reflects lack of compassion, whereas some degree of humility along with subtle confidence can be a reliable sign of compassion and tolerance. We can assess this factor as well.

Awareness of Commitment

Partners should make their business to understand, and think of, commitment as an essential part of marriage. We cannot think or make promises of commitment without really knowing what it means, how it can be achieved, and what its *real* objective is. Once this basic requirement is understood, we must actively look for 'sensible commitment factors' that have been discussed in this chapter and measure them in ourselves and our partners.

Expressing Personal Expectations

It is essential for partners to know before wedding about, i) each other's expectations from marriage, ii) their marital objectives, iii) personal ambitions, and iv) likely sacrifices required to run their relationship smoothly. Thus, it is important to make a habit, from the outset, to share our expectations from marriage frankly and seriously with our partner and insist that s/he does the same.

Expressing their expectations honestly helps partners cross the bridge between *love* and *understanding*, while there is a bridge to make this crossover possible. The difference between love and understanding is usually unclear to partners, and it remains vague before marriage. Partners believe they know each other already and that nothing would damage their wonderful impressions of marriage afterwards. They neglect to think practically due to their misperceptions of marriage. They assume they would understand each other's expectations even better and easier later just because they are married. They think that cohabitation would raise their mutual understanding and sensitivity, so discussing and resolving expectations would be easy and a routine process. They may even imagine that their understanding of each other's expectations and needs would be somewhat natural, and thus unnecessary to discuss in advance. This wishful thinking is a common, natural feeling, but in reality, it almost never happens. In fact, partners' level of understanding and responding to each other's needs and expectations usually diminishes fast after marriage.

The six noted personality attributes, i) patience and flexibility, ii) forgiveness, iii) handling anger, iv) compassion, v) awareness of commitment, and vi) expressing personal expectations comprise the third set of compatibility measurements that make partners' commitments to each other sensible and possible. If one or both partners are weak in many of these areas, soon alienation and frictions build up. Making a marriage proposal or accepting it without serious consideration of the compatibility factors listed in Table 8.1 and reviewed in this chapter would be a big mistake, In fact, partners' mutual grasp of these basic, but important facts, can save them lots of hassles later. Compatibility measurement process by partners would take months to complete realistically; it is not a simple exercise to undertake quickly just to get married. The present sloppy attitude only leads to many years of anguish and alienation before partners realize the need for separation and then face the pains of divorce as well.

Is Compatibility a Dream?

We usually think that we can assess our partner casually based on things s/he does or says. Seldom do we make direct and designed efforts to measure the crucial aspects of compatibility, such as a person's ability for teamwork or keeping his/her commitments. This is because we do not know how and it is not part of social norms yet, although we judge people hastily, anyway. While indirect and casual assessment has some value, it is not useful like a direct and designed test that we can apply actively. These direct tests can be done in a stealthy, rather playful, manner when partners are not stressed or hostile.

Casual customary assessments are based on our perfunctory judgments (and possibly even hasty emotional justifications) of our partner's behaviours or calculated actions. People often lie or use Model to portray a made-up personality, whereas in direct (but secretive) testing we can try to create situations and ask questions that disable Model to play a major role and confuse us. Thus, we give our partner's deeper, hidden, personality attributes a chance to emerge.

A hurdle for measuring partners' compatibility lies in the fact that they mostly meet by accident and get attached rather quickly after an initial attraction, without any training about compatibility factors or prior planning to look for certain qualities in each other. At the same time, we also expect personal perfection from one another, as our rigid standard for compatibility, while most of us are not even good enough beings, which means hardly any two people can relate naturally! The reality is that at best only a tiny minority with no or minimal psychological flaws, who are well aware of their own and their partner's needs, might meet and be compatible on many grounds. The rest of us, with psychological defects, driven by our Egos, and naive about our own or partners' needs, are hardly compatible with anybody else. We have little chance of building a peaceful relationship, since humans are not compatible in general. We ruin everything fast personally with our egoism and insecurities, even if we happen to meet a perfect person. In the final analysis, it seems as though our own shortfalls make every one of us incompatible with the rest of the world.

Sadly, not even basic professional help is available these days to measure partners' incompatibilities and give them at least a heads-up about their incompatibility areas and levels, and likely headaches. They could at least prevent many mismatched unions that are ruining people's spirits and damaging social structure. The current compatibility tests are ineffective and flawed in terms of their designs. More depressing, however, is our persistence to ignore even strong clues or perceptions of incompatibility, which further reveals the low potency and value of our logic and the dangers of relying on our intuition these days, too. Sadly, most couples prefer to rely mostly on their raw intuitions, emotions, and arbitrary criteria that society and their parents have injected into their minds about relationships' success factors.

A common mistake, which becomes evident only after getting married, is that one or both partners assume and perceive they are getting into a normal marriage that would be ideal. Accordingly, they seek, and insist on, the *perfection* they had imagined for a 'normal' relationship, and instead only get more disappointments, distress, fights, retaliations, and alienation. Partners do not realize at the outset that most likely they are surely not a perfect match, but more importantly why and in what respects; and how they can make their marriage work, despite the known, and potentially a lot more, imperfections.

A *normal* relationship is, in fact, full of inconveniences and quarrels, so far from perfection. We should also be careful with our personal definition of perfection. We often expect others to be perfect in the way we define perfection for our convenience and according to our personal values in life. In addition to this naïve, narrow demand, we allow ourselves to be and behave any way we like—supposedly perfect—again, as it suits us. We look at the world and people for our convenience, interests, and out of pure selfishness. Meanwhile, we just trust our crude judgment of a person and romanticism to choose a partner.

Nevertheless, seeking compatibility is a big challenge due to 1) our idealism and high expectations, 2) the immensity of our peculiar idiosyncrasies augmenting humans' innate inability to relate, and 3) our lack of knowledge about relationships' needs, compatibility factors, and personal efforts and patience required to keep two people together in a teamwork setting.

Humans' Inherent Incompatibility

While we keep seeking an ideal partner without knowing how to gauge compatibility, no one can fulfil our needs realistically. In the end, mainly our own shortfalls make us incompatible with everybody else, anyway. These facts suggest that most of us are doomed to suffer of incompatibility syndrome throughout our lives, mostly by our own faults. Then again, how can we accept such a harsh truth and admit humans' inherent, incurable flaws?!

Someday, humans may be able to find better ways of looking for and studying compatible partners, instead of relying only on accidents and emotions to get married. Maybe sufficient research (sometime in the future) can reveal which personal shortfalls of couples are possibly sharable between them, if possible. For now, however, we remain mostly at the mercy of luck to find the right match for our unique, often flawed, personalities. Therefore, we (scientists mostly) must find tools for helping even less perfect couples live within specific relationship models by staying vigilant about their moderate incompatibilities forever and learning how to be mutually tolerant of each other's unique idiosyncrasies. A more challenging task, of course, is to find out how couples with severe incompatibilities might be helped, mainly psychologically, for a rather courteous joint life with minimal frictions and pains —or by designing and applying particular relationship models along with some practical guidelines.

Sometime in the future, couples might find access to reliable compatibility tests that specify exactly where they stand in terms of the kind of relationship they might be able to build together within a specific relationship model. For now, basic compatibility tests might at least help couples pinpoint those areas of their clear incompatibilities with dire potential problems at least. The goal is not to assist only fully compatible people marry, but rather help most couples who feel attracted towards each other build a viable relationship for themselves through self-awareness, compatibility tests, and choosing a relationship model suitable for their peculiar needs and personalities.

Naturally, compatibility tests are useful mostly before marriage for predicting the obstacles and the likely outcome of a proposed relationship. It might help couples choose the right partner and relationship model for them. However, once the decision is made, couples should strive to make their relationships work in the best ways possible rather than whining and arguing. They should be educated and get ready to handle the foreseeable headaches of relationships in general. For example, they must understand and work actively on the success factors suggested in this chapter. They must keep themselves alert and proactive in terms of their tough roles to keep their relationships healthy within the general guidelines and in line with their specific relationship model's needs. They must learn to honour certain rules, instead of insisting on their exaggerated personal needs and expectations the way it has become customary in modern societies.

In all, it is wise to doubt and postpone marriage until partners have had a chance to understand marital demands and risks, their compatibility, and their union's special circumstances, especially partners' personalities. If, at the end of their long evaluation, they still have doubts about some aspects of their compatibility, then most likely something is missing. That kind of union would fail. The least they can do is to review the list of relationships' success factors again to determine the areas that need partners' sincere deliberation and decision. Most important of all, however, is our ability to learn patience by admitting that our crude mentalities in modern societies worsen humans' innate faulty nature and make it very hard to build satisfactory relationships. Especially, couples should know relationships' specific needs and goals, compatibly factors, and the guidelines for relating.

At the same time, couples must also gauge the sources of their doubts regarding the viability of their relationship. Many factors might have made us tired or unrealistic about the potential and nature of relationships, especially in modern societies, nowadays, including our natural (or obsessive) search for compatibility, our high expectations from companionships, the lack of teamwork, and the difficulty of getting our partners' consensus over personal and joint objectives.

Unfortunately, an ideal marital relationship is unlikely and not suggested here, either. A complete match and compatibility is unrealistic. The sole goal is to learn about the *practical* forms of compatibility for various relationship models and evaluate our unique situations against it to gauge the level of discrepancy and potential for headaches in the future.

Nonetheless, it is also essential to spend ample time to study the main attributes of our prospective partner patiently, instead of deciding hastily, either positively or negatively. We must learn, in particular, about those flaws and incompatibilities we must cope with a lifetime, while we would be under so many other career related and social pressures. Despite all our love for a person, we must know realistically whether, and how, we might tolerate his/her quirks and small nuisances, which might be evident already, for many years to come without losing our sanity. Even small irritants and issues most likely hint about deeper idiosyncrasies that could lead to marital conflicts and 'divorce.'

Therefore, time for a right decision is now, before making a commitment, although we also remember that no couple can be fully compatible! If not enough compatibility or agreement exists about the main factors for the success of a relationship, it is wise to stop. In particular, it is crucial to gauge partners' compatibility factors for a specific 'relationship model' that might best fit their mentalities and personal needs, especially for their desired level of personal independence.[§§]

[§§] See footnote on page 129 about 'Relationship Models.'

CHAPTER NINE
Sources of Marital Problems

Humans' big difficulty to relate is a natural phenomenon that any wise person should expect and learn to accept. It causes partners' *innate* incompatibilities and deep marital problems, as discussed in the previous chapters. Then, couples' *peculiar* idiosyncrasies raise their incompatibilities so much more when they attempt to share their emotions and life aspirations. Accordingly, studying any relationship situation—to grasp the depth of issues and find solutions—is too difficult due to its uniqueness and complexity. Moreover, spouses are usually too dogged, dogmatic, and spiteful to agree on the causes of their particular conflicts or suggested solutions even if ten most qualified marriage counsellors tried to help them. The impotency of human logic reveals itself in full force when partners merely shrug off all the evidences and logic before them about the main causes of their relationship problems. Many books have offered insightful solutions regarding marital conundrums for decades with no tangible results. Marriages are in fact getting more unreliable and sadder every day, because we do not know anything about relationship demands and the right factors for partners' compatibility in the first place when we have a chance to make a proper decision. Some shoddy factors, like love and loneliness, usually make a couple jump into a marriage and then suffer its repercussions for many decades. Anyway, finding the unique issues behind each couple's marital conflicts remains a big challenge that smart couples must strive to sort out mostly on their own. The compatibility measures discussed in the previous chapters along with the general roots of marital conflicts reviewed in this chapter can help couples get a sense about their *odd* conditions and partners' *unique* idiosyncrasies largely. They can at least identify and beware of the general conflicts in most marriages and ponder the solutions suggested in this chapter.

Communication Hurdles

Communication breakdown is surely the main cause of marriage problems. While couples seem to grasp and bear the content and method of their partner's communication relatively well before marriage, they usually have great difficulty communicating after marriage. It is safe to assume that if communication had been lacking or feeling problematic, partners would have wisely not married. If this is true, then something goes terribly wrong after people get married! Some of the possibilities are as follows:

- While partners might have assumed that they had had good (or at least bearable) communication before marriage, they had not understood its required depth, importance, contents, and goals.
- We all have a tendency to think positively before marriage about the way we know our partners and how we understand the contents and means of our communications. Then, we are shocked more every day after marriage when we realize our naive initial optimism. We realize our erroneous assumptions about understanding our partner's expectations and the way we interpret each other's simple words, thoughts, and method of communication. Communication breakdown is because we do not grasp, or misinterpret, each other's intentions and needs.
- The level of listening, giving, and forgiving, which are all parts of communication, diminishes after marriage, since partners'

Part III: Companionship and Marriage

initial intentions of impressing (and maybe manipulating) each other subside after marriage.
- The level of partners' sensitivity towards each other's feelings somehow diminishes, often inadvertently. While our premarital communications seem to be tailored for luring our partners, post-marital communications are more focused on domination of the situation and our partners.
- At the same time, partners become oversensitive and impatient more everyday about the way their partner treats them.
- Partners refocus on other issues of life that feel more pressing again after marriage, thus they find less time and need to spend on proper communication. Partners do not appear to be paying enough attention to each other's needs and words, although they might continue to be mentally and physically attracted to each other.
- Often, the level of respect declines as partners learn more about each other's vulnerabilities. The idol they had expected in a partner proves to be quite defective. The contents, means, and level of communication are, of course, a function of respect.
- Partners often overestimate their tolerance level and put a great level of faith in the power of their love.
- Partners assume they know about relationships' unique needs, but almost nobody knows the real purposes and complexities of relationships in the new era. Thus, their communication channels collapse, while other relationship deficiencies press on and demand some form of cooperation and understanding.
- Partners face family or personal issues and they cannot see things the same way, or they are not prepared to accept each other's conclusions and solutions, just out of spite or perhaps with good personal reasons. Differences of opinions, values, and lifestyle make communication incoherent and lousy.
- Partners had not noted the idea of using a relationship model suitable for their personalities and needs. (See the footnote on page 129 about 'Relationship Models.')

When communication hurdles emerge and get out of hand, it becomes increasingly impossible to bring it back under control. Some basic communication issues grow into major relationship obstacles where no single problem can be discussed and resolved. It appears as if all other aspects of the relationship have stopped functioning. The moods and feelings change and partners start to be suspicious of each other. We stop expressing our needs to our partner, as we find it a waste of time, since we feel our partner is not listening or we do not grasp our communication contents. We merely try to minimize our conflicts and arguments by keeping a safe distance. Things we say to each other sound senseless and contrary to everything we thought we had agreed on implicitly and perhaps even explicitly in our earlier communications.

We can analyse the contents of communication to find out the causes of frictions or the lack of interest to discuss seemingly contentious issues. We can also observe how quickly partners' insecurities and unsatisfied needs always interfere and override the context of communications. In many cases, communication is convoluted by the hidden personal agendas, fears, insecurities, and other psychological defects that are not obvious or admitted to by partners. In such circumstances, we always revert to the same old crooked personal perceptions and draw on our inherent idiosyncrasies to express our anger and blame our partners for everything regardless of the subject or content of communication. Any topic of conversation becomes only a prelude to raise the same old grievances, which may be well founded or a product of hasty retaliations. Nevertheless, the results are always the same as far as communication problems are concerned. Unless these basic issues are somehow resolved, communication contents would not be of any relevance in harmonizing the process, partners' needs and intentions, and outcomes.

The method of communication also affects partners' reactions largely. For example, showing interest, concern, and compassion stirs a favourable atmosphere for dialogue, and enhances partners' trust in each other as well as their personal confidence. Of course, this approach works as long as partners appreciate each other's concerns and respect the rules of a good communication process. Acknowledging the conflicts and our partner's feelings usually helps the process. However, on some occasions, one partner keeps raising his/her demands despite all the compassion s/he receives from his/her partner—a symptom of severe psychological defect that hinder the advance of communication process permanently.

A similar communication hurdle emerges when we think we are giving more to our partner than s/he is ever able to grasp and repay. We believe we are more attentive to his/her needs, show more concern and compassion, thus feel deprived of receiving equivalent attention and appreciation. In fact, we are baffled by our partner's rising demands despite everything we do for him/her already. A partner's feeling about the imbalance in exchange of affection and care always emerges in their tone and texture of communications and results in muddled exchanges of charged feelings instead of a dialogue.

The problem of inadequate affection and understanding in family relationships is recognized widely. The customary remedy prescribed by many books is that partners should become more conscious and show extra affection. This suggestion often means that partners must make even more use of their Model to produce and present more affection beyond what they naturally feel. They sense a pressure to play an unnatural role, to show extra affection even when they do not feel affectionate for so many reasons. It is necessary and nice that partners recognize each other's problems and show empathy. Yet, in reality, most of us cannot resolve our psychological shortfalls by a mere exchange of affection. One partner's unconditioned and superficial show of affection only boosts his/her partner's Ego and leads to even more demands for recognition and attention. This feels and appears like rewarding our partner's unjustifiable demands and manipulations. This may continue to the point of complete submission of one partner and domination by the other. Ironically, in some cases, extra affection would actually hurt partners' chance for logical communication.

Besides, some people are incapable of expressing affection or even developing their Models altogether. For some of us, the use of Model, above what we can naturally handle and believe in, feels untrue and torturous. We eventually drop the act or show our discomfort in other ways in our subsequent communications. The problem is that, even with extra affection, communication deficiencies would most likely never get resolved. For example, when the sources of problems relate to partners' personalities, never-ending selfish needs, or psychological defects (e.g., Ego, insecurity, and fears), extra affection cannot remedy any of these flaws in the long run. Despite some temporary improvements, the original unrest, demands, suspicions, and all other insecurities in partners resurface soon.

When partners' customary communication *methods* cause confrontation, they feel the chaos and disappointments. Their Egos get hurt and agitated as soon as the communication begins, because they anticipate the regular abuse and arguments. The atmosphere creates hurdles and resistance to tackle the *contents* of the communication, because the method is not reliable and trusted. For example, (A) starts to talk about something and then (B) interrupts impulsively and makes a hasty point or correction, which is unrelated to the main intention of (A)'s communication. (A) becomes upset and tries to correct (B) for unsolicited and irrelevant comment and then their intense arguments prevent the substantive and pressing matters of their marriage properly. For instance, they agree to discuss budget and financial plans for the upcoming year. (B), maybe stressed or struck by a recent thought, reminisces some of his/her past hurts. S/he uses the occasion to relieve the frustrations of, let us say, (A)'s carelessness and lack of passion, *or perhaps regarding not having enough shoes!* S/he hastily jumps in to express his/her dissatisfaction with (A) being secretive, maybe about the amount of money s/he makes. When (A) shockingly asks for explanation, (B) replies, "Because you have kept your financial activities a secret." Most likely, other reasons are instigating this outburst, but it reflects the general mistrust between partners. Most of all, though, the main intention of discussing the budget is ignored completely.

Therefore, the disagreement over an unrelated point prevents partners to remain within their initial intentions and contents of communication. Often, a partner might realize his/her destructive interjection and/or a mistake in his/her opinion. Yet, s/he does not want to change his/her position because of false pride, or just to prove s/he never makes a mistake. S/he does not want to set a precedent for being wrong even once.

A lack of good communication often reflects partners' fear and anticipation of clashes anytime they try to converse. This is the result of many years of negative experiences, and partners' reactionary and defensive attitude towards all communications between them. Most often, before partners get a chance to discuss the main contents of the communication, compulsive reactions and anger disrupt the whole process.

When communication is tense, both partners only push their ideas and Egos without any attention to communication contents and the intentions of the other person. Eventually, they would be arguing about irrelevant issues only for blaming each other and making noise. In these situations, a possible solution is to enforce a one-way communication method for a while. In this method, (A) raises and explains his/her points, *about only one selected topic,* while (B) merely listens and makes notes. Partner (B) must leave the meeting with an understanding of (A)'s concerns and spend sometime to reflect on them. If (B) is genuinely interested in improving their communication, s/he can make real efforts to see (A)'s viewpoints without becoming too defensive and upset. When (B) is ready to go back in a few days with answers and suggestions, this time only (B) speaks and (A) listens without interfering or making gestures to provoke unrest and anger. (A) would have his/her chance in a few days again to reflect on (B)'s comments and ideas. This process continues until one topic is relatively resolved. And then to the next item on the agenda, which is prepared by both partners' contributions. In this process, partners apply their negotiating skills, *to solve one issue at a time,* except that they do not talk simultaneously and spontaneously before having the chance to contemplate their partner's problems and proposed suggestions.

One-way communication feels long and stressful, especially for the partner whose turn is to only listen. The idea of restraining our rage and egoism for a day or two to only ponder our partner's words is too tough. However, for couples with communication issues, but genuine interest to improve the situation, one-way communication method often helps. It focuses on communication contents to control anger and avoid jumping from issue to issue and losing track of the intentions of the communication. The ideal would be to have a third person mediate and moderate the process at least until partners learn to follow the communication rules and control their reactionary attitude and anger.

Withdrawal and avoiding dialogue to prevent confrontations may seem the only option to us, and in fact, it might prove to be the case at the end other than separation. First, however, we must try to keep communication channels open as long as possible. If a two-way communication method does not work, we can always resort to the one-way method and extend genuine efforts to learn to communicate, because without it any marriage is doomed. We must embrace this (more sensible) hardship to deter the chances of bigger agonies that withdrawal and confrontation cause.

Understanding the depth of communication hurdles and the importance of dealing with them effectively become even more evident when referring to the discussions on pages 145-8 about the significance of 'Communication and Negotiation Abilities' as a vital success factor and compatibility measure for relationships.

Expecting Our Partner to Change

Expecting our partner to change is another common mistake and source of relationship conflicts. When we are young and naïve, we take our partner's declaration of love a kind of submission to (or at least acceptance of) our way of thinking and living. Thus, immediately, we assume that not only we understand each other, but also love would motivate our partner become the image we have nurtured for a perfect spouse. Therefore, we get married. Initially, we expect our partner to guess and sense our thoughts and needs and adjust her/himself accordingly. We expect change in all matters and levels. We want change of attitude, thoughts, beliefs, talking, way of dressing, etiquettes, relationships and friends, personal needs, eating habits, things we like or dislike around the house, the way and time we choose to do things, life philosophy and outlook, political views, tastes in things, on and on we can go. When this does not happen automatically on the power of our love per se, we eventually lose our patience and *ask*, directly, through subtle manipulation, or sneaky retaliations, for changes that we believe are overdue. And, again, when we do not see true changes, we get frustrated and angry with our partner for being so stubborn and unwilling to cooperate (change). We now *demand* change or try to manipulate our partner to get the results we need. In particular, as our insecurities emerge, e.g., when one partner gets possessive, s/he would demand her/his partner to change drastically in terms of being too friendly, charming, or flirtatious around other men or women. This becomes often a big challenge when some people do all these things on purpose just for raising their partners' jealousy or as a means of retaliation for other conflicts in their relationship.

In all, our first mistake is to assume that the strength of our love would overcome our partner's natural resistance to change. Our second mistake is our assumption that s/he can change and is deliberately resisting it. Mostly the appearance of resistance and carelessness towards our requests and expectations agitates and frustrates us. Thus, we continue to get into arguments. Naturally, we also blame our partner for being the cause of these arguments, especially for refusing to admit his/her stubbornness amidst many other faults.

The fact is that people hardly change, since their personalities are shaped mostly by their unconscious urges, which drive them to be who they are. They cannot even control their thoughts and attitudes, which are driven mostly by their subconscious minds. Merely for social adaptation and acceptance purposes, sometimes we can draw upon our Model to portray an attitude of change. Yet, this tentative change fails to stabilize and we revert to our original form soon, because change is not internalized and we cannot subdue our old habits and needs. Permanent and stable changes require substantive psychological motivation or personal convictions through experience and enlightenment. We do not change since others ask us to, and not even by a mere personal choice, but only because our mental capabilities have reached the level in which we believe that only real mental 'change' might bring the truth we can trust to make us a better being and happier.

Our unrealistic assumptions and expectations about 'changing our partner' stir many marital conflicts. If we admit change is not automatic and controllable at the level we desire, we stay cautious about our marriage decisions. Then, we can also become a little more understanding and flexible with our partner on this matter after marriage. We must evaluate our intentions for expecting our partner to change, but also remember they cannot do it readily even if they worked on it hard. Then, we may stop attributing our partner's lack of change to spite or his/her purposeful resistance. Of course, some attitude changes are possible, even at noticeable degrees, when a person keeps his/her Model at full alert to play certain expected roles. Yet, these changes are mostly superficial. Personal changes are simply unattainable without a person's full intention and a long process of self-awareness.

Why Do We Expect Change only from others?

Because we believe we are perfect as we are, but everybody else needs urgent, major changes to fit our views of tolerable persons! We want our partner to change for many reasons. For one thing, we desire a routine that is most convenient for us, or because our partner's habits, values, or ethics irritate us. Another reason is our strong tendency to dominate others and make them do things our ways. Most of us have strong inner urges to control people and events. We must dominate others or else feel dominated and lost. We attempt to change our partners' attitudes to make them more subservient, dependent, and agreeable to our frame of mind. We imagine we can save our marriage only by making our partner change before the situation gets out of hand. Still another major reason for demanding change is our 'need for feeling loved and testing our partner's devotion.' It satisfies our urge for possession, too. Our partner's dependence on us (for love) gives us a sense of security (because we feel wanted, needed, and in control of our marriage). We want to be *spoiled* to curb our insecurities.

We demand change obsessively to satiate our need for Elove, too. When our partner refuses to change, our Ego is threatened and our need for being loved feels under attack. All along, we think we are honest and true in terms of our love for our partner, while s/he seems more careless every day. 'Love' and 'being in need of love' are different concepts, though. While 'love' is a mythical expression of beauty, devotion, giving, and forgiving, 'being in need for love' reflects our selfishness, needy attitude, and the overall dependency urge of humans. We think love, but in fact are influenced and driven by our selfish 'need for being loved'—to be spoiled, as a new fad in relationships.

Thus, we take our partner's inability to change to heart, as not only his/her vindictive persistence to contradict us, but also not loving us anymore. We often think s/he resists change only since s/he does not care about us enough, and not because s/he cannot change. Love and need for love are good topics for understanding the self, ego, and model aspects of our personality. Even when we attempt to invoke our Self and inherent spiritual need for love, often Ego interferes with its 'need for love.' All the expressions and pretences of love are reflections of Model manifesting the feeling of love without really grasping the true implications of selfless love. Clearly, all three aspects of personality reflect some type of love when we express or demand it, but it is mostly Ego driven.

Sometimes, we may try or pretend to change to make our partner happy or show that we care. Therefore, we activate our Model to portray the change. We force ourselves to make the best use of our Model to display a change of attitude. We do it for a while, but most likely fail to bring about a real change. Model is the least stable aspect of personality and forgets its promises, and in fact rarely concerns itself about commitments. It can be swayed easily by strong incentives to adopt a different position or role, or just drops an existing role when Ego begins to interfere. Then, when we fail to keep our promise to change, our partner becomes even angrier and takes our apathy as a direct insult and rejection of his/her love. His/her anger reflects how deeply his/her pathetic need for love is threatened, thus causing him/her pain. S/he takes our seemingly broken promise as a rebellion, retaliation, or loss of love depending on the circumstances.

Overall, we hope love and marriage per se give our partner enough incentive and power to change. Our egoism and naivety force us misjudge our power and the possibility of making our partner think and act according to our life outlook. We believe if s/he loved us enough, s/he would change to prove it. We like to test our partner's ability and sincerity in his/her declaration of love and devotion. Thus, we expect her/him to change quickly, often drastically. If s/he does not, we take it too personal, as a sign of her/his inadequate love, devotion, and commitment, if not sudden hostility and rebellion altogether.

Why Cannot We Change?

We cannot really detect and control our Ego easily in order to affect a real change. We may change our attitude, a bit, mostly temporarily, but not our essence, which comprises our way of thinking, convictions, habits, preferences, pride, etc. To prove this point, we can refer to experiences when we faced our partner's retaliation for something. We may remember how quickly we reverted to our Ego in spite of our effort to portray our 'changed attitude.' We got angry, even when Model had meant to keep us tactful, or our Self had meant to be compassionate and patient with our partner's innate flaws. This shows that 'attitude change' is often a superficial act with no deep meaning and conviction for the person displaying a change. All along, our inability to change makes our partner conclude that, not only we do not love her/him because the change has not been internalized, but also s/he has been fooled all this time by our phony display of change. Thus, relationships deteriorate further by partners' tentative and shallow changes, while partners become more disappointed and furious. The only exception is when one partner makes some vital mental changes as steppingstones to explore a new lifestyle, which might lead to self-awareness and deep changes in their relationship over time as well. Tentative attitude changes are helpful in calming turbulent situations, of course, but partners should remember why change cannot be deep and permanent unless it occurs gradually through self-awareness, personal conviction, and experience. We should not depend on our partners' fake changes to satiate our 'need for love' or as a level of his/her real 'love.' These tentative changes are unreliable, and their values and purposes are highly questionable, although they might help in stabilizing relationships atmosphere during critical situations.

An interesting scenario usually occurs after we go through a few rounds of temporary changes without success. In our next round of negotiations for change, we decide and demand that this time we would compromise (change) only if, and only after, our partner has demonstrated authentic changes first. We expect our partner to prove that his/her change is real and permanent before we adopt and express the changes s/he is expecting from us in return. Interesting and comical enough, hardly anybody agrees with this demand. This scheme (blackmail) cannot motivate us to change, anyway. In a similar scenario, sometimes we may not discuss our demands for change explicitly with our partner, but implicitly contemplate the possibility of changing our attitude in some respects if our partner changes his/hers first in the areas of our desire. All these scenarios show our high frustration with broken promises, thus resorting to desperate means of bargaining. These situations, which often sound very much like blackmail and threat, prevail when partners lose their trusts for effecting change.

Promising to change, but more so hoping to convince our partners to change, happens quite often in the early stages of most relationships when partners try desperately to save their marriage. On the one hand, the mere intention to change (when one partner promises to change first or both partners do it simultaneously) reflects their sincerity and deep desire to make their relationship work. On the other hand, it shows how hollow and naive our promises for change can be and how little we know about the possibilities of change due to humans' intricate psychological and genetic construct shaping their mindsets that are often irreparable. It also shows our struggles to play our Model as much as possible to portray a personal change that we do not believe in truly, or cannot control. Sometimes, partners consent to a mutual change of attitude, while they dislike the demanded changes in principle, anyway. They often call this a compromise. Yet, deep down, they might not be convinced of the purpose and value of their efforts. They are agreeing to change (cooperate) merely to get something they need or just to calm the situation, but not that they believe change is good for them personally, or even for improving their relationship. The effect of this kind of compromise is discussed in the next section.

The Effects of Demanding Change

Partners' difficulty to change might lead to over-activating their Model when they try to compromise or pretend they are making an effort, which then affects other aspects of their personalities indirectly, too. We make these efforts in organizational and social relationships in order to cope with tough situations and possibly accommodate others as well. People's influence over one another has both positive and negative implications. A positive impact happens mostly when Model strives to show compassion, maybe overcome Ego eventually, or even internalize compassion as a deep 'self' trait. Under this special condition, the individual really grasps and believes in the *purpose* of change and practices it with an open mind and heart. His/her efforts and Model's role are commendable and have positive effects.

On the negative side, we often begin to resent our partner and marriage even more when playing Model is solely for the sake of stopping his/her endless nagging. Increasing our Model requires a comparable reduction of either Ego or Self. Ego is rarely reduced, and it happens *only* when change is internalized in the long run as an accepted target for improving personality. Thus, our Self and integrity is sacrificed usually in the form of lower 'self'-esteem, and 'self'-image, when we keep playing a sharper Model without believing in it as a right attitude or thought. As long as a change is not essential or at least fruitful (in our minds), we know that our phony 'attitude changes' are bound to collapse when we get tired of playing a particular role, find other priorities, or revert to our domineering personality and let Ego rule above the model again —the way it normally does and feels more natural, too.

Another side effect of using Model regularly is that it should be constantly kept active and alert, or it would lose its focus and direction. For example, we may inherently nurture a lot of love in our Self, but are unable to express it freely. Therefore, we use our Model to show love as part of a relationship therapy. This therapy makes us attentive on the surface, but the process feels odd and tasteless to our agitated nature and integrity. Thus, we feel tense due to this inner conflict. An added problem is that after a short while our partner's expectations get used to our heightened level of attention to her/him. Our improved attitude may gradually feel inadequate to him/her again, thus s/he makes new demands for even higher attention, while we feel pressed to play our Model too much already. If we forget only once to express our love in a particular and timely manner, it would be conceived as a loss of love again.

Some interesting suggestions in John Gray's book, *Men are from Mars, Women are from Venus,* might help men and women adjust their attitudes and become more acceptable and pleasing to their partners. On the other hand, the above discussions about the instability of 'attitude change' suggest that we need a reliable technique to bring partners closer together. We need changes in relationship mechanisms, to encourage *sensible commitments* between partners naturally (instead of relying on role-playing to get along superficially, while raising each other's frustration and inner conflicts). We need only one major change in our common mentality: To grasp the role and needs of relationships in the new era. Although men and women seem radically different mentally, they have the same basic need, i.e., for companionship—as their most urgent and essential need. Although men and women might seem to have come from different planets, the only possibility for achieving harmony and peace is to invent and grasp a common language. Sometimes, it seems that perhaps women have become homesick due to many years of exploitation by men on the Earth. Thus, now these two genders have real difficulty understanding each other's language, especially due to all the ambiguities that new lifestyles, role-playings, and modern values have brought about. For any possibility to resolve the existing marital problems and miscommunications, better guidelines and a basic language must be developed. Perhaps we succeed in a couple of centuries or so! That is, if women have not already returned to Venus by then, *which could be one kind of a solution. Or maybe we could send men back to where they came from!*

The problems is that, despite John's firm claim, we still do not know where men and women have really come from, considering their dire tendency to argue, instead of learning to relate a bit for their mutual benefits, torturing their kids less, and saving their families and societies.

The principles for relative success in marriages, e.g., need for ongoing teamwork, are not hard to pinpoint, but are difficult to believe in and implement. Accordingly, reiterating the bottomline about people's ability to change is useful: The first rule is to not make naive assumptions about partners' potential or motivation to change. Second, often only tentative 'attitude changes' may result from 'our demand for change,' at best. Essential changes can only happen from within a person and not through an outside force or someone else's demands. Third, love and being in need of love are contradictory and neither of them can play a role for change, anyway. Only our misperception about the relationship between 'love' and 'change' is causing so much marital conflicts. Fourth, we must focus on changing ourselves to grasp and accept the challenge of satisfying marital relationships' specific needs, nowadays. And finally, remember that relationship conflicts arise mostly when a partner strives to change the other, knowingly or inadvertently, while the other partner is not genuinely motivated to change. Why change anyway, when the reason for change does not feel natural. Deep down, a rebellious inner voice keeps nagging, "I do not want to (or cannot) be like you or anybody else." Knowing that change cannot be easy, we can revise our level of premarital optimism and stop hoping that we can make our partner change. Even worse, it is merely too naïve to believe that marriage by itself makes our partner change for the better, anyway! We usually make these odd assumptions mainly during initial courting and gauging our partner.

As another conundrum, while marriage partners have taken the position that 'change proves love and love justifies change,' they are only abusing this belief subconsciously. That is, they mostly want to change their partner, instead of themselves, at least for becoming less demanding and selfish personally. Thus, they impose extra burden on their marriages and communication, which raise both partners' pain and stress in their relationship due to their misperceptions about 'love' helping or stirring people to 'change.'

Blaming and Nagging Syndrome

Having a spouse appears to be the most convenient, but idiotic, means of relieving our tensions by blaming someone for our life deficiencies! After all, humans' tenacity to look outward to blame something or somebody for offsetting their distress and agonies is such a deep natural urge. However, the result of this pandemic is shattering when partners get carried away, mostly unconsciously, with their routine naggings and 'tension-releasing' schemes.

If spouses trust and respect each other enough and have good communication skills, they reduce their life burdens and tensions by discussing their concerns, while exchanging compassion and empathy. However, without trust and respect, partners feel lonely and spiteful towards each other. Their ideas and suggestions often erupt in hostile tones and their marriage turns into a battlefield for firing blames and nagging at each other.

Partners share many responsibilities and decisions. Then, they blame each other even for the outcomes of their joint decisions and for things that neither partner has been involved with directly or meant to do. They look for an excuse desperately to attribute a failure or flaw to each other often unconsciously and sometimes as a kind of retaliation for something else they are angry about. Sometimes, they are miserable due to their personal problems or deficiencies and then find a convenient occasion to blame them on their partners somehow indirectly or directly. They may even arrive at general conclusions to blame their partners, for example by making comments like, "I have lost my confidence because of the way you have treated me!", or, "I have become old because of you!", etc. Often, one partner is suffering from his/her incomplete life, thus finds all sorts of reasons to nag at his/her partner and blame him/her routinely even when no specific issue to bug him/her for exists.

The irony is that if by a miracle we could be unmarried again, most likely we would be as much, or even more, miserable and full of failures, and nobody would be around to blame it on or nag to. It is our own self-inflicted misery that we condemn our partner for so relentlessly and irresponsibly. And usually we feel, express, and expect love at the same time! In fact, we still expect to be *spoiled,* while we keep blaming him/her and nagging all the time! We either nag directly for not being spoiled enough, or find something to complain about merely for irritating him/her. Are not we modern humans too spoiled already and totally out of sync regarding life's realities?

Often one partner has no self-fulfilling activities to keep him/herself amused and happy, then keeps blaming his/her partner for not finding interesting things to do together and not giving this matter enough thought and time. The blamed partner may believe s/he is doing a lot already, and is willing to participate in other joint activities whenever possible, too, but also has some personal interests that the blaming partner does not care for. One partner's personal interests become the source of envy for the other partner and an excuse to nag constantly. S/he just hopes that, by nagging and blaming, the other partner would eventually give up his/her personal interests, which seem to be drawing all his/her attention (love), and thus a perceived conflict and threat. Sometimes, the whole point of our nagging seems to be merely for wearing out our partner and making him/her as miserable as we are. We hate his/her relative peace.

Conflicts arise when one or both partners cannot separate their personal and relationship (joint) needs, so raise their expectations of each other idiotically. Thus, even a partner's basic interests (as simple as listening to music or watching sports), makes the other partner feel neglected and mentally insecure. One partner may prefer to do everything together when the other has less patience for some aspects of his/her partner's activities, or prefers to do some activities alone. This shows that they have not discussed and agreed upon a workable relationship model suitable for them.

Partners' blaming and nagging attitudes are often deliberate or unconscious reactions due to their inner pains and conflicts, but either way, they exhaust partners and ruin their relationship with no benefit to them. Often, applying Model can help in expressing one's sufferings and needs in a calm, passionate, and convincing manner, hoping for some tangible and productive communication at least, and perhaps some sympathy. 'Model' is often capable of making peace offerings in a nice package and this is one of those times when Model can really prove its value. On the other hand, with nagging and blaming, we lose the opportunity of showing our honest feelings through Model or Self to keep the situation under control, or maybe even boosting our relationships. Instead, our Ego makes us keep nagging and blaming our partner with no sign of Model's flexibility to soothe even the basic frictions in all relationships. Surely, Self is absent when nagging and blaming goes on. In all, blaming and nagging reflect our inner sufferings due to either our failures to change or manipulate our partner, or our unrelenting need for attention.

With our blaming and nagging, we actually put our partner on notice to prepare for a battle. We merely agitate the relationship without concern or conscience about causing many conflicts and confrontations mainly due to our own insecurities and personality flaws. Both the nagger and naggee recognize this and put up their defences. The nagging partner is most likely empty of Model, at least temporarily, and is forcefully attacking with an inflated Ego. Thus, the other partner is left with the options of surrendering and leaving the battlefield, igniting a fight, or trying to initiate a peace negotiation. If s/he uses the last option, which is in most cases the wisest one, s/he draws upon his/her Model and Self to bring his/her partner and situation under control. We can do it to invoke the softer emotions of our partner if we know how and if possible at all. Once we normalize the situation a bit with compassion and maybe other Self attributes, we can reduce Model and focus on peace terms and means of keeping it in the long run. We cannot expect things to work out permanently with one or even dozen negotiations, since nagging is a deep habit that partners do not give up easily. However, our patient efforts for peace provide the only chance left before we lose our total confidence in our partner and marriage.

At the same time, distinguishing constructive criticism—as part of teamwork—from blaming and nagging is very important. We need both courage and patience to make this fine distinction. Sadly, some couples have difficulty in expressing their intentions properly. A constructive criticism by one partner may be received as a blatant blame and nagging if it is expressed in a wrong tone of voice. But often a partner is so arrogant and insecure that even simple suggestions sound like blaming and nagging to her/him. Thus, partners get into needless arguments and enmity, instead of benefiting from each other's wisdom and insight. The borderline between blame and objective criticism may become a blur when expressed harshly or when the recipient is psychologically avert to any type of consultation and teamwork. Overall, both partners should realize one fact sooner or later: Blaming does not help or solve any problem, thus it does not matter how forcefully we condemn our partner or a situation. In the end, it does not matter whose fault it is that a couple cannot communicate or solve their problems. Pointing fingers of blame to each other only damages their relationship further. Partners could instead try to define and discuss the causes of their frictions regardless of whose fault they are.

We must stop taking marriage problems personal and getting offended quickly, even if we believe our partner is more in fault than we are. Instead, only concentrating on objective thinking, goodwill, and solutions may resolve marital problems, and it can happen only through calm negotiations, and not personalizing the issues and blaming each other.

The Evil of Domination

Domination and exploitation are two other innate human evils that have spread like plagues despite our dire pretences of civilization. Even in marital relationships, the need for domination has become intense because of the high level of emotions involved and the proximity of couples' activities and decision-making processes. It is bizarre when couples (especially women) insist on equality, but seem capable of implementing this presumed sense of equality only through domination!

In fact, need for domination and egoism are usually behind all marital conflicts. When we communicate with one another, we set out quickly to dominate (or manipulate) the situation and our partner by insisting on our position and points in order to win. When we try to convince our partner to change his/her attitude, again it reflects our inner urges to dominate and turn him/her to a personality of our preference. And when we search for excuses to blame and nag, it is partly because we feel we do not have as much control as we like to have in general, and partly because we just cannot quit our urges and intentions of dominating the family structure and our spouse. Ironically, we just want to ensure our relationship works in the way we like! Blaming and nagging are partly personal war tactics to wear down our partner in order to take over the situation and decisions.

Of course, signs of teamwork and cooperation emerge from time to time mostly through Model. However, soon enough, our Ego takes over and proceeds to dominate the situation and our partner. Naturally, we all try to hide our urges for domination and manipulation, especially before marriage when we use Model to manoeuvre and soften the person we like. Then our urges for domination and manipulation eventually erupt with full force, out of either mere egotism or for saving our marriages.

Our urge for domination often reflects our good intention to prevent our relationship from going the wrong way, but it is also for controlling our destiny and independence. On the one hand, we strongly believe in controlling our family's attitude, decisions, and actions even for their own good. On the other hand, when our family's reactions and interferences threaten our needs for control and independence, we quickly see the need to dominate them and the situation. We hate surprises, risks, and headaches. We like things to proceed smoothly as we have always planned, possibly under the influence of social and parental teachings. We simply feel a need to control family issues and situations. Thus, when our spouse interferes, we are left with no option but to control him/her, too. Nonetheless, the logical tactic in our minds is to control all situations and persons that might affect the outcomes of our plans and expectations for a kind of life and marriage we prefer, along with our independence. We expect our partner to grasp and agree with our perceptions of life, values, and logic. We think our vision and lifestyle are the most sensible ones, thus everybody should agree with us after we explain our viewpoints to them, in our often-crooked language. Yet, if we cannot come to some agreement, we plan and persist to stay in control one way or another, or else we become agitated and retaliatory all the time.

Our urge for domination also emerges from our desires to possess our partner like a personal property. Possessiveness is by itself a rather natural psychological defect that inflicts everybody at some level. Possessiveness and jealousy induce our need for control and domination over not only the physical aspects of our partner's life, like what s/he does, where s/he goes, or what s/he wears, but also his/her thoughts. We want our partner think in certain ways for our convenience, but also because we want to be in charge and possess him/her totally.

Our urges for domination and possessiveness hurt our partner and relationship, but also annihilate our individuality and peace. They trigger rivalry, jealousy, retaliation, nagging and blaming, and many other negative psychological reactions. The amount of time and energy we waste to handle these personal idiosyncrasies are quite substantial. Our onerous jealousy and possessiveness cripple our brains and deprive us from pursuing rewarding and relaxing activities. Many people grasp this fact in the latter stages of their lives when the futility of their jealousies and retaliations become clear *too late*.

Instead of letting our need for love drown us deep in a state of helplessness and raise our humiliating urges for possessiveness and domination, we could concentrate on our essential personal needs. We can also pay attention to the joint needs of partners (especially for independence and equality) in modern marriages.

The Significance of Marriage Decision

In the author's opinion, marriage is, nowadays, the second most critical decision in a normal life circumstance—*ironically* after the matter of separation and divorce. The decision process 'to marry or not to marry' a specific person is quite delicate and difficult. This is because we are not aware even of our own psychological needs and defects, and do not know our prospective partner's deep emotions and needs, either. We are not familiar with the complexities of marital life, due to our inexperience and naivety during the courting stage. Therefore, we are not prepared for the demands and commitments that marriage places upon us. We do not know much regarding relationships' specific needs or how to evaluate partners' common objectives, unique idiosyncrasies, and personal needs and expectations. We do not know how to prepare ourselves for new challenges and changes in our lives.

In all, marriage demands deep and difficult changes, contrary to our imagination of a wonderful world that it would bring. We must realize that some changes are necessary and useful, though perhaps not the ones that our spouse would like to impose upon us. We must test our sense, ability, and willingness to change, since after marriage 'independence' is no longer a feasible feature of our new identity as a spouse. We must prepare ourselves by acknowledging and understanding the need for major personal adjustments, and also learn how to do them and why. We must change our attitudes and expectations and learn to use our Model (the personality aspect for coping) perhaps more than what we have learned or believed in. We should learn quickly to defeat the evil of domination and possessiveness in ourselves, or else expect a life of misery, contradictions, and quarrels. If a person does not recognize and accept these facts and the need for major changes, s/he should avoid getting married. Or, at least, s/he must prepare him/herself for a big shock and lots of frustration.

Unfortunately, most people make their marriage decision spontaneously instead of systematically with proper knowledge of relationship needs and demands. Couples may court for years, while making all kinds of judgments and assessments about each other and a marriage, too. Yet, the final decision to get married usually happens within days, if not hours or minutes, with one partner proposing and the other accepting, and viola, we have a *shoddy* commitment and a *risky* marriage. What happens at this moment for such a crucial decision is often unclear to the partners making and accepting the proposal, but it is mostly a matter of sentimentality and a hasty, spontaneous response to a surge of sudden personal urges. They just cannot live without each other! Fine, but why marry before all the issues noted in this book are quite clear to them and worked out patiently? Anyway, partners' spontaneity and approach for marriage decision is problematic and risky in relationships, nowadays. Of course, partners imagine they have studied their marriage scenario long enough already, maybe even for years, but most likely they have not yet analysed the right factors realistically.

We all seem to realize that **Marriage decision should always follow an educational process, instead of a spontaneous act (like an outburst of dormant emotions).** Yet, most of us do not know how to do it even if we were not often pressed for a quick decision due to our sentimentality or feelings of loneliness. The long educational process consists of a fine plan of analyses and negotiations between partners until all the details of their future relationship are examined and worked out in line with the success factors suggested in this book. It would be almost like assessing a business venture, which is usually the true nature of marriages, nowadays. The process might take a few weeks, months, or more to complete, until partners are comfortable with all the details of their scrutinized pending marriage, including a basic partnership agreement addressing the issues raised in this book. Only at the end of this process, their marriage decision becomes somewhat clear automatically without the need for one partner proposing it spontaneously and the other feeling pressed for a decision equally unprepared. Instead of making a proposal, partners should only reach a point where they feel the need for a decision and know if it is time to ponder the marriage option. If yes, let the process begin, which includes studying the points raised in this part of the book as well as the matter of learning about *'divorce' at the time of marriage,* as explained in Chapter Ten. Partners must also learn about potential marriage agonies besides the hassles of divorce, which is a highly likely outcome of most marriages these days. Only a thoughtful plan should determine their decision, only after couples have spent ample time to sort out all the angles fully. The present mode of marriage decisions is outdated and problematic for such a highly critical *romantic* business. Sadly, our marriage decisions, nowadays, should be viewed and handled strictly, very much like signing a treaty after enough negotiating and planning within a friendship atmosphere.

Universal Relationship Problems and Solutions

Solutions for our marital conflicts are rare and relative. Most of us do not even understand the problems, or make our selfish (and naïve) diagnosis quickly. However, we can start by recognizing the universal problems that inflict most families. They are similar in nature and causation and have become epidemic in the new era. We must believe that miscommunication, incongruity of partners' needs, high expectations, and personal idiosyncrasies play major roles in causing intolerance, misunderstandings, and alienation. And we must seriously doubt the possibility of finding a partner even remotely compatible with us or able to build a relatively quiet life together, as experience definitely proves to all the optimistic couples. We must know what kinds of personality adjustments, mainly through Model, are necessary and what kinds of sacrifices we are expected to make. Another vital point people miss is that for sharing a joint life with a partner, we must first have a purposeful life of our own. Instead, we expect our spouse to create a fantastic life for us.

Marriage problems and partners' low patience and tolerance —mostly caused by their high expectations— are universal and all these deficiencies would keep soaring. No remedy seems in sight and not enough research is underway to find a cure, either. The ideal would be to develop a screening process to prevent at least clearly unfit marriages at the outset. Furthermore, we need an effective process to educate partners initially about the specific needs and hassles of relationships in the new era. And we need substantive therapeutic procedures to help those marriages tainted by destructive germs and viruses. Relationship diseases, evident from disproportionate marriage deaths and rising family torments have already damaged the entire social structure. Meanwhile, people continue to suffer and live with this epidemic helplessly. Unfortunately, the situation would get worse in the 21st century.

Accordingly, special attention and commitment for research are urgently needed by scholars and authorities to revamp social and people's mindsets about the real purposes of relationships and find practical mechanisms to deal with this matter. Governments, universities, and legal systems have so far been causing more problems than solving them. They are only concentrating on the symptoms of this social pandemic, instead of detecting and curing its roots. In particular, we need a new approach to revise current social and personal mentalities that have been mostly responsible for such fatal marital diseases. Our educational systems must take on a more active role in teaching social issues in new societies, in particular marital affairs, to new generations.

Couples must spend a few months to pass certain educational requirements before rushing into marriage. Maybe they must take a few courses in conflict resolution and negotiation techniques. This surely sounds quite unnatural, yet no longer natural laws drive marital relationships in modern societies. Marriage turns into a cold, calculating enterprise too often, nowadays, thus needs proper contemplation and education.

In addition, there should be special recognition of individuals who make major contributions in the field of family relationships. After all, family relationships set the foundation of social life and we are doomed to fail in all fronts if the problems originated in family nucleus are not resolved. We have all sorts of prizes for science and literature and even Oscar and Emmy for acting in fictional roles. Yet, we neglect to acknowledge the wisdom and level of tolerance that every person is extending to act in real life to make a marriage successful. We should recognize those who succeed, because a naturally liveable marital life has become so scarce and astonishing. We should strive to develop procedures and cures for marital problems, but also honour couples who can demonstrate the secrets of a successful marriage in a documented way. We need lots of theories and guidelines to bring objectivity back into relationships. In all, this nucleus of social life needs an overhaul to inject some kind of optimism and positive energy in society. Our random thoughts and sporadic raw theories about relationships are not enough. A focused approach is needed now to rid societies of the negative effects of marriages. We must stop dealing merely with the symptoms of relationship failures and instead view the deepening chaos in relationships as a big social pandemic. There should be a way to get smarter! In particular, the roles of governments and judicial systems must be curtailed drastically. For now, **'Think divorce at the time of marriage'** as a potent precautionary vaccine.

Part IV offers a good summary of divorce causes and pains as a start for reflection.

PART IV
Alienation and Separation

CHAPTER TEN
A Time for Thinking Marriage

The toughest decision, under normal life circumstances, happens when a marital relationship breaks down, especially if young kids are involved. Not only the agony of separation and legal hassles, but also deep scars hurt partners and their children for years. Most divorced people relate to this assertion. Then again, married couples gauge their options regularly, while their alienation pains rival their gloomy perceptions of separation and divorce agonies. When partners' flaws are extensive and obvious, the decision is easy. However, a separation decision often gets tough, since most people have borderline psychological flaws—which still make them wicked and incompatible—and yet the decision becomes only a matter of partners' tolerance level.

Partners' imperfections, which often seem normal personally, clash in relationships severely, thus the degree of incompatibility and malice increases many folds very quickly. At the same time, partners are unable to set their tolerance levels realistically, since they have no reliable view of the expected (acceptable) level of relationship conflicts. Without enough wisdom and self-control, including the criteria for tolerance level in a typical marriage, they let their Egos drive all their decisions. In fact, many people are reluctant or unable, nowadays, to endure the inconveniences of marriage, mainly because of their drive for individuality and a misguided sense of self-importance, not to mention their growing zeal for sexual liberty in modern societies. Thus, with the first signs of conflict, they seek a way out. Conversely, another group takes lots of abuse, but lacks enough guts to gauge their options realistically. Most of us fall between these two extremes, though. We have adequate tolerance to bear some of the shortfalls of marital life, but also have enough pride to consider the option of separation if things REALLY do not work. This large group has the hardest time in making a decision, though, since it is never clear when to quit tolerating and depart, while the repercussions of divorce or separation feel enormous to these sensible people already. As a result, we, the majority, should live with marriage and life difficulties, but also struggle with our incessant doubts about the validity and viability of our marriages and the future of our confusing, sad relationships. These doubts are overwhelming and last a lifetime.

This social dysfunction has obviously accelerated since we no longer know how to relate to one another in society. Especially in marriage, we walk into a trying trap, because most of us do not know enough about relationships' unique needs to manage our marriages, while getting out feels awkward and depressing, too. It is a trap because the alternatives in most cases do not seem too lucrative, especially when our youth is wasted and there are many opposing factors to consider. **This is the kind of knowledge (point of reference) we should rely on for thinking divorce when contemplating marriage**—before getting trapped in a position where the alternatives to our miserable marriages appear even more depressing.

Separation is the hardest life decision (within a normal life setting), since we often end up in a less favourable position than we like to be (or imagine initially). Opting for divorce carelessly or living with the agony of indecision about separation has its own stressful outcome. In either case, when we seek divorce prematurely or when we struggle to save our marriage futilely, we cause sufferings for ourselves and our children. Judging by the statistics, too many of us choose the divorce solution, since it seems easier and most appealing to our Ego. In this state of mind, we consider divorce the only solution because we have tolerated enough already. Our false pride, in particular, has been damaged. Our senses of equality, individualism, and independence are also threatened. However, perhaps we still have a chance for saving our relationship if we just stop being antagonistic and reckless in arriving at such a negative conclusion. Therefore, this becomes **the point of reference (the reason) for thinking marriage when separation appears more viable and easier.** Thinking about marriage is merely the idea of creating an atmosphere for relaxing our minds to mull over things more clearly and work out sensible solutions.

Now, we *think of marriage* in order to revive the romantic mood that had started this relationship, which is needed now more than it had ever been. We *think of marriage* also to pinpoint the issues that have contaminated a relationship that had seemed so logical at the time of marriage. What promises and factors had made the strength of this relationship? We want to explore what and how things have changed our relationship and us. We want to imagine whether we might come up with a different solution if we could set our Ego aside a few days. We wish to evaluate the viability of forces that can keep us together to satisfy the *real* purposes of marriage, instead of focusing on personal whims or fussing over irresolvable human issues. The question to ask is whether it is possible to remarry our partner after we have drifted apart, often inadvertently, because of ignorance or egoism. Have we tried to communicate in a constructive manner to resolve our differences and express our ideas in a logical manner? Have we become so alienated that separation feels like the only solution? And for those of us who might still have a chance to save our relationships, we should learn about alienation causes. Moreover, we want to know how we have drawn the borderline between tolerance and divorce. We want to reset our expectations and list the criteria and rules that feel useful for relating with our partner within a new relationship model in order to salvage our marriage. We like to know the possibility and conditions for remarrying our existing spouse if starting again was a viable and sensible option under new terms. Can we adopt a different relationship model for living together (maybe even more independently and passively if necessary), instead of opting for divorce?

Many divorces can be avoided if partners show a little more patience and flexibility through their Self, rather than letting their Egos guide (deceive) them during a crisis. Our wild imaginations fool us about a more caring and smarter partner waiting out there for us. We let our false pride and obstinacy dictate the decision of separation and divorce, whereas compassion and forgiveness could have saved a lot of hassle and misery for both partners and their children. Conversely, we could have found at least some peace of mind and regained our independence if we had made a decision to separate from our spouse in a timelier manner when the relationship had seemed doomed, despite our sincere efforts to reconcile our personality differences and marital deficiencies. To reiterate, the main question partners should ask themselves is whether another relationship model exists for them to adopt for living together (maybe even somewhat more independently and passively if necessary) as a wiser alternative to divorce.

The decision of separation and divorce is quite easy, and least consequential, when partners believe *sincerely* and objectively that alternatives to their existing marital affair are definitely more promising and separation is to their advantage. A decision under this circumstance is easy as long as partners are in a sound mental condition to make an honest assessment of their needs. Yet, it is usually hard to be sincere in our judgments and beliefs (mostly about separation), since we do not know how to curb our Egos and fantasies even a few days to gauge the situation realistically without bias and spite. The decision gets tough when our Ego takes charge of the situation and ruins our objectivity even if we were a logical person. Ego abolishes our ability for tolerance and reflection. Consequently, partners get engaged in endless pursuit of power struggles and petty shows of individualism (based on their shortsighted definition of individualism and independence, of course). And when egoism is not blocking the communication, partners do not know the mechanism of cooperating to resolve their problems, thus resort to the option of separation.

In some extreme instances, one partner has special personal plans or affairs, or simply makes a unilateral decision regarding separation regardless of his/her partner's needs and desires. In these situations, separation would most likely be inevitable and the other partner is doomed to accept an imposed decision. It would be too late to convince the demanding partner to change his/her mind, and the chance for reconciling their differences is usually very little. One partner has already made the decision for both of them in such cases.

The Road to Separation

Usually a long, rough path leads to separation. From the early days of honeymoon and love, we embark upon a jerky journey in search of intimacy and a friendly relationship. However, like any journey, the road is full of hazards and turmoil. *Sneaky storms* erupt after we set sail so enthusiastically on this journey. Some obscure and adverse currents crush our enthusiasm and redirect our focus towards a new, ambiguous destination. Our search for intimacy fails and we enter a new phase of relationship, which feels more like an alienation course. Every day we feel a bit more estranged and drifting further apart from our partner until we hardly see or feel each other. Naturally, everybody abhors this looming destination and the depressing idea of 'separation.' This option had hardly crossed our minds when getting married; or we might have recklessly dismissed the chance to study it. Somehow, however, we have now arrived at this destination unexpectedly. We are shocked and confused, yet the reason for arriving at this point is clear: Estrangement happens when we lose sight of our initial destination (marriage purposes) and drift away mentally to a point where we cannot see our partner eye to eye; we cannot help each other steer the boat in the same direction. It happens when we do not recognize or work proactively on 'Relationships Success Factors.' Thus, we arrive at an odd destination we had not sailed for, and we feel lonely, confused, and tired. We have just gotten there because we had drifted away from our original targets mostly out of ignorance, stubbornness, and spite.

The long, lonely journey of 'alienation' brings us deep hurts, disappointments, disagreements, turmoil, anger, and anxiety. Soon the time comes when our sweet dreams and love are gone and our relationship enters a new phase of constant doubts and evaluation. We assess our marriage, our partner, our expectations, and the prospect of the existing arrangement. A deep sense of doubtfulness and an urge to assess our options overwhelm our minds gradually, as we live in a daunting daze with our pressing life responsibilities and struggles. We question the sensibility of our life and relationship and seek a solution. Our doubts about, and search for, a refuge intensify during marital conflicts or when we withdraw temporarily in a state of shock. Naturally, we are disappointed with the consequences of married life and develop deep doubts about the value and validity of marriage. The more we are disappointed and discouraged about our relationship and unfulfilled expectations, and the more we become doubtful of our sanity to live in this condition, the more we feel alienated towards our partner. Our initial attraction and trust are essentially replaced by doubts, suspicions, and resentment.

If these thoughts and feelings sound familiar, you are most likely on an alienation course and now is time to do something about it fast. Maybe it is actually a very good time to ponder marriage—i.e., remarrying your present spouse after finding a viable relationship model to bear each other's idiosyncrasies better. Can you find the nerve in yourself to ponder the notion of approaching your partner for a possible, calm renegotiation and does s/he seem capable of cooperating? Is there still time?

The Road with No Return

Partners are often unaware of their marital atmosphere and how poorly they relate to each other. Thus, they do not notice their alienation journey until it is too late to return. Perhaps when we are in the early stages of this journey, we could return to the main road, but not after we have travelled a long distance and fallen apart from our partner completely. We would simply not have enough stamina and motivation to travel back even if we could find the road to return. At some point and time, eventually the road to return is eroded by severe storms and upheavals. Some of us might be lucky in avoiding the alienation journey due to our personalities without even realizing it. However, a large majority is susceptible to embark upon this journey fast when their marital relationships start to decline. If we are unaware of the hazards of this journey and unprepared to fight alienation traps actively, we soon find ourselves in a no-return territory merely able to move forward where the journey often ends in separation, or perhaps a lifelong of desolation at best.

Naturally, alienation is mainly the outcome of unmatched or faulty personalities unnoticed or ignored before marriage. When we discover our partner's shortfalls, and when we finally realize our naivety in trying to change him/her, we get discouraged and adopt an attitude of resistance or carelessness that leads to more conflicts and misunderstandings. We would rather withdraw than fight on issues that we accept as irresolvable and irreconcilable at last. Misunderstandings, poor communication skills, and other marital problems also contribute to alienation even if partners had been partially, or even totally, compatible. Our withdrawals fuel the process of alienation as well. In addition, initial respect and attraction fades away after a period of cohabitation and learning about each other's idiosyncrasies. Thus, it gets almost impossible to reverse the course of alienation and separation. All that initial love and enthusiasm seem to vaporize and one or both partners wonder about the fast turn of events and loss of passion.

Reversing Our Focus

While it is wise to prevent mismatched marriages, our focus should reverse after marriage. That is, the burden of proof resides on partners' shoulders to show why their differences cannot be worked out if their psychological defects and Egos are not drastic and uncontrollable; and if the logic and some flares of love that existed at the time of marriage is still intact. Even unmatched partners might have a chance to reconcile their differences if they remain aware and resist the temptation of going deeply on an alienation journey. Most importantly, they must know about and work proactively on Relationships Success Factors listed in Table 8.1 on page 144.

Another major problem is that we do not recognize the hidden traps in marriage and how they lead to alienation. Thus, naively we leave our marriage's future to chance and destiny, instead of playing an active role in recognizing and eluding alienation traps. Most alienation cases relate to partners' inability to communicate civilly, although they might be rather compatible. Actually, even incompatible partners with mutual attraction and basic abilities to communicate succeed better than compatible couples who cannot learn to communicate. This is unfortunate because partners trap themselves on the alienation journey needlessly and wastefully. Another large portion of separations is due to spouses' innocent miscommunications, which exhausts partners' patience and level of tolerance.

The process of alienation starts with small disappointments. However, these letdowns accumulate quickly when partners do not deal with them collectively and promptly. Staying conscious of the destructive power and outcome of alienation, partners can learn to fight the circumstances and personal urges that induce alienation. They can learn about those interactions and situations that cause misunderstanding, hurt feelings, and alienation. They must also recognize the repercussions of their forbidding attitudes (including misperceptions, idiosyncrasies, harsh tone of voice, and hasty judgments about their partner) as creators of alienation conditions and torments.

We can find many examples and typical situations that lead to alienation. For one thing, our (changing) image of our partner initiates the process of alienation. Our fantasy about a perfect partner and our unfulfilled expectations of marriage create major misgivings. We compare our partner's behaviour with our image of a perfect mate who can satisfy our needs. We merely focus on our own needs and convenience. When our partner cannot match that image, we get vastly disappointed and angry with him/her. Our inability to curb our Egos, as we face such inconveniences, plays a major role in developing alienation.

Marital high demands and responsibilities create alienation as well when the concepts of teamwork and sensible commitment are not understood and observed. Partners might still have the potential of building a good relationship together if other hurdles did not stop them. Yet, they cannot fulfil the main requirements of a successful marriage, since they are not trained for married life properly. Their inexperience regarding marital circumstances and its communication hurdles also make them incapable of making the right judgments and decisions, at least in their first marriage. Usually our second and third marriages—if we dare to remarry—have a lesser chance of failure. Is this because we learn a few lessons about relationships' intricacies and alienation entrapments from our first marriage? Or, we simply give up and decide to be more patient and tolerant, perhaps due to aging and feeling more vulnerable? Or, maybe because we have now become wiser and realized that marriage can never be even slightly perfect, the way we like it to be? Or, because we are now more careful and wise about choosing a companion? Perhaps a combination of all these factors makes us wiser at some point. Yet many of these lessons could be learned beforehand and practised in the first marriage as well, if we just invest some time and patience. It is just a matter of pondering our marriage and divorce decisions more seriously —possibly in the reverse order if we can!

Alienation as a Reflection of Global Mentality

We usually use simple examples to make general interpretations. Now, let us do the opposite by studying the global mentality and chaos to detect the roots of marital conflicts and family mentality. The rising social unrests amongst races, people and authorities, political parties, genders, religions, etc. reflect the annihilation of ethics and logic in the new era. The global chaos is accelerating, as nations, ethnic groups, religious fanatics, and ordinary people fight and kill one another for all sorts of foolish ideological goals. Endless wars around the world, especially in the Middle East, e.g., the Palestine's struggles to get back what Israel has captured as its own with the support of some hypocritical superpowers, show who we are as human beings. They reveal how our pervasive attitudes towards others surface from our deep convictions and egoistic perception of 'us versus them.' The attitude that 'I know everything, I am the best, but the rest are evil and stupid' is the rule of our planet now—a fact we nurture and believe in very strongly. We always think we deserve more than the rest. Thus, we draw a line to signify our borders, to isolate others and to keep everything for ourselves even if what we have is something we have borrowed or captured by force from somebody else. It is ours now. It is hard not to wonder about some Quebecer's zeal for sovereignty and independence from Canada, considering the relatively civil life for Canadians. Merely the image and dream of being *distinct* is probably provoking them to fight for separation. So, what is behind this dire need for 'distinction' that drives us blindly and forcefully into this path and the feelings of alienation? Has our increasing disappointments with human encounters and relationships brought us to such obstinate position? Is merely our inner urge for independence pushing us to be so controversial at all social levels? Or, is it just our egoism to attest our existence in the most retaliatory manner?

Obviously, these very same urges and forces that contaminate and stir our social thinking and patriotic struggles are ruining our personal lives, too. In fact they both are derived from the same source—the egoism dictating our personal beliefs and needs. The vile forces and egos that define and run organizations and our work habits, as explained in Part II, dominate our marriages, too.

Our selfish needs are reinforced by prevalent social values and pervasive attitudes and expectations of other fellow humans. We reinforce each other's Ego to strive for foolish and pointless means of building and expressing our individualism, identity, and importance. These very same fundamentals of human nature, now augmented by demented modern thinking, drive the alienation process in marital life as well.

We get married with false expectations that are bound to fail, anyway. We burden our marital relationships by many demands and a haughty display of individualism, as if carrying the torch of separation from day one in our heads without realizing it. Even marriage itself is often considered only an exercise for separation from bachelorhood, which we feel is constricting our identity as someone who can (and must) be loved and needed. We think of marriage as an exercise to portray our individualism. We just do not know or ignore that marriage is not a platform for expression of individualism and personal Ego or for satisfying our personal needs. This mentality actually defeats the notion of developing personal independence. As noted in Chapter One of Volume II, 'individualism' demands humility and selflessness. However, in society and marital life we abuse 'individualism' as a means of showing off our Ego and expressing personal power and abilities, instead of humility, teamwork, and objectivity. Ironically, our obsession for a companion and marriage is mostly a sign of our inability or unwillingness to grow up and live as an independent individual! Most of us are too needy to bear independence or grasp the true meaning of individualism. Still, we hypocritical humans do not stop pretending otherwise, anyway.

Our initial, inflated expectations of marriage create the basic hurdles in building our relationships properly. Our first thoughts in marriage are about all those things that we expect from our partners and all the great things that should now start to happen. We are unaware of marriage requirements and all the new things that we should do for our partner and relationship. We have no vision of the demands on us to cope with the new way of life. We do not realize the sacrifices that are needed just to stabilize our relationships and how our personal Ego must be managed more tightly. We do not know or ponder the responsibilities we must carry in a relationship and the delicate role we should play. Thus, we do everything the wrong way by playing a false personality in hopes of asserting our individuality and dominating the situation. Only when we realize the implications of an alienation journey, how it starts, and what triggers it, we might grasp the damaging roles we play in instigating alienation. We play a forbidding role when our attitudes and values make our partners feel alienated. And we play another negative role when our partners alienate us and we quickly resort to retaliation, instead of dealing with the situation calmly and effectively.

Alienation Characteristics

Since alienation is the main road to separation, it helps to realize its characteristics and prevent it from overtaking our relationships. We can beware of alienation symptoms that creep up gradually in our marriages and ruin our relationships eventually.

Alienation is a *feeling* of dissociation with our partner and his/her ideas. It is a feeling of loss of influence on the direction of our relationship, and a lack of strength and motivation to do anything about it. We see our partner in a different light all of a sudden. Our new image of our partner is unfamiliar and causes internal unrest when we think about him/her. We feel as though we do not know our partner. We do not grasp her/his reasoning and logic when analyzing the facts of life and our marriage. No common ground exists for discussing our interests and needs, we do not trust his/her judgment, we feel falling adrift from him/her more every day, and we become doubtful about the prospects of our relationship. The level of intimacy appears to decline along with our respect for him/her, and we feel uncomfortable and strange in his/her presence.

In addition, alienation is a *state of mind* in which we give up arguing about issues and changes that we sought from our partner before. We prefer to stay passive and keep a distance from our partner in order to eliminate or reduce conflicts and arguments. We stop reasoning and often surrender to our partners' whims, just because we doubt if our viewpoints have any value or effect for restoring our relationship. We feel emotionally overwhelmed and exhausted by even the thought of approaching our partner to discuss or ask something. We fear our partner and hate arguments that erupt at any point and time we are together. We fear the games, blaming, nagging, and intimidations that often erupt when we are together. Our contacts are unpleasant, and thus we try to minimize and control them. Without enough inner strengths and a healthy self-image, we might eventually feel miserable with no control of our life on top of the relationship itself.

Gentler alienation trips start in our marriage before we get to the real alienation journey. We all walk on and off the alienation path anytime we feel despair or disappointment with our partners. The severity of conflicts rises only when we advance further out on this journey. Otherwise, mostly subtle and mild alienation trips set us off during our lighter, innocent arguments before we return to our main journey of togetherness and cooperation. Still, while the effects of these alienation trips may be much less dire, so many trips, however short they may be, eventually exhaust us and infect our relationship. Frequent trips eventually instigate the big journey of alienation.

Partners' depression caused by short alienation trips naturally affects their sense of physical attraction and enjoyment. They engage in sexual relationships for lust instead of a feeling of love. The analogy of 'men going to their caves,' which John Gray uses in his book, is a reference to this alienation process. However, it seems that both men and women are equally moody regularly, thus withdraw from their partners emotionally and physically on a cyclical routine. On some occasions, in fact, women show a higher tendency for withdrawal, especially during menstruation. The mood cycles are reinforced, nevertheless, when partners are on an alienation course, however mild or subtle the alienation may be. In all, men do not seem to 'go to their caves' more often than women do, considering the latter's natural tendencies and the effect of their hormones. Actually, it happens more to women also due to their higher intuitive and emotional personalities—often for sensing and proving their higher need for autonomy these days, or perhaps for being from the planet Venus with a very peculiar mindset. In all, women are often more sensitive and demanding, thus show a higher tendency to withdraw. There is a significant difference in the nature of withdrawals between men and women, though. Men's withdrawal is usually passive as they merely hide in their shells. Women's is often showy, retaliatory, and spiteful. Ironically, however, women's withdrawals also feel rather sneaky or diplomatic most often!

Several factors, including lower Model and higher Ego, make men more abrupt in their withdrawal, when their pains and sense of alienation reaches its height temporarily. That is, when either men or women are on an alienation journey, maybe even without realizing it, they would be inclined to keep a distance and avoid unnecessary contacts that would cause arguments. However, gradually the force of sexual needs begins to take over. At this stage, either men or women begin to crawl out of the cave and approach their partners for the eventual goal of satisfying their lust. Since men are usually more aggressive (but more needy and vulnerable) regarding their sexual urges, their emergence from cave is more apparent, thus, for the same reason, their withdrawal might also appear more transparent and crude. In all, the intensity of alienation sends both men and women to their caves according to genders' prominent personality aspects, and often their high urge for sex brings them out of seclusion. Women's higher urge to grasp or re-establish their positions in their marriages brings them out of the cave faster than men, too.

Alienation makes partners see each other as aliens from two different planets. They see and interpret things differently. They do not seem to relate to each other's viewpoints even when they try to explain or listen to each other for making their own lives more bearable. Sometimes, we feel that our partner is resisting the chance to learn teamwork or anything else, and s/he is fighting our suggestions deliberately. So oddly, s/he seems to prefer spite even to a chance of making her/his life easier! *What tenacity!*

Being from the planets Venus and Mars, we would expect men and women to see each other as aliens at the first sight. Thus, the fact that we initially meet so naturally and peacefully, fall in love, and express our intimacy and feelings towards one another so generously is puzzling and contradictory. This is how and why it becomes difficult to make a real judgment about the root and emergence of subsequent problems. If men and women are good and nice to each other at the beginning, with no sense of being aliens, something makes them perceive each other's real personalities after marriage so differently, in a way that had not been obvious before, or at least had not felt so unbearable. Only partners' new perceptions after marriage result in partners' views of each other as aliens, if not mean enemies. Thus, it appears that men and women are from the planet Earth, after all, as they set out so naturally to get married and make all kinds of woes and commitments to one another so convincingly.

Yet, everybody has unique perspectives and priorities in life, which also change all the time. Surely, people are different in terms of their visions and aspirations. When these differences are not recognized as innate human nature, and when we insist on equality in all respects (including partners' intelligence level), we get into trouble with our naïve expectations from marriage. And when marriages are not bound by simple, sensible guidelines and commitments, it falls into alienation traps easier because of our unclear and unfounded perceptions of marriage.

We may eventually get fed up with our marriage and think time has come to separate. We are usually aware of a process and a period of alienation before we reach this final point. Yet, we are often not consciously aware of how we are travelling on this alienation path and then suddenly reach the end of the road and feel fed up. Or we keep living in a state of alienation for the rest of our lives without ever making the final decision to separate. The decision is hard, because we usually do not know where we stand in our relationship and cannot gather enough clues from all the signs that appear regularly on the alienation road. Yet, we are filled with huge doubts about our conclusions, relationships, and existence as a whole, and do not know how to deal with them.

Alienation Seeds and Growth

During an initial graceful period after marriage, partners strive to adapt to the new routines and expectations, assert their views of marital life, test each other, and prove themselves. They cleverly gauge their positions in their relationship and play with all aspects of their personalities to look cordial, express love, and, most of all, mark their territories. A lot of passion and compassion is often exchanged, while partners follow certain routines to raise their life enjoyments. The freshness of the experience allows partners forget their other engagements, personal interests, and obligations temporarily to put stress on pleasant activities and conversations. Optimism and cooperation prevail and future looks bright and full of promises. Oh, how much we all miss that sweet period! *For some lucky couples this exhilarating period might even last a whole year or so!!!*

Soon, however, the reality kicks in and partners remember the importance of their other activities and responsibilities. They miss their personal interests and friends. Therefore, they return to their old habits and activities gradually, and take marital life as a new foundation for accommodating other activities and life objectives. Real life issues feel serious again, thus our degree of attention to our partner and his/her interests stabilize at a level convenient for us; not the level that s/he expects in his/her sensitive mind.

Strangely enough, while we balance our activities and level of attention to our partner's needs according to our needs and sense of practicality, we continue to expect our partner to give us the same high level of love and attention that we need and imagined prior to marriage. We see our balancing act a practical move, but conceive our partner's adjustment a loss of his/her interest, thus a threat to our relationship. We start doubting our partner's love, intentions, and commitment. Thus, we cultivate the first seeds of mistrust and alienation. Alienation is not serious at this point, but it grows fast, unless partners learn to align their mentalities and activities with stringent relationship requirements in the new era. Accordingly, both their own cooling down and their spouse's adjusted attitude baffle partners. The change and the confusion lead to hurt feelings and reactions, openly or indirectly. Perhaps some hints and casual chitchat about their hurt feelings come up occasionally, each partner striving to justify his/her intentions, but criticizing his/her partner's cooling attitude. Partners' quirks and anxiety erupt in the form of insecurities, possessiveness, jealousy, withdrawals, etc., especially for couples who have depended too much on love to carry their relationships. Egos are under pressure and partners' frustrations erupt in many ways. Their reactions set the pace for the next level of struggles, where hostile discussions and never-ending futile arguments make their lives miserable. Those who are less tolerant, or perhaps more practical in their minds, may give up already and ask for separation at this stage. Yet, the majority of us continue with our fights, withdrawals, and doubts, with hopes that someday our partner would understand our needs and demands and stop resisting our request to change.

We do not know that change is impossible even if our partner had all the best intentions to change. Meanwhile, the conditions keep deteriorating, because we do not know how to handle the situation and our injured Egos. We doubt even the value of our arguments and the likelihood of our partner ever caring for us enough to change, yet we keep pushing him/her in different ways, anyhow. Especially, if a mutual attraction exists, we keep going through cycles of arguments and fights - hostility and withdrawal - make up and sex - logical confrontation and justification - back to the beginning of the cycle - a new round of ferocious fights. Yet, every time we go through this cycle, a little bit of intimacy is scraped off our relationship. We lose confidence regarding our relationship and wonder whether our efforts would ever lead to any tangible results. We feel more alienated towards our partner and less interested to discuss the contentious issues. We start to doubt our decision to marry this person. Sadly, we find that the number of issues we avoid discussing grows gradually until not much is left to say to each other outside a few very essentials, and in a hostile tone. Especially, alienation process accelerates fast if partners have not discussed and chosen a particular relationship model to moderate their needs, attitudes, and expectations.

We are alienated somewhat, maybe a lot even. However, we still do not give up. Beneath all those doubts about the viability of our marriage and the value of our struggles, still some glimpses of optimism and hope keep us going. Both partners feel the pains of alienation and the heaviness of their silence, but neither dares or cares to initiate a conversation that would most likely stir more fights and disappointments. They feel helpless in the depth of their doubts and despair, yet no other options seem promising, either. Simply, no remedy seems at hand but tolerating their relationship, for now at least.

The alienation grows gradually even with small, unintentional tactlessness, conflicts, and insensitive comments. Often, partners' idiosyncrasies expedite the alienation, usually in an early stage of marriage and proceeds hastily towards its final destination, as if they were travelling on a supersonic plane rather than a sailboat. Surely, partners' personalities, particularly their patience, affect the process and speed of alienation substantially. However, in effect, the outcome and eventuality of separation do not change much if couples' alienation reaches a point where return becomes insurmountable. Therefore, if partners are so drastically different in personality and cannot find the means of cooperation to elude alienation, they are better off following the speedy process of concluding everything fast with minimal bloodshed. Painful, long alienation journeys are suffocating and excruciating.

Couples feel alienated toward each other for many unintended and innocent gestures that get out of hand. We hurt each other with our passive/aggressive attitude and crooked communication methods. We forget that our rising idiosyncrasies are responsible for inducing many miscommunications and alienations either deliberately or innocently. Of course, many non-psychological and external causes of alienation also burden relationships, such as financial hardship, social norms, health issues, etc. However, the bulk of alienation problems are created, and allowed to get out of hand, since we are not aware and in control of our small flaws, including our persistence to use sarcastic tone and vague messages in our communications. Common causes of alienation among couples are listed below:

Common Causes of Alienation
- Inability to communicate
- Miscommunication, intentional or due to carelessness
- Nagging and blaming
- Hostile or irritable tone of voice during communication
- Reluctance or inability to share information and cooperate
- Lack of trust or respect
- Deceit and insincerity
- Egoism and intimidation
- Lack of passion and compassion
- Personality clashes and incompatibility
- Insecurities and deprivation of personal needs
- Financial or social burdens, and other external factors
- Unbalanced and unsatisfied expectations
- Perceptions of the above, especially the lack of love
- Etc.

Innocent Causes of Alienation

Even minor personal idiosyncrasies and miscommunications can cause alienation. A simple communication may be misinterpreted and reacted upon antagonistically. Partners often raise old issues in hopes of clarifying a particular point or solving an outstanding issue. Soon, however, this seemingly logical attempt makes them anxious, especially when the main topic of discussion is lost. For example, (partner A) raises an old incident only as a general idea or for noting a weakness in their relationship that needs attention. Yet, (B) uses the occasion to fight by questioning (A)'s hidden intentions to raise this particular topic again now. By itself, (A)'s point is just meant to signify an old event or a life experience that might have educational value. However, since (A) has brought it up, the argument is swiftly redirected towards a deeper marital problem that neither of them had even meant to discuss again. Merely, (A) is blamed again for his/her insensitivity and dragged into a faultfinding exercise that leads only to more confusion and stress for both partners.

Ironically, partners do not even understand the causes of their outbursts from simple points or observations, except that they get into lengthy arguments over issues that no longer really matter. They end up sleeping in different rooms and do not talk to each other for perhaps a week or two with no logical reason to support such childish behaviours. Some couples may get a bit smarter at last and study their conversations and the causes of their conflicts. They may realize how they allow their spouses drag them into needless fights based on simple conversations or opinions, which have no direct relevance to, or importance for, their marriage. Eventually, partners may learn to avoid raising points that trigger faultfinding arguments regarding past events, which means they would never give themselves a chance to learn anything from their experiences. The funny thing is that when a partner talks about a new issue, the other partner usually interrupts him/her and asks, "Like what? Give me an example." However, they both know better now that reiterating contentious experiences could merely open the can of worms all over again for a new round of arguments.

Understanding simple conditions that trigger arguments and fights in marriage (such as the example noted above) does not mean that we can always avoid such explosive situations. Rather, this knowledge may raise our awareness of many conditions that lead to numerous miscommunications unique for each couple. Still, couples can try to pinpoint those special topics or situations that trigger most of their miscommunications. Strangely enough, often miscommunication causes are quite simple and irrelevant to the issue at hand. They usually reflect the hidden problems and neglected needs of one or both partners, awaiting an opportunity to erupt. If not, it relates to the poor way each person handles the communication process and how information is sent, received, analysed, and reacted to. The tone of our communications is also a big alienating factor too often.

In John Gray's book, *Men are from Mars, Women are from Venus,* Harpercollins; Harperperennial, 1992, he refers to some simple and straightforward examples of miscommunication, such as:

"Women say: 'We never go out,'

men hear: 'You are not doing your job. What a disappointment you have turned out to be ... , you are lazy, unromantic, and just boring.,'

they mean: 'I feel like going out and doing something together.'" Ibid., page 62.

"Women say: 'Everyone ignores me,'

men hear: 'I am so unhappy, I just can't get the attention I need. Everything is completely hopeless. You should be ashamed. You are unloving.,'

they mean: 'Today, I am feeling ignored and unacknowledged. Would you give me a hug and tell me how special I am to you?'" Ibid., page 63.

> *"Men say: 'I'm fine,' and*
> *women hear: 'I don't care about what has happened. This problem isn't important to me. Even if it upsets you, I don't care.,'*
> *They mean: 'I am fine because I am successfully dealing with my upset or problem. I don't need any help. If I do I will ask.'"*
> Ibid., page 74.

These interpretations are not necessarily complete or precise, but they reflect how our miscommunications trigger our senses of insecurity and oversensitivity. Some interesting conclusions can, however, be deduced from these miscommunications. First, they indicate that we hide our real needs and meanings in the context or tone of our communications. Second, we expect our partner to be sensitive and intelligent enough to grasp and interpret our real meanings from miscommunications, moody attitudes, and hidden messages in our dialogues. Third, we have gotten used to this kind of incomprehensive communications and believe it is all right. Fourth, it suggests the necessity of building a sixth sense for interpreting 'intentionally ambiguous' communications, and that people should be blamed when their brains cannot learn to do so all the time. We have become too selfish to recognize and accept that miscommunication occurs because we express our intentions in strange and irrelevant manners, or that we are oversensitive, too demanding, or use a bad tone of voice. Once we start this game (the process of miscommunication filled with futile hints and hidden expectations) between a couple, it becomes a norm and normal routine for both partners to confuse and torture each other with their sarcastic, enigmatic communications.

John Gray seems to be suggesting that we should get used to this type of communications in marriages and learn how to read between the lines when our partners talk. If so, I disagree!

Miscommunication erupts deliberately or innocently for many reasons. Especially, the increase in individuals' stress level due to preoccupation with many tasks and problems, including personal and business priorities, substantially reduces the amount of time and patience needed for communication. We are always in a rush to go somewhere else and do something else, and we expect our partner to know and respect these facts. We expect our partner to not only understand our meaning in a communication even when it is not expressed straight, but also adjust his/her communication style and personal needs to accept and accommodate our bizarre way of communicating. The problem is that the more partners try to accommodate these kinds of infantile expectations, the faster and more convoluted the communication norms become, and the more the chances of miscommunication and alienation get. We never seem interested in solving the sources of problems, but merely deal with their annoying symptoms *superficially*. These perceptions and perfunctory solutions only create more confusion and stress, not to mention all the extra efforts that people must put into even their simple communications, while ruining society, too.

Learning about the alienation process and its causes is important for detecting and acknowledging both our personal and marital issues before it is too late. It helps us view marital *relationships* more consciously as a dynamic environment highly susceptible to (mostly self-induced) destructive alienation factors (as listed above). Nonetheless, we are personally responsible for allowing these forces interfere and shape our mentalities and relationships. Self-awareness helps us recognize the causes of alienation, adjust our attitudes and expectations, and curb our debilitating habits that promote alienation.

Fighting Alienation

Normally, nobody imagines leaving his/her spouse when s/he is just getting married. We all *assume* and imagine only a smooth, fruitful relationship growing gradually into a prosperous, happy partnership. This innocent assumption shows how things usually go wrong despite our *supposedly* good intentions. Occasionally, a partner might change his/her mind about marriage, thus actively causes alienation to get out of it. When a partner is adamant about separation, hardly can any person or advice help the situation and partners.

However, alienation usually starts inadvertently against our good intentions. We prefer to stay married if external forces and partners' quirks do not ruin things. Yet, always things go wrong and alienation begins early in most marriages, nowadays. Many of us realize how our own sense of insecurity might have ruined our marriages, which shows just one common example of genetic deficiencies we bring to our marriages and stir endless struggles. Therefore, we can search seriously for factors, especially personal defects, that lead to our alienation after marriage.

Alienation is mainly a symptom of some real or perceived threat (mainly our spouse) triggering some of our psychological flaws, which we do not know about or cannot control. Usually, an external stimulus, e.g., our partner's flirting with someone else, provokes our hidden quirks. It triggers our sense of jealousy and insecurity beyond our control. In many situations, the outside stimulus may not be even real. Rather, only our (mis)perceptions of external events often trigger our quirks. Our imaginations can drive us crazy if we let them. And, of course, in many situations, we become the subject of abuse by our partner without any fault or provocation on our side. We simply receive different kinds of abuse, perhaps even without our partner's direct intention to hurt or alienate us. Conversely, we sometimes act in a provocative way (intentionally or inadvertently) that annoys our partner. In this case, our action becomes an external stimulus for our partner whose reaction we observe and respond to (again) with another rude reaction of our own. Naturally, this endless series of actions-reactions can lead to more misperceptions, retaliatory exchanges, and of course alienation.

If partners are REALLY serious and sincere for sustaining their relationship, and only if they are not badly flawed beyond repair, they could search for, and find ways of preventing, the causes of alienation, as explained in detail in the next chapter.

CHAPTER ELEVEN
Alienation Preparedness

Regretfully, the alienation growth and its dire consequences are too tricky to explain in one book. Nevertheless, it is always wiser for any smart couple to prevent alienation from the beginning if possible. Thus, this chapter's main intention is to help the readers learn enough about alienation preparedness process and apply some steps diligently to monitor and improve their relationships, then make right decisions about their marriage, especially when alienation or the separation likelihood is growing.

The goal of the 'alienation preparedness' process is to curb the rotting relationship conditions that cripple partners' judgment, while they stagger and struggle on an alienation course. Through self-awareness process, we also learn to make our judgments and decisions about marital problems only when we are in control of our thoughts and emotions, and not when we have lost our senses in the heat of arguments. We should remember that our judgment is sound only if it is free from prejudices, Ego, and raw emotions.

Smart, caring couples can take some preventative measures against alienation process, though it is a tough task. They should become much better persons by, i) recognizing and stopping their alienating behaviours, and ii) learning to bear more hardship and psychological insecurities that usually persist in all relationships.

Surely, by expressing and intending to be a 'good' and 'patient' person, we do not actually turn into one over night. It would take many years of conviction and faith to make it happen.

Acknowledgment and Awareness

To remedy alienation, we should become a conscientious and conscious person with higher patience and compassion. This means acknowledging our personal flaws and realizing their role in causing alienation. We should distinguish our personal needs from relationship needs that often do not coincide, and then find the right balance in favour of relationship needs. We must also find the roots of our idiosyncrasies, crude mentality, and relationship issues without getting into deep analyses or drawing conclusions right away. We are only looking for some clues regarding the causes of our clashes and crude attitude to draw a general picture about the health of our relationship and the chance of saving it. This fact-finding routine that is mainly for self-assessment demands total sincerity, commitment, and objectivity. This means no fast judgments and conclusions.

At this stage, in particular, we are better off not acquiring our partner's participation or consent. We should not ask our partner to sit with us, argue, blame each other, get our Egos worked up, and accomplish nothing at the end. Rather, problem diagnosis is merely a personal awareness exercise. We do this alone, at least initially, without the involvement of our partner. For example, if we have lost our love or interest in a relationship, we must admit it honestly, instead of looking for excuses as to 'why I have lost my passion or respect for him/her.' The reasons are only useful at the next stage, only if the possibility of regaining our love and respect for him/her still exists. We do not even have to admit our faults or loss of interest to our partner if we do not want to, but at least we should become aware of our own erratic emotions, and eventually start working on them.

We may think that we are aware of all the factors contributing to alienation and we are aware of the process and the rest of it. Yet, this fundamental superficiality, and our ignorance, about the meaning of awareness make us flop. In addition, we often *think* that we are aware and proactive in strengthening our relationship, but our partner's ignorance and faults negate our efforts, anyway. We might even believe that our awareness efforts and practising certain roles to prevent alienation are just a waste of our time or not fair, since we are doing all the work and showing interest to save our marriage, while our partner seems more careless daily.

While we can aim for both partners' awareness and support to elude alienation, we can only be in charge of our own awareness process and progress. We are just responsible for playing our role consciously and conscientiously without being too discouraged or disturbed by our partner's apathy. Our awareness means that we accept our partner's resistance and prepare for the possibility of negative attitude and psychological defects of our partner, which may interfere and hinder our attempts to spawn awareness in our marital relationship. We must keep playing our role calmly.

Boosting our consciousness and awareness requires activating Self slowly to become a more selfless and compassionate person for both finding personal peace and possibly saving our marriage. We focus on the alienation process itself, rather than our partner's faults, while we learn and play a proactive role to prevent our marriage breakdown, if possible. We avoid using awareness as another level of scrutiny on our partner's lack of understanding, love, or goodwill. Otherwise, we cannot attain the meaning and purpose of awareness. We would only keep blaming our partner and sink deeper in depression and our egoistic personality. That kind of crooked approach to awareness would only create more alienation and friction than help. In these circumstances, we also get frustrated and give up quickly when we face our partner's retaliatory actions and spite. Our insincerity and egoism would only confuse us subconsciously and alienate our partner further, too. In all, the only objective of boosting our consciousness and awareness is to turn inwardly to detect our own flaws and build our strength to fight alienation. Then, we might be ready to study those relationship hurdles that reflect partners' incompatibilities and lower their communication abilities.

One essential fact to remember is that, in most cases, we must prevent alienation on our own. Like all other types of awareness and enlightenment experiences, relationship awareness is also a personal objective we pursue mostly for our benefit. It would prove to be a useful way of calming ourselves and reducing the stress caused by the unknown sources of marital conflicts and quarrels. More importantly, marital awareness is just a personal endeavour, because, in the final analysis, the information and wisdom we gain in the process is mainly for soothing our nerves and preventing a lifelong quarrel with our doubts about the nature and prospect of our marriage. The idea is to gain enough clues and confidence to make an objective decision about our relationship and future. We cooperate with our partner and show interest in pursuing a joint awareness process as much and long as possible, but then we would be responsible for our decision, especially if it must be 'separation.' This awareness would also be vastly useful if we ever have to choose another partner in case our marriage falters eventually. We would know much better what factors are essential for us in choosing a new partner.

When we speak to our partner from an awareness platform, it does not necessarily mean that s/he understands or agrees with our views and approach for solving our conflicts. We must create common grounds and communication about our intentions about marital awareness with our partner after building our regimen for self-awareness first. Often we think we are aware of the situation and problems when in fact we are only focusing on our partner's faults and blaming him/her for everything. In such cases, our self-exploration is not objective and honest, but only a faultfinding endeavour. Our persistence to convince our partner regarding relationship problems, and blaming her/him, merely shows our egoistic mentality and our self-awareness failure so far. However, this is the most common approach that partners pursue naively. Focusing on our partner's faults and flaws is often the easiest way of copping out, instead of learning to cope with relationships' sad realities in modern societies through self-awareness. We refuse to admit our responsibility in causing conflicts and the role we must play to prevent alienation. We have not learned that a great deal of tolerance is required these days to maintain a relationship and enjoy its potential benefits.

The bottomline is that we pursue an awareness exercise only because we sincerely care about our relationship as well as our life. That is a significant motive and target. The goal is to help ourselves by remaining objective to identify the real issues and set the course of our lives in a proper direction. We should admit that awareness is more about finding our own faults and share of conflicts. It is more a process of bringing our Ego in check. And it is mostly a search of our inner strengths for enhancing marital communication. Only as a secondary objective, we strive to find other sources and external factors that also cause alienation. At this stage, we only try to learn about (become aware of) the roots of the problems and our role in creating them. To the extent we can work on problems unilaterally, we might initiate plans and programs to improve our attitude and approach in line with the details offered below. To the extent we must address other facts, including our partner's attitude or perceptions at least, we cannot demand them fast without establishing a mutual understanding and drawing a sensible plan to gain his/her trust first.

Ultimately, we must choose the path of our lives with utmost intelligence and sincerity. That is the only way we can survive in society and our marriages. That is also the ultimate goal of both self-awareness and marital awareness.

Alienation Preparedness Factors

'Alienation preparedness' is merely a precautionary antidote for marriage breakdown if partners have not drifted apart drastically.

It is a potent preventative measure—vaccine—even if partners are inflicted by the symptoms of alienation somewhat already. With alienation preparedness, we plan to maintain the health of our relationships by:
1. Acknowledging potential relationship problems
   (as well as unique issues in our relationships)
2. Dealing with our psychological defects
3. Measuring and improving our tolerance
4. Recognizing our opportunities and fears
5. Admitting, planning, and playing our roles
6. Making objective judgments and decisions

These six steps are partners' perpetual responsibilities starting on the wedding day, while they keep working on the 14 success factors listed in Table 8.1 on page 144. Thus, ask yourself whether you have the patience and interest to study and apply the issues discussed in this book, especially Part IV, sincerely. If not, your relationship's chances of alienation and failure are high. Surely, your partner's participation in the process would be useful, too, but you must practise alienation preparedness factors personally first, with the intention and hopes of including your partner in this learning process soon. Surely, your partner's commonsense and goodwill to join you later is also useful, after you explain the goals and benefits of alienation preparedness process to her/him. Yet, you should prepare yourself for this ideal never materializing.

Alienation Preparedness - Factor One
Acknowledging Potential Relationship Problems

Unfortunately, we can no longer take our marriages as a *stable* support system (platform) for performing our more tangible life duties. Most of our perceptions of marriage, especially about its stability and partners' commitments, are flawed, nowadays. We do not recognize that marriage is an ongoing responsibility and challenge for fulfilling special objectives, while partners should play specific roles properly and perpetually. Nowadays, marriage stability requires constant control and engagement. Even then, relationships remain forever quite vulnerable as a symptom of new social disorder and people's obsession for independence and identity. Unfortunately, relationships' stability was the luxury that old generations enjoyed so casually, but no more.

Similar to an earthquake, we can never anticipate the eruption of marriage fatal turmoil. We can never foresee when one or both partners reach the end of their alienation journey so unexpectedly and their marriage tumbles under the pressures of alienation, as if a major earthquake had shaken the foundation and structure of their relationship rather fast and unexpectedly. And similar to an earthquake preparedness program (to foresee and prepare for its severe repercussions), the 'alienation preparedness,' is just a basic plan to enhance our awareness about alienation and to learn how to be prepared to face and defeat it; or at least minimize its effects on ourselves and our family. Some general plans and guidelines are drawn in this chapter, but everybody can do his/her planning best. Understanding and respecting our marriages' peculiarities and partners' unique needs give everybody the insight to prepare his/her astute and customized alienation preparedness plan.

The first step is to study marriage environment, relationships' unique needs, and circumstances that often lead to alienation, as noted in the last chapter. Most of us take our marriages for granted subsequent to a short period of honeymoon—after our passion settles and we touch life's realities again. This does not necessarily mean that we lose our love or enthusiasm fast. On the contrary, we feel secure and comfortable in our marital environment. This gives us the psychological security and a platform to ensue our life aspirations more actively. This is consistent with Maslow's theory, which speculates we move on to search and satisfy our higher needs once our lower needs (e.g., belonging and love) are satisfied. However, the problem is that we assume our marriage is as safe as we feel, rather relaxed, about our love and belonging needs. This may not be true. Actually, we often have a wrong perception of marriage at the outset, since we assume a normal (average) marital relationship would be problem free, despite all the stories and statistics that suggest otherwise. We think marital problems emerge from those exceptional circumstances where partners are either abnormal or cannot handle their marital affairs logically. Thus, we see no reason to worry, because we consider both ourselves and our marital conditions normal. The problem with these crude assumptions is that, nowadays, even a 'normal' relationship gets entangled and tainted quickly by many complex circumstances due to the overall malfunctioning of social systems and partners' misperceptions, stress, and untamed expectations. No 'normal relationship' exists in society anymore. Therefore, we must study and acknowledge three categories of information in our marital relationships:

i) Partners' compatibilities and quirks.
ii) Marital environments, with the objective of learning about relationships' specific needs and keeping the peculiarities of our unique relationship at our conscious level permanently. We must also learn about relationship models and determine which model best suits partners' personalities and needs.
iii) Main alienating sources in relationships (as listed on pages 213) and how to avoid them.

The above three important topics have been discussed throughout Part IV, but will be delineated further in Chapter Twelve.

Alienation Preparedness - Factor Two
Acknowledging Our Psychological Defects

After acknowledging the sources and severity of our relationship problems, the next step in 'alienation preparedness' process is to recognize our idiosyncrasies, which taint our relationships often. The main goal is to admit that everybody is loaded with defects and then learn how to deal with our psychological flaws best. Our imaginary standards of human beings regarding their intelligence and morality vastly surpass their instincts and nature. We imagine ethics much better than we can ever attain it as a human. Only when we accept that nobody is even half-perfect as our Ego likes to suggest, or our Model pretends, we might acquire the wisdom to better ourselves as a person and a companion, exude patience and compassion, and prevent alienation.

We must grasp our martial and personal issues, as outlined in the previous chapter, to learn about our defects, learn who we are, and gauge the personality that portrays us to others. Volume II of this trilogy also offers many ideas about self-awareness. We learn that our psychological flaws are mostly not created or controlled by us. Thus, acknowledging them is not intended to cause shame and guilt in our minds. On the contrary, merely our persistence to ignore them shows our naivety and arrogance. We should be only ashamed of, and feel guilty about, our naïve stubbornness, and sometimes our inability, to accept the universality and depth of human imperfections. We all still have a hard time grasping the essence of our being—both our dire impurity and nothingness.

Only by soul-searching and self-assessing, we might finally grasp the depth of our psychological defects, and then decide to what extent we wish to control them or let them control us. We need enough maturity to gauge these defects and their impacts on our own and other people's lives. We always resist criticism and change, as we believe we are perfect already, and that we know everything about ourselves and everybody else. This primitive psychological barrier hinders our search for wisdom and peace. We are addicted to our phony personalities and lifestyles, thus resist the idea of becoming natural and purer persons, which we often find unattainable or futile. This is like expecting a smoker to give up smoking just because he knows the hazards of his habit. Perhaps assuming that the goal is not to change ourselves—not initially at least—eases our natural resistance to discover the finer aspects of 'self' and who we really are. Detecting our defects does not stir an automatic commitment for change, yet our new knowledge of self may lead to a gradual transformation from within without too much effort to bring change about.

We must pinpoint our personality aspects that dominate our relationship with our partner—to establish how we relate; how much of our contacts and relations are driven by Ego, Self, or Model. Especially, when a majority of partners' demands and attitudes are Ego driven, they may learn how, and how much, they are contributing to their relationship's demise. They should be fair and unbiased when monitoring their attitudes and roles in undermining each other. Similarly, they should beware of their partner's main personality aspects and learn how they might be causing more alienation and less opportunity to reconcile, often unconsciously and helplessly.

Naturally, it is harder to see and accept our own defects than those of others due to our Ego standing in the way, while we set personal standards of normal behaviour unilaterally, too. We are selfish in the way: i) we truly believe that whatever we do is right and justified, ii) we use our self-serving beliefs and standards to judge and treat others with prejudice, and iii) we apply double standards for ourselves and others shamelessly. We impose our double standards when we use one criterion to judge ourselves or someone we like, and use a different criterion for judging others, especially our adversaries. We are hardly aware of our quirks, anyway. When, on occasions, we notice clues of our wickedness and weaknesses, we find ways to suppress our thoughts fast and intentionally support our defective perception of life and our role in the midst of it all.

In all, we can at least learn that our psychological flaws consist of, i) those we simply cannot see, and ii) those we face from time to time, but push into our unconscious swiftly in order to justify our selfish actions without a sense of guilt and remorse. Even this basic awareness can make us more conscientious and conscious of who we are. Meanwhile, our psychological flaws keep causing sufferings for others and us, as long as we remain not serious or compassionate enough to do something about them.

By acknowledging our own and humans' natural flaws we can i) heal our obvious flaws, ii) deal with our partner's defects more compassionately, and iii) always remember the wide scope of simple psychological flaws that cause alienation. These three objectives of healing, handling, and remembering our flaws are elaborated in Chapter Twelve (Page 256).

Alienation Preparedness - Factor Three
Measuring and Improving Our Tolerance

Without **great** patience and flexibility, we do not last long in a marriage. Most of us learn this fact the hard way eventually. What we perhaps do not fully recognize, however, is that *high* 'tolerance' is an inevitable reality of marriage, a general rule—an absolute necessity. Rather, we perceive patience a major sacrifice and inconvenience (maybe torture) that only we seem to endure. We are all becoming less patient and flexible in our relationships, in fact, due to our misperceptions about the purpose of marriage, obsession for individualism and love, and rising stress from our other life responsibilities. Moreover, we doubt the definition and level of tolerance that can be considered normal and practical in a marital relationship. These doubts often increase impatience (and inflexibility) all by themselves.

Another problem is that we mostly rely on our Ego to decide on the tolerance level that feels normal to us—what ego! Usually, during arguments, not only our offended Ego becomes in charge of viewing, analysing, and tackling the issues, but also we rely on this impatient and selfish aspect of our personality to decide on how much more we can (or must) tolerate the situation. Thus, we hurry for separation and divorce, get entangled in an alienation process, find ourselves a lover, spend more time with friends and do things away from our spouse and family, get dissolved in too much work or personal hobbies, become spiteful, etc.

Therefore, a main test for a couple contemplating marriage is to gauge their tolerance levels—especially their own—carefully and remember that no marriage survives these days without high patience and tolerance. If partners are not mentally and logically prepared for this crucial need of relationships, they should avoid that marriage at all cost, even despite their great love. Partners must know how to cope with severe deficiencies of relationships, including deep conflicts and quarrels, and still show good faith and intentions, while also hope that mutual understanding grows gradually. Many of us might realize at last that most relationship problems remain unresolved and we must somehow learn to live with them through wisdom and tolerance. Accordingly, the main questions are, 'Am I the type of person who can go through life in a conflict-laden environment and make the best of it patiently somehow? Why would I do that?' Then, remember our answers forever whenever we face relationship conundrums.

Tolerance depends on personal virtues (or defects) reinforced by social norms and partners' level of expectations from their relationship. Most of us imagine that a perfect partner and ideal relationship are within our reach and a most natural expectation. We assume tolerance would hardly be required, because we can find an ideal companion and atmosphere to nurture our personal needs. With such grand misperception, we do not learn that a marital relationship is built mainly around patience and evolves merely out of flexibility. Our parents and society do not teach us what tolerance means and requires. In fact, many recent social norms advocate low tolerance while pushing for individualism and equality. We all think that *we deserve better*, and that there is something more interesting and peaceful out there awaiting us as soon as we get out of our existing marital relationship. Sadly, our popular social guidelines are misleading us more than helping us, nowadays.

Since partners cannot change themselves quickly and easily, their only hope should be to create an atmosphere where they can nurture an *enduring* level of faith and compassion. Tolerance is the foundation for building such an atmosphere, within which personality adjustments might be goaded and nurtured. Tolerance means allowing our partner express and pursue his/her interests without our interference. Developing such atmosphere, perhaps as a last resort in some conflict-ridden cases, may in turn instigate the process of personal awareness and change. Simply, the idea is that, with tolerance, partners allow each other evolve as a person first (and then as a partner) on his/her own terms, until eventually (soon hopefully) they grasp each other's needs and ways. Again, choosing the right relationship model is crucial to force this issue.

Then again, tolerance does not mean accepting our partner's abuse or living with a selfish spouse in alienation. This attitude is a sign of helplessness and desperation mixed with one's inability, or indecisiveness, to break away. Tolerance is unadvisable for cases where partners are narcissistic or highly incompatible.

Acknowledging the oddities of our marital relationships and the inevitable impacts of partners' psychological defects improves our tolerance level directly. It helps us recognize why tolerance is a prerequisite of any marital relationship. In this sense, tolerance becomes an inherent product of our awareness. It grows rather automatically in line with the gradual growth of our wisdom. The reason this happens should be obvious: With awareness, our Ego subsides vastly and the decision about tolerance level is entrusted to Self. Self not only is more patient and passionate by its virtues, but also grasps much better the helplessness and limitations of our partner in handling his/her defects. We can learn to manage our Ego, instead of letting it control and ruin our lives.

We can also learn why telling somebody to be more patient or flexible cannot help him/her or the situation at all. Tolerance is mostly a function of self-confidence and learning how people's psychological defects control and render them helpless too often. Only then, we can increase our tolerance. For example, at some stage in their relationship, a couple may realize that they often end up fighting when they have opposing views on a topic. They just cannot wait to prove their points and save their Egos at any cost. When partners learn how their Egos jump out to control those situations, and when they learn how useless winning or losing an argument is for saving their relationship, they become more tolerant of each other's disagreements even when they think they are absolutely right regarding something. They merely learn to let it go. Soon, both partners reach the same conclusion and become less argumentative, if they are not too egoistical. Partners' awareness changes them directly, but also helps create an atmosphere to improve their attitudes and stop insisting on always being right. This helps them to calm down and recognize the silliness and uselessness of their egoistic arguments.

Alienation Preparedness - Factor Four
Recognizing Our Opportunities and Fears

A big difference exists between tolerating out of confidence or fear. We are acting from a position of confidence if we tolerate the harsh realities of our relationship according to the 'alienation preparedness' points noted here. We are monitoring and fighting the alienation process with a logical plan. We are confident that either the situation would improve soon, or we know how to exit calmly when it deteriorates beyond our preset tolerance level—without regrets for not having tried enough or separated sooner. On the other hand, if we tolerate out of fear of unknown future, a less desirable lifestyle, or whatever else, we are only delaying the act of separation while immersing deeper in the self-defeat and alienation process. In this case, we are unable to help ourselves, our partners, or our relationships in any way. The only possibility to help the situation and perhaps reverse the alienation process is to turn our fears into authentic confidence (but not false pride). How we can achieve this, of course, depends on the nature of our fears and the strength of our personality.

Managing our tolerance level on a consistent basis is difficult, so it is discussed further in Chapter Twelve (Page 264).

People's various fears, insecurities, and vulnerabilities are too numerous and peculiar. We should list our own for ourselves as part of self-awareness. They affect our decisions, perceptions of life, and relationships. Yet, behind any fear, an opportunity awaits to be tapped. For example, behind the fear of separation (and loneliness) stands the great chance of finding 'who we are' away from our debilitating urge for a companion. We merely need courage to tap the opportunity that exists behind our fears. If we reorient our minds only slightly to break out of normalcy and the freezing effect of our fears of change, most of us find a new world. We find courage to confront, and go beyond, the apparent limits within our crooked societies, thus seize new opportunities. New life dimensions present themselves as we embrace the new opportunities. The joy of new discoveries and the relief from old fears would redefine our identity and create a refreshing sense of existence. Exploring every new opportunity also brings us a higher level of self-confidence. For example, we might have been tolerating our humiliating relationship out of fear of loneliness and inability to find another companion. Some of us in fact prefer an annoying partner to no partner, and we might have a good rationale for it as well. However, behind those rationales could be our weak emotions, lack of confidence, self-pity, and other fears that turn into excuses and justifications. The truth is that without confidence we can neither succeed in our relationships (present or future ones), nor capture the essence of individualism. We also lose life's immense opportunities, including spirituality, that any intelligent person must explore on his/her own.

Our doubts about the viability of our relationships intensify our fears; not only the normal fears of loneliness and emotional breakdown, but also the fears of being wrong in our judgment about the state of our marriage and the possibility of reversing the alienation course. We doubt our partner ever understanding our needs and being able to provide a chance for a relatively peaceful companionship. We have doubts about the wisdom of staying in this convoluted marriage. We think we should leave our partner before it is too late and we lose our youth and attractiveness. These kinds of doubts and fears could deprive us from exploring the opportunities to save our marriage by fighting the alienation process head on, gaining self-awareness and tolerance, making our relationship work in a creative manner, etc. Both our fears of either leaving our partner prematurely or staying too long in a doomed marriage make us suffer.

The bottomline is that we may conquer our doubts and fears only by building our confidence and faith, and by redirecting our negative thoughts 180 degrees. Confidence gives us a precious opportunity for independence and individualism that lies beyond our fears and void our false pride and arrogance. The chance of doing the right things is much higher when we gauge our options from a platform of confidence with patience and intelligent faith in ourselves and our partner. We would do the right things when we confidently overcome the fears of loneliness or making big mistakes, which we also realize could always happen.

Still, we must ensure we do not get carried away quickly and abandon a relationship that could have been saved had we just followed the guidelines for 'alienation preparedness'.

After living with a companion for a while, we learn to view life from only one general dimension. We judge our lives' values mainly by the level of our success in maintaining a relationship supported by a rudimentary career. We ignore or undermine the value of an inherent relationship we (can) have with 'self.' With our fear of loneliness, we deprive ourselves of grasping our inner 'self' that can show us the finer opportunities of life, starting with the mere recognition of our identity and spirituality. We never realize and utilize our innate potentialities, which can provide us with the greatest secrets of our existence. If only we bypass our fears of losing our existing relationships and never finding others, we approach a divine dimension of individualism much beyond our customary definitions. This does not mean that we rush out to leave our spouses. Rather, we learn to embrace our relationships with some confidence built around total humility and respect our families for not only their own values, but also the strengths they could give us to explore our spirits as a supplementary feature of human existence.

Learning more about the meaning of individualism and power of independence, as explained in Volume II of this trilogy, can help a person build his/her mindset and the confidence needed for making an appropriate decision in line with his/her unique needs and personality. Individualism and independence, which we all brag about and cherish personally and socially, largely evolve around our ability to stand alone, which implies both the divinity and necessity of loneliness as a precious human characteristic.

The bare minimal benefit of recognizing the inherent power and potentiality in our 'self' is the confidence we gain to repair our damaged relationships through tolerance and wisdom. On the other hand, we should beware of the high chance of growing a false confidence or overconfidence, which merely indicates our neglect to ponder the facts reiterated in this chapter adequately. Overconfidence shows low consciousness and high insecurities that stir intolerance. People's misperceptions about equality and individualism give them a false sense of overconfidence, thus a low tolerance level, while they become more arrogant daily, too. This misleading overconfidence, or false pride, destroys both our chances of having a good relationship and finding 'self.' It shows our immaturity and neediness. Conversely, authentic confidence makes us humble within or without a relationship.

Thus, we are facing another major life dilemma: Our doubts and fears prevent us from boosting our confidence, and without confidence, we cannot conquer our fears and doubts. It is like the trite chicken and egg dilemma again—the old cliché. Most of us grow up with low self-image or often lose our self-confidence during life struggles. As a form of psychological defect, with our compromised confidence we suffer from our fears and hurt our partner in so many ways, including our aggression, low tolerance, and suspicions. Therefore, we should somehow gain our humble confidence to overcome our fears and bring it to the rescue of our relationships. Initiating a self-awareness regimen is probably the best way to do that. We cannot merely buy or learn confidence even by taking confidence lessons and listening to expensive positive thinking lectures. Psychotherapy may help when pursued for a long period. On the other hand, the humble confidence that we need evolves automatically, though gradually, in line with the rising level of our consciousness and compassion. This appears to be a much easier and cheaper option for gaining our confidence and all the good things that come along with it.

Alienation Preparedness - Factor Five
Admitting, Planning, and Playing Our Roles

We must play an active role to suppress the process of alienation. We can just watch our relationship go sour, worsen the situation by our retaliations or egoistic manoeuvres, or play a positive role to prevent it from collapsing altogether. It does not matter, at this stage, if our partner does not understand how s/he is at least partly responsible for the problems. Any effort centred on blaming or changing our partner's attitude would surely fail. S/he would not even care to grasp the scope of problems, while we most likely get trapped further in the same games of faultfinding, arguing, fighting, and challenging each other's Ego. Now, it is time to do something different if we care. It is time to play an active role.

The role we should play is different from everything we have been doing so far. The logic is simple and clear. If we had been doing the things right, we would not have been in such a messy position now, after all. Although we might think that only our partner's faults are causing our alienation, we often have doubts about this conclusion in our subconscious and conscience if we just defer to them. Contacting our subconscious and conscience regularly is a small part of the role we must play.

Now, it does not really matter who is wrong or how much, anyway. Those who have blamed only their partners for their troubles are already divorced! They have somehow convinced themselves of their own perfection and never assumed their Egos were responsible for at least some of the problems. They have already decided about the futility of their relationships and do not want to keep struggling and suffering any more.

Often, however, most of us have doubts, because deep down we feel that maybe some of our flaws inflame the raging conflicts inadvertently. After all, we cannot be perfect, in spite of what our Ego keeps telling us non-stop. Another possibility for still being in a doomed relationship is that we have very low self-image and confidence. Alternatively, we might be still too optimistic naively about eventually forcing our partner to change. Nevertheless, we somehow entertain these possibilities, thus reinforce our doubts about the potential and viability of our relationships. In the final analysis, however, it does not matter which partner is guiltier if we are wise enough and keen to correct the situation.

Then again, trying to play an active role all of a sudden, in particular when we have already drifted a long way along the alienation path, is not an easy task. We may feel embarrassed in front of our partner to suddenly appear much softer and more compromising than s/he ever thought we would (or could) be. The changes in us, if real, would definitely come across quite vividly, even though they might happen gradually. Our efforts to change our personal vision and approach to life (and marriage) would normally emerge slowly. However, our partner usually notices it at one instance when our attitude suddenly looks odd or different in his/her eyes. We might have discussed our new ideas with our partner or not, but it is only his/her perceptions and our actual performance that s/he can believe, most likely with great scepticism at the beginning. Anyway, our new role in defusing the process of alienation grows along with our grasp of our true 'self' for our benefit in terms of boosting so many dimensions of our lives as reiterated throughout this trilogy. If so, it feels rather natural to stay humble and play our marriage-saviour role as well.

However, we should be cautious about the way we approach this sensitive task of preventing our marital alienation, since we are a novice; and because our doubts and fears, which still linger in our subconscious, make us look hesitant and vulnerable.

Initially, we may depend on our Model to play the new role, while we become completely convinced of the merits of our new mission and become committed to it. Model can be instrumental in containing our Ego until we learn to draw upon our Self for facing our partner's persistence to make us fail. S/he might be resentful of our calmer approach to solving conflicts and ignoring many topics that usually cause arguments and faultfinding urges. Yet, s/he would eventually get used to the new person we have become, appreciate the change, and possibly even join in with us to make things better, although perhaps not initially, because of her/his doubts and suspicions as to what we are up to now.

Nevertheless, understanding our new role and playing it well is a major step for slowing down and defusing the alienation process. We accept this challenging responsibility only with the aim of helping ourselves, and perhaps our relationship eventually. The most important role we should play consists of those steps listed about acknowledging relationship needs and personal flaws —Alienation Preparedness Factors One and Two. We must learn about ourselves and our marriages' peculiarities, set our tolerance level, and all the rest of it just to ensure we have played an active role in shaping our attitude for running a workable, fair marriage —maybe even by finding a more suitable relationship model. We want to be certain that when we surrender to alienation, or opt for eventual separation, we have extended our best efforts to avoid it (considering our own defects). We want to wait until no chance of communicating and understanding exists, although we have set our Ego aside and dealt with our relationship only thru Self. We raise our tolerance and faith with commitment and persistence, as part of 'alienation preparedness' regimen.

Taking all these initiatives is hard. Yet, showing initiative is the main idea behind tolerance as part of the scared role we must play. Only by flexibility, we can *learn* to give up our egoism and use our Self for saving our marriage. We want to play our role effectively. Of course, we must also remember that most likely we would fail despite our sincere efforts to implement substantive changes. We admit that the alienation process would most likely keep deteriorating beyond repair, despite our good intentions and efforts. We know that our only reward is to bring our marriage to a tolerable level, if possible, as a last resort. The objective is to regain our relative independence (in and out of our relationship) without having any regrets later on. We want to be sure we have made our best and honest efforts to fix the mess that marriage partners usually create for each other. We should recognize the complexity of people's psychological defects, which play a big role in causing marital problems. We also admit that we all have extreme difficulty in realizing and defeating our idiosyncrasies. We acknowledge that tolerance is crucial for living with another individual. However, we also set a rational level for it based on the characteristics of our relationship and our partner's depth of defects and goodwill. We realize our efforts to make big changes in our approach and attitude by being an active agent of change, but more importantly by being a true example of change.

Once we understand all these facts about our role and their wide implications, we set out to implement our thoughts slowly. We plan about discussing some of the issues with our partner, how, and when. We plan about the areas of personal flaws that require more care, awareness, and improvement—i.e., contacting our subconscious and conscience regularly. We plan about the needed changes that we should pursue actively, personally and perhaps with our partner's help later. We plan our steps, measure our progress, learn from our mistakes, and hope for the best. If necessary, we revise our plans later and devise more challenging, detailed ones in line with our newer refined thoughts.

Playing our role diligently and patiently with compassion would be tricky, but vital for salvaging our failing relationships.

Alienation Preparedness - Factor Six
Making an Objective Judgment and Decision

To live or leave: That is the doubt!

A highly annoying dilemma in a marriage is couples' 'doubt' about its quality and viability. Should we continue to *live* with our inconsiderate partner, or time has finally come to *leave* him/her? This doubt persists even when we have set proper tolerance criteria and follow the alienation preparedness process and goals discussed in this chapter.

We suffer needlessly when issues (and doubts) stay unsettled in our minds. We recognize this primary dilemma and tolerate it consciously or subliminally as a necessity for social adaptation. Yet, we also believe that every problem needs a resolution. If we cannot get rid of the problems, we should at least come to terms with them. In fact, it is usually more practical, and even more effective in the long run, to come to terms with problems rather than solving them or destroying their sources—, which appears to be our partner often. We try to accept a problem as an inevitable fact in modern societies when it is not possible or practical to eliminate it. For example, if we learn to accept marital problems as a social pandemic, we might be able to take relationship pains less personal. We might learn to handle them in a rather passive 'relationship model' perhaps, hoping to create a tolerable, fair relationship despite its irresolvable problems. The point of a good judgment and decision is to settle our marital problems in our minds, especially when they cannot be solved. Ignoring marital problems—on an alienation course towards divorce—appears the fastest and simplest way out. It is a solution, but it is neither a creative one nor an effective way of measuring and settling a problem.

Often problems have no solutions, nor can we come to terms with them—like our declining socioeconomic condition, or an evil, nagging spouse. A major problem may break a person to the verge of committing suicide as the only option for coming to terms with the problem. Or a terminally ill person might prefer a decent, quick exit to avoid pain and degradation. At the other extreme, smaller problems that remain undetected might cause incessant suffering and stress. We must look deep down in our psyche to find the reasons, and their legitimacy, for our lacklustre life and failing relationships. At least we might realize the scope and sources of our problems, which might be major, minor, or mediocre. Conversely, we might feel that we cannot identify their causes on our own, although we at least believe that we certainly have problems.

Another quandary is that no reliable criteria exist, nowadays, for measuring the degree of our marital problems. We wonder about the degree of our problems in relation to a typical marital relationship in our mishmash culture. Are they real or imaginary? Of course, we may explain our problems in general terms, such as the lack of communication or understanding, but these typical diagnoses cannot help us see the roots of problems. We can seek professional help and marriage counselling, but at the end, we cannot quite locate and feel our problems unless we make a point of measuring and judging them personally with patience thru self-assessment. We should take on the responsibility of defusing the alienation process merely in hopes of resolving the problems and salvaging our marriage somehow eventually. Otherwise, the most reasonable, easiest solution would be to end the doomed relationship as soon as possible.

Partners could drag a dead relationships on their backs until death do them part. However, a relationship contaminated with irresolvable problems would only cause more sufferings, and may restrict access to opportunities outside their relationship. We know these facts when we face our doubts about an unsettling marital situation. However, before pronouncing our relationships dead, we wish to examine them for any vital sign to ensure there is no chance of revival.

To make a judgment of any value for such a crucial decision, we should obviously step outside our Ego barrier and defeat our silly false pride. After all, our impartial judgment about marital problems is ONLY for our own benefit, thus we ought to become more altruistic and realistic about the level of personal egoism we can allow for such a serious judgment.

Being a good judge of our relationships is not easy, of course. Impartiality is impossible when our Ego is the judge, which is often the case. Ego has become the nucleus of our individuality and identity and the dominant force in our relationships. It has overtaken most of us to the extremes of perceiving and assessing the world and events only from Ego's point of view. Still we let it judge and decide for us all the time so adamantly and ruthlessly. We let it control us totally. In this largely tainted world, it would be extremely hard (but wise) to delve into our true 'self,' at least partially, to mitigate our Egos, fears, and biases.

Surely, some obstacles often obstruct our objective judgment about the state and content of our marriages. For one thing, the lack of adequate information always raises our doubts about our partner's intentions and the sources of our problems. Sometimes, we want to give our partner the benefit of our doubts, especially if we finally become partially aware of our own flaws, prejudices, and biases. Sometimes we remain optimistic about our partner smartening up and changing his or her attitude and approach eventually. Sometimes, we are too much attached to our partner emotionally. These erratic perceptions or facts merely raise our doubts and delay our relationship decisions, which we should eventually make, still with patience.

Alienation preparedness is for helping us mitigate our doubts as well as our prejudices by utilizing our newly earned awareness and wisdom. During this process, we accumulate all the relevant information, including the intensity of partners' flaws and the depth of their *(possibly failing)* good intentions. Then, we set our tolerance criteria and level. We grasp and acknowledge our fears and opportunities, and we play our reconciliatory role actively. If we take all these steps properly and faithfully, our judgment is bound to be more rational and impartial than ever.

CHAPTER TWELVE
Alienation Awareness Essentials

The big causes of relationship conflicts were discussed in the last three chapters, while it was stressed that no 'normal relationship' exists in society anymore. This chapter will elaborate on the first three 'alienation preparedness' factors discussed in the previous chapter under the following headings:
1. Partners' General Recognition
2. Coping with Human and Relationship Flaws
3. Managing Our Tolerance Level

The goal is develop finer mechanisms for facing our own and our partners' idiosyncrasies mostly by grasping marriage's innate needs and possibly agreeing on a 'relationship model' suitable for partners' particular personalities.

1. Partners' General Recognition

Partners' recognitions of the following three areas are particularly crucial for gauging and managing their relationships sensitively:
  i) Relationships' unique needs
 ii) Partners' (in)compatibilities
iii) Marital environment's hidden threats

i) Relationships' Unique Needs[***]

People still believe that marriage can satisfy a big variety of their personal needs and bring them happiness, as if relationship needs were just the same as, or an extension of, partners' needs. These are wrong expectations and assumptions. Actually, it is the other way around. That is, partners are responsible for satisfying the specific needs of relationships first, before it can fulfil even a few of partners' needs in any way. Realistically, marital relationships in modern societies should be viewed as independent entities with complex needs.

Accordingly, learning about relationship needs and setting can help couples not only with their marriage decision per se, but also staying vigilant about the high risks of marital alienation these days. They can learn about alienation preparedness purposes and success factors in relationships. They realize that staying vigilant about their relationship's peculiarities (and relationship needs in general) is not a casual exercise, but rather a lifetime obligation. They would remember all these sources of alienation and discuss them regularly in a natural manner for both partners.

Besides the mandate of grasping relationships' *general* needs in the new era, partners should also try to understand and work on their own relationship's *unique* issues as a regimen, especially regarding their (in)compatibilities, personal needs, and aspirations. Nevertheless, the underlying objective of all these education is to avoid alienation by keeping these general marital needs, issues, and commitments at a high level of consciousness. However, this marital awareness affects other aspects of couple's personal lives as well, including their self-awareness and self-realization.

In particular, couples had better assume that even their small idiosyncrasies would most likely taint their relationship quickly and gravely. Partners' personal needs, including the rising modern obsession for individualism, also usually hinder their capabilities to understand and address relationships' basic needs, nowadays.

[***] See this author's book, *The Relationship Needs, Framework, and Models*.

Thus, marital environments become tense and agonizing quickly, even when partners share enough strengths and compatibilities.

ii) Partners' (in)Compatibilities

Partners' knowledge of their (in)compatibility areas is crucial for avoiding a wrong decision, despite their attraction and love, or at least remaining vigilant and working on those noted weaknesses forever. They can use the compatibility factors noted in Chapter Eight or take some reliable compatibility tests that are possibly available. Even minor incompatibilities might cause conflicts, so partners must decide how they might handle them effectively if they still wish to risk marrying. Actually, more incompatibilities always erupt only after marriage along with unexpected couples' eccentricities and demands. Thus, partners must predict so many potential sources of marital conflicts and be ready for the likely risks with open minds and patience. They may also learn to draw on their compatibility powers to offset the burdens of their known incompatibilities and manage their relationship.

Recognizing and using partners' unique qualities, especially for teamwork, is also crucial. The time and effort partners share for this exercise would by itself enrich their relationship. In most relationships, however, partners do the opposite. They waste their energies to whine about each other's weaknesses, retaliate, and compete to boost their own Egos, manipulate each other, and control their relationship. They exhaust and depress each other, instead of recognizing, and benefiting from, their compatibilities or complementary qualities. They ignore the need for teamwork and appreciating each other's qualities that could maximize their relationship's strengths and synergy.

Obviously, if partners do not have enough compatibility and unique personal qualities to offer, they should have not started their relationship to begin with. More importantly, if they have major or irreconcilable incompatibilities, they should not marry on the premise that their conflicts can be resolved or tolerated *somehow*. Nevertheless, the goal is to seek ideas and methods that promote their compatibility, while they stay alert about their areas of incompatibility begging for ultra attention and sensitivity. Learning to use their compatibilities is crucial for bringing order into their marriage consciously and actively to avoid alienation.

After discussing their strengths and compatibilities, partners might try to share their objective (unbiased) evaluation of both partners' quirks that often annul their compatibilities and increase alienation—usually due to partners' endless miscommunications and egoism. Yet, the focus should be on detecting and resolving *our own idiosyncrasies,* instead of stressing on our partners' just for criticizing them. In particular, alienation awareness requires partners' efforts to recognize miscommunication causes, which were discussed in Chapters Eight and Nine.

We can build a 'marital awareness checklist' that reinforces our purpose, logic, impartiality, and attention to both marriage and self-development needs. Some items on this checklist may look like the following:

- Separation is the result of a sneaky alienation process that reaches a boiling (no-return) point unexpectedly.
- Alienation repercussions can be severe, even before it gets out of hand and leads to separation.
- Alienation is a process that grows gradually, so watching for the clues diligently is essential.
- Only partners' knowledge of the alienation process and clues can prevent their relationship from falling into this trap.
- Partners must be proactive in playing certain roles (Factor Five noted in the previous chapter) to alleviate or prevent alienation.
- Alienation is mostly caused by partners' psychological defects aggravated by misperceptions and miscommunications fast.
- Partners must be ultra conscious of how they convey, receive, and judge their communication, including their tone of voice.
- Partners must be ultra careful in the ways their oversensitivity and false pride may cause alienation and negative reactions.
- Many simple issues and judgments can cause alienation.

- Without due sincerity, objectivity, and fairness, partners cannot stop the process of alienation.
- Etc.

iii) Marital Environment's Hidden Threats (Alienation Sources)

The main roots of marital failures were listed on pages 213, yet specific events, situations, and attitudes in marriage often point to one or more of these main alienation sources, plus a variety of smaller issues. Together, these sources of alienation complicate the mood and content of a relationship beyond all the standards that partners had imagined. Partners get confused, lose track of the real sources of their clashes, and sometimes fight over trivial matters idiotically just out of spite. Even when minor conflicts are resolved, partners quickly find something else to nag about all the time. Deep down, they are often worried about many irreparable conditions and do not like to even think about them, e.g., their loss of love and respect for their partner.

Often, a seemingly small irritant may in fact reflect a major problem. Partners' naggings may be only small excuses to hide major problems in their personal lives or relationships, e.g., when one partner is having an affair. Nonetheless, studying even small incidents can help them pinpoint and acknowledge deeper issues. Some minor arguments might indeed be symptoms of one or more larger problems hidden or ignored all along, most likely due to partners' inability to find workable solutions for them. At the same time, even unresolved small conflicts can gradually turn into big alienation sources. Through awareness, partners might learn to become somewhat more sensitive regarding some issues that require more attention, while fussing less about intangible ones.

Some marital problems could become overwhelming and we simply cannot resolve them, thus we ignore them, hoping they would go away by themselves. Meanwhile, we continue to suffer their consequences, while approaching marriage breakdown, too, because we refuse to take a firm action. For example, a gambler or alcoholic has a major problem without him/her admitting to it, or worrying about its consequences on his/her marriage until it is too late to do anything about it. The difficulty lies in pinpointing and admitting to problems that demand immediate attention from amidst the bulk of trivial issues. Often, we create new problems for ourselves and our partner just for avoiding the main one. We waste most of our times and energies on faultfinding, retaliation, and creating more headaches for each other. Therefore, we hardly have any energy and motivation to deal with those few major problems of our relationship. When our minds are preoccupied by blames and demands all the time, no incentive or creativity remains to work on the main problems.

Again, we should remember that 'alienation preparedness' is an ongoing process. It evolves gradually and leads to incremental wisdom about our relationship and ourselves. We cannot expect to identify our relationship's main problem(s) and recognize its circumstances and flaws fast. Rather, we might discover better explanations and solutions for our alienation problems only by spending time and efforts to understand the dire intricacies of all relationships in the new era. We realize the demands and needed resilience to pursue the related learning process objectively and gain the required wisdom to save our marriage.

Once the main problem(s) are identified and brought into a high level of consciousness, our tensions would subside, even though the problems are not solved yet. Just the mere knowledge of the real sources of relationship conflicts relieves a great burden from our shoulders and reduces our confusion, stress, and sense of helplessness. The process would be more productive if both partners agreed on the roots of their problems. Then, by focusing on major problems, they would get creative in finding solutions, or configuring the hidden causes of problems. They would realize that often a mix of major and minor issues causes complications, conflicts, and alienation.

Studying alienating sources in relationships often points to partners' unique psychological defects, which are discussed in the next section. However, a typical situation, which usually leads to conflicts and alienation between couples, happens when partners go through a period of cool down—may be a few days of withdrawal—before a specific or subtle mechanism brings them back together. Most often partners' sexual urges push them to reconcile. One partner usually takes the first step, though, not based on who feels guiltier or in need of sex, but rather his/her psychological vulnerability during that specific period. On the other hand, a partner may have a stronger, forgiving personality, thus initiates the process of reconciliation. His/her goodwill and intelligence goad him/her to work on their relationship conflicts proactively and wisely, instead of letting alienation destroy their relationship. Nevertheless, often a sense of power struggle and relative domination seems to prevail in almost all relationships. Maybe it is not intentional, but this inhibiting pervasive condition contaminates almost all relationship atmospheres somehow. These are small signs and symptoms of alienation that we can be more conscious about, while boosting our awareness level.

Partners' psychological vulnerability fluctuates based on their daily experiences. For example, when a partner is unemployed, struggles with office or health issues, etc., s/he feels mentally weaker than normal. His/her depleted confidence and need for affection make him/her vulnerable to all kinds of manipulation and abuse. During such times, this partner is usually subdued and eventually forced to initiate the makeup process after every fight or even small conflicts. This unjust approach eventually leads to resentment about self for being such a loser. Conversely, one partner may wish to have everything under his/her control, to the extent that s/he may even create a fight only to humiliate his/her partner, just for enjoying his/her partner's defeat and maybe even getting a direct apology. S/he is usually attempting to justify and affirm his/her position about their marital conflicts while refuting his/her partner's viewpoints.

Only an alienation preparedness process might help partners see the vanity, unfairness, and destructiveness of their games and approaches. They might develop a sense of fairness and learn to become less dogmatic for reconciling their regular skirmishes. They do not need to agree on a mechanism for reconciliation, as it would happen automatically while partners strive to grasp the intricacy of their relationship. The main objective, of course, is to disallow a variety of inevitable conflicts between partners linger too long and deepen their alienation.

The best reconciliation mechanism is when partners try to stay both ethical and fair by taking turns to initiate a makeup after going through a cool-down period. The trick is to recognize and respect each other's equal needs for building their confidence and self-image for, and thru, strengthening their relationship. Through 'alienation preparedness,' partners learn to increase each other's confidence, instead of traumatizing or hurting a partner's sinking spirit at a specific time. They appreciate how humiliating it is for a vulnerable person to become also a subject of his/her partner's apathy and blackmail when s/he actually needs lots of support and understanding.

The above noted simple examples of alienations prevail in most relationships, but partners are not quite aware of them or do not know how to face them. Sadly, our own psychological needs and insecurities cause these small problems or misunderstandings and quickly turn into fundamental sources of alienation. All these points naturally make sense to couples if they decide to become objective and show goodwill, and share their ideas and concerns for keeping their marriages is intact.

Sharing our thoughts and commitments with our partner also helps other goals. First, by mere discussion of contentious issues we show how serious we feel about our relationship and how patiently we should work together to pursue and exercise our *sensible commitment* to our marriage. Second, calm dialogue per se boosts comradeship and teamwork. Finally, through dialogue we may be able to raise our partner's interest about the merits of 'alienation preparedness' and perhaps joining in with us to make it a permanent facet of our relationship.

Besides the task of stirring a relaxed relationship environment, it is important to grasp and then show 'how much we care' about our marriage and how we fear of alienation ruining our marriage. It is crucial to understand the importance of a serene relationship environment and then commit to developing it actively before it loses its momentum on an alienation course. Yes, relationships must build and sustain a momentum rather than being left alone to dry out or get sluggish. Knowing the negative consequences of alienation can help us focus on the task of finding out 'how much we care.' Still, we often have some doubt about 'how much we *really* care.' We have doubts regarding the quality and viability of our marriage, often even from the start, rather intuitively or possibly *thanks* to our awareness about marital risks.

Worst of all, we have doubts about 'how much we care about our spouse.' We might actually care about him/her, but we do not know 'how much.' We do not have a standard for measuring our level of 'caring.' We often feel, or express, love without realizing what we mean or what love is supposed to imply! Instead, we trust our emotions, which are often too soft, hard, or vague, but also tentative and driven according to our recent perceptions of our partner. We do not know how our 'caring' can, or should, translate into a measure of tolerance of our partner's hidden or already-known defects.

We often gauge our affection for our spouse intuitively by comparing him/her with people we really love, like our children or parents. Accordingly, our spouse usually gets a lower score on that scale, which then heightens our doubts about our level of caring for him/her, the purpose of our marginal relationship, and our real options. Especially for romantic people who crave love, their normal caring about their partner often feels inadequate and a cause for worry. We always long to love someone and be loved. Yet, real caring is different from, and does not necessarily need, love, but mostly compassion. In all, the more realistically partners care for each other, the more actively they care about keeping their relationship setting peaceful through logic and compassion.

Usually when couples separate temporarily, perhaps because one partner goes on a long trip or lives alone after a fight, they get a chance to figure out how much, and why, they care about each other and their marriage. However, we do not know whether this caring, during our partner's absence, is our reaction to loneliness or special passion for our partner—perhaps a little bit of both. This knowledge is valuable for the information it provides about 'how much we *really* care,' but mostly because it goads us to learn 'why we care,' by measuring the *content and features* of our relationship. We must know why we care about the health of our relationship with this particular person. We also get a good chance to learn about ourselves in terms of, a) the actual degree of independence we can handle or prefer, and b) our true sense of compassion and our capacity to express it to elude alienation.

After we learn 'how much we care and why,' we like to know 'how much our partner cares.' This is even a harder task, because it is difficult to imagine what goes on in our partner's mind. Even when our marital relationship does not seem to work, most of us still give our partner the benefit of a doubt and find all sorts of excuses to justify his/her random displays of carelessness. (This is because we wish to believe that we are still being loved and lovable. And sometimes because we need him/her so badly.)

On the other hand, some of us are usually overly pessimistic about the health of our relationships. We interpret our partner's slightest impatience and neglect as a concrete sign of apathy and carelessness. Then this misunderstanding affects our image of our relationship and partner. However, many reasons might exist for our partner's seeming apathy. We can try to find out the truth behind the appearances, i.e., his/her actions and behaviour, if we care. Nonetheless, for pursuing 'alienation preparedness' goals, it would be useful to establish whether both partners genuinely care for each other and their relationship deep down, regardless of what their words and appearances might suggest.

Another crucial factor to learn about relationship environment is that many types of relationship models are becoming prevalent to fit our modern lifestyles and needy personalities. It is wise to study these models and adopt a suitable one based on partners' personalities. Instead of fantasizing an ideal relationship that can satisfy both partners' needs and aspirations, usually a more liberal relationship model, where partners have higher independence, can minimize alienation and raise the health of their relationship. Discussions about relationship models are extensive (see footnote on page 129). Overall, the idea is that with partners' demand for higher independence, nowadays, their expectations from their relationship must be reduced, so that partners would not interfere with each other's personal affairs or get on each other's nerves too much all the time.

Naturally, it would be difficult to improve a relationship very much without both partners' cooperation or while one of them is highly careless. However, it would be even harder to interpret the meaning and purpose of our partner's seeming apathy regarding our relationship and the growing alienation. His/her indifference feels like a major blow in our face any time we attempt to assess the flaws of our relationship. It may be a sign of her/his apathy towards us and our ideas of any kind, including our suggestions about self-awareness and alienation preparedness processes.

Often one or both partners remain careless, since they do not know how to go about discussing relationship needs calmly and objectively. Sometimes, our partner may appear careless because s/he has lost faith in our abilities to reconcile our differences, or perhaps s/he has even lost interest in our marriage altogether. S/he might have lost his/her trust in, and respect for, us. However, apathy may be a sign of frustration, as her/his efforts to prevent alienation do not seem to be effective, perhaps because we are not responding favourably to her/his efforts to fight alienation, or because we do not understand his/her approach or meaning.

Apathy and carelessness might be a sign that our alienation has grown beyond repair. It can also be only a farce, a Model presentation, for a partner's hidden inner turmoil and conflicts. S/he might be angry, jealous, or insecure regarding the situations surrounding our relationship, but plays an apathetic role in order to protect his/her Ego or to avoid unnecessary fights. Sometimes, indifference is merely for drawing our partner's attention to us or unresolved relationship conflicts. Thus, the trick is finding the right cause of our partner's apparent apathy, which might include one or more of many possibilities noted in this chapter.

Another scenario may be that our partner cares enough about our relationship, but does not feel necessary, or does not have time or patience, to get involved in an alienation preparedness regimen. Surely, convincing him/her to share the responsibility for alienation preparedness raises the chance of success drastically. However, this may prove to become a frustrating challenge. On the other hand, if we often face our partner's resistance to join, we should eventually decide personally whether and how to fight alienation alone as much as possible. The fact that our partner does not show cooperation or share responsibility for saving our marriage pushes us into a state of isolation and alienation. Still, that is not necessarily a reason to give up yet.

It is possible that our partner has reached his/her conclusions already. Maybe s/he thinks we have already travelled so far on our alienation journey that discussing marital problems would not help. Sometimes, one partner does not talk about his/her concerns and expect the other to grasp her/his meanings automatically and perhaps even show some kind of concession. And sometimes, the excuse for his/her silence is that s/he is not listened to, or cared about, or that their communication often leads to arguments and useless fights. Nevertheless, when a partner refuses to discuss his/her views, the process of mutual awareness is hindered.

Our partner's seeming disinterest to participate actively in the process of awareness and alienation preparedness confuses us. It is frustrating to keep guessing various reasons for it. Is s/he quiet because s/he is agreeing with some of our suggested solutions, thus silently and slowly changing her/his approach and attitude? Is it because s/he is not willing to accept our suggestions out of spite, or only trying to avoid giving us a reason to brag about how right or smart we are? Is it because s/he is careless inherently and we are wasting our time and breath? Is s/he in full disagreement, but afraid to say so because of possible retaliation or not having any alternatives to offer? Or, is it just because s/he does not want to get into arguments and useless awareness efforts? Would not s/he have shown more enthusiasm and spoken up already if our efforts were working? May be yes, may be no.

Nevertheless, to grasp the depth of our problems and assess the process of alienation, we eventually need our partner's input for gauging our position. Yet, making both partners believe in the *value of alienation preparedness* for keeping an active, peaceful relationship environment is often unrealistic, although necessary.

We normally emphasize the importance of communication for keeping the relationship atmosphere open. However, in fact, it is mostly the underlying *awareness property* of communication that makes it so crucial for preventing alienation. Communication without the objective of 'learning and acknowledging' would be a waste of time and a cause for more arguments and conflicts (and another form of losing sight of relationship unique needs).

Sometimes, communication is merely for creating and sharing joyful moments with our partner. However, a more crucial aspect of it is to goad and grow a relaxed environment, while partners enhance their awareness about themselves and their relationship. Conversely, when partners communicate with the aim of 'raising overall awareness,' their relationship environment improves a lot, too. For example, one-way communication, just to listen to our partner's concerns and needs, can be considered an awareness-oriented exercise. However, we should understand the gist of the information we receive through listening to our partner's words. Our communication should have useful contents and objectives. We should try to grasp the roots of our partner's concerns. Are Ego, insensitivity, and careless attitudes hindering the sincerity of our relationship? Or, is it mostly those unfounded demands and whining of our spouse that make us feel alienated and unable to communicate naturally? Often, it is a combination of both. Or, perhaps the tone or mechanism of communication has been weak and caused these side effects.

2. Coping with Human and Relationship Flaws

By simply acknowledging our own and humans' natural flaws as debilitating factors for both communication and self-realization, we can boost our stamina and chances to, i) manage our obvious defects, ii) handle our partner's flaws easier, and iii) remember the immensity of simple psychological flaws causing alienation.

i) Managing Our Obvious Flaws

If motivated to do anything about our psychological flaws, we can start with those we already know about and face regularly. For example, our sense of rivalry, jealousy and selfishness are not too difficult to spot in our feelings and dealings with others. We can recall these flaws in our conscious mind and witness them appear and interfere in our relationships and decisions regularly. By remembering them, we can tame them a bit, although getting rid of them completely requires super power. Yet, we normally find an excuse to abandon our chances for learning. We quickly forget our commitment to monitor and assess our behaviour with an unbiased mind. For example, if we are jealous, we blame it on our partner who instigates it in us.

It feels more natural to us to control others—in this case our partner who makes us jealous—than to control our own defects. For one thing, we consider our partner's behaviour provocative, which raises our doubts about his/her intentions or innocence. Is s/he a devil or just a gullible? Since we cannot control our doubts (or misperceptions) about her/his intentions, we try to control the source of our doubts and provocation—our partner. After all, if we did not doubt his/her intentions, we would not be pained for everything s/he does. Still, regardless of her/his intentions, wicked or naive, we feel the urgency to handle the cause of our suffering in the fastest way—by controlling him/her. As another obstacle for learning about our defects, some of them—e.g., competition or greed—have become such a dominant part of our personalities now, like fully innate and normal behaviour beyond our control. Heck, the whole society propagates them actively as valid social norms and positive traits. Thus, we manipulate and hurt others in many ways, e.g., thru rivalry or out of greed, instead of grasping our own personal defects, which we seem unable to control.

Many of these pervasive, misguided norms (defects) are, however, reversible habits acquired through social conditioning. Our life experiences, humans' cruelty, and universal unfairness, sometimes even by destiny and God Himself, make us cynical and callous. Yet, our seeming helplessness against our defects is not completely true.

Although receiving professional help is wise, we must mostly depend on ourselves to learn about our defects. Recognizing our obvious defects and many likely hidden ones gives us a chance to defeat them gradually. We can strive to find the strength in our psyche to curb and turn them around. The only trick is to believe in our inner power and the chance of drawing upon it once we become sincere to detect our deeper flaws.

The significance of our attempt to learn about our defects and fighting them is in *the way* it improves the quality of our lives and relationships. Conversely, our relationships offer a good setting to explore our defects, while we test our new convictions in the way we relate to people less selfishly. We learn about both our own and humans' natural defects, especially people we seemingly care for. Thus, we also learn about caring and showing compassion—maybe as a start for self-cleansing and soul-searching that bring us higher values and rewards beyond the basic benefit of curbing our flaws.

The way we would eventually view and judge our defects, and subsequently the defects of others, would be quite significant. Instead of blaming others and ourselves and paining everybody in the process, we view our psychological defects as a mirror of sour experiences that we can try to break through in order to enter a healthier lifestyle beyond our existing routines. We can view our struggles to defeat our defects a healing process, which may expand our lives and thoughts to such magnificent planes beyond common imagination. In fact, we could take a negative aspect of our lives and turn it into an exercise of tranquility and beauty. How easy it is to grasp the meaning of true existence, and yet how difficult we have made it for ourselves to even appreciate the divinity we can attain by defusing our simple defects, such as egoism. We can forgive ourselves, instead of only ignoring and denying even our obvious flaws. Once we focus on forgiving, instead of forgetting, our defects, the process of healing begins.

Acknowledging our most obvious defects, and their impacts on our minds and souls, also provides a good chance to test our willpower and wisdom. Mitigating those direct, incessant sources of our suffering, such as rivalry and greed, gives us huge strength and tranquility to challenge our less obvious, deeper flaws. Then, our awareness about our defects and attempts to control them give us the opportunity of learning more about our 'self' and living within its boundaries somewhat naturally. Accordingly, our new wisdom and sense of our 'self' makes the alienation preparedness process smoother and easier.

Acknowledging our defects does not threaten our identity, pride, or psychological security, contrary to what our sneaky, challenged Ego wants us to believe. It only opens a window of opportunity to observe our inner hurts and insecurities and delve into our subconscious and more complex nature after working out our most common and obvious flaws. Thus, we gradually get into the deeper aspects of our psyche and explore our 'being.' In the process, we encounter the devil that stands between who we are and who we want to be. We would also find the courage to accept input from our spouse about any of our flaws that have remained hidden from us. By the strength of our soul, we would stop rejecting the information that flows readily through people's view of us and about how we hurt others. We would welcome the information, as we now have ways of assessing its viability and value to us without getting offended and defensive. We listen to people's comments open-mindedly, although they may be, and often are, wrong. Yes, we still make unselfish, compassionate, and objective judgments about others. People's normal hang-ups and attachments make us sad about their obsessions and helplessness to live in such a phony world. Yet, these observations only make us more compassionate with reserved attitude about preaching them, despite our loathing for their idiotic lifestyle and mentality.

ii) Handling Our Partner's Defects

Only after recognizing the depth and effects of our defects, we are ready to assess our partner's psychological flaws. However, now our assessment of his/her flaws is merely a compassionate exercise and vision, as debilitating factors largely outside of his/her control. Our basic challenge is to acknowledge our inability to do anything regarding our partner's flaws directly. We can do something about our own, but not his/hers. Thus, our view of his/her flaws is **only** for assessing our own ability to face them as part of our 'alienation preparedness' exercise per se. We could hope and wait for a miraculous transformation in her/him (which might happen thru personal life experiences), but usually requires his/her interest to adopt 'alienation preparedness' systematically). Instead of blaming and trying to change our partner, we become now more understanding of people's difficulty in controlling their flaws. We can play a role—as will be discussed shortly—but our expectations differ from what we have had before our awareness. Our awareness is only for re-examining our marital expectations to curb our anger and anxiety. We would suffer less personally, cause our partner less pain, and use our energy to find productive initiatives that often produce the same results—mainly peace—that we were after in the first place, i.e., when we were struggling hard to change our partner to accommodate our needs.

Knowing the type and extent of our partner's shortfalls and their impacts on us is useful *only* for improving our judgment and tolerance level. The goal is to become fairer and more objective in our judgments about her/his intentions and control over his/her attitude. This knowledge can help us mitigate our doubts about the viability of our relationship and build tolerance, at least for a short while, without always making a big issue quickly about our partner's conflicting personality and flaws. The question is how much efforts are required on our part to live with relationship flaws without blaming or arguing with our partner about them indefinitely. That is, since s/he cannot change, how much time are we willing to devote to saving our relationship before asking for separation? The next question is whether we have played our role properly to mitigate alienation. If there is, in our minds, any time that we can spare to view things from a new perspective, before asking for separation, it may be the most productive time in our marriage, hopefully.

With our new approach for dealing with our partner and her/his flaws, s/he notices our 'attitude change.' This would prove a basic positive step in reversing the process of alienation. By not nagging at or criticizing our partner, s/he might put down her/his guard. Then, we use our energy to appreciate the new opportunity opening up in our relationship. S/he would try to figure out what has made us change our attitude and approach. This provides a chance to use the one-way communication method or similar mechanisms to voice our concerns logically without pressing our expectations or asking him/her to change. We would only talk about our concerns and various issues that hurt us or weaken our relationship. Our change of attitude and growing patience most likely show in our sincere, diplomatic approach automatically. We can assume that our partner also realizes at least some of his/her flaws, yet his/her fat ego is stopping him/her to ponder and do something about them.

As noted above, we can do certain things about our partner's flaws without aiming to change her/him. We can raise, *indirectly and tactfully,* our partner's awareness about his/her psychological defects, the impact they may have on our relationship, and how they are reinforcing the alienation process. We do this in different ways. For the most part, showing our non-blaming attitude and patience would lead to positive reactions, in most people, in due time. REAL patience implies (and requires) waiting for some months or even years before its significance are established in our spouse's eyes. Yet, this basic awareness and patience (waiting) by itself would change us and our expectations in terms of seeing and handling relationship conflicts. Thus, even our partner's tiny compromises start to feel pleasing and noticeable. Then, with our subtle gestures about his/her efforts, some tangible changes might also ensue, since s/he would find them satisfying and rewarding, too, compared with our old method of demanding and nagging.

While working with our partner to mitigate the effects of our flaws, we might notice the positive changes and progress in each other's attitudes. Exchanging feedbacks about positive changes would be helpful. Most improvements are probably insufficient, yet a move in the right direction. They should be acknowledged and encouraged, so that partners realize that they have understood each other and have meant to curb their irritating habits. Waiting for an ultimate result before giving feedback and encouragement to our partner would cause further alienation. This is because our partner is doing his/her best to overcome some of his/her defects, which is a very difficult task to accomplish. His/her efforts per se are valuable even though the result may not be apparent for a long time. Partner (A) would perceive (B)'s lack of feedback a sign of (B)'s apathy or a sign of (A)'s futile efforts to change, which appear to have no tangible benefits for their relationship. We do not have to get into a formal expression or appreciation of the improvement. In fact, doing that might have adverse effect on some people. Rather, we should give our feedback by implied gestures of appreciation and maybe an emotional reward as simple as a warm smile in a right moment, or an invitation to a romantic dinner at the proper mood and time. Then, making some hints, perhaps indirectly, can also help.

Our efforts help us directly, and we can also help our partner indirectly by our attitude, then possibly introducing her/him to alienation preparedness process when s/he seems ready to hear about our experience. The ultimate success comes when partners begin to trust each other's judgments about their personal and relationship's weaknesses, especially the ones causing alienation. This would help them recognize their less clear defects gradually and overcome their doubts and hesitation to admit them. We cannot necessarily elude our defects because we have detected them. Both partners realize this fact and take it into consideration in their dealings and expectations from each other. Still, the mere attention to our flaws, as well as knowing that our partner also recognizes and works on his/hers, at least slows the alienation process. It transcends us to a higher level of understanding and compassion slowly, then healing, and finally an effective control of partners' personal flaws.

iii) Remembering the Enormity of Simple Psychological Flaws Causing Alienation

Fortunately, the psychological defects of majority of us are not *all* too extreme to make us totally useless and require specialized attention and cure. We are mostly inflicted with small, common defects, but also usually one or two deeper ones. Sadly, however, these simple defects, such as lying, deceit, rivalry, and greed, have become an inherent part of our personalities. They manifest in our Ego and Model driven attitudes and emotions, such as the ones listed in Table 11.1 as 'Simple Psychological Defects'.

It is easy to conceive how one or more of the simple personal flaws noted in Table 11.1 can turn into many alienation factors. These common personal defects are actually spreading fast and ruining our relationships and societies with dire consequences for humanity altogether.

Clearly, an alienation situation has many other causes besides psychological defect, too. For example, a misunderstanding or weakness in expressing oneself can create miscommunication, which is not *necessarily* a psychological flaw. Yet, even these small irritants and weaknesses may lead to deep alienation issues.

Table 11.1: Personal Defects Causing Alienation

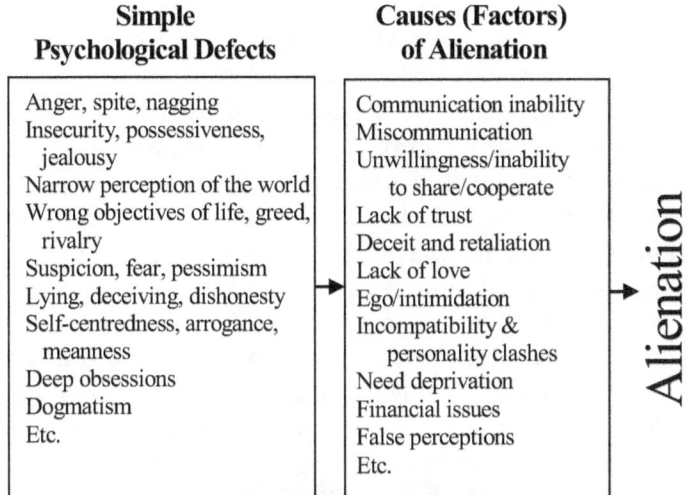

Simple Psychological Defects	Causes (Factors) of Alienation	
Anger, spite, nagging Insecurity, possessiveness, jealousy Narrow perception of the world Wrong objectives of life, greed, rivalry Suspicion, fear, pessimism Lying, deceiving, dishonesty Self-centredness, arrogance, meanness Deep obsessions Dogmatism Etc.	Communication inability Miscommunication Unwillingness/inability to share/cooperate Lack of trust Deceit and retaliation Lack of love Ego/intimidation Incompatibility & personality clashes Need deprivation Financial issues False perceptions Etc.	→ Alienation

A real story about communication weakness may help here. It occurred when a woman asked for her husband's help:

One Sunday morning, an unexpected snowfall covered the streets and driveways. He is in the middle of a job when his wife comes around and asks him about his plan to shovel the snow in the driveway. It is around one p.m., snow has stopped, and it seems to him that it may rain and clear the snow in the driveway. He looks at her with surprise and asks her, "Why?" The confused wife replies with angst, "Because we must go to work tomorrow! If you don't clean the driveway, it might freeze overnight and make the driving out of the garage difficult in the morning."

To avoid needless arguments, he agrees, "Yes, ok. I will do it this afternoon." Only when she leaves with stress, he realizes the weakness of his communication. Without telling her his reasons, his wife had no clue about his resistance and the idea of helping her, *like usual,* so she took it as a blunt rejection. He could have instead said, "Yes, I will. But let's wait a couple of hours to see if it will rain and clear the snow." Sometimes, we try to economize in our communication, or assume our partner can read our minds. Therefore, a simple weakness of communication can cause big, lasting misunderstanding for both partners, which can stir further arguments, retaliations, and alienation. *By the way, it rained and cleared the snow before the lazy husband shovel it!*

"I was right," he whispered giddily, but then was either smart or had no guts to provoke his wife by *hoping* to prove his point.

On the other hand, we do not always have a presence of mind and excellent communication skills to be precise enough in our interactions to avoid misunderstanding. Even if we did, it would be too exhausting and time-consuming to be precise with all our communications. Thus, we should always also think that what we hear and understand from our partner's comments is most likely not all the facts that s/he had meant to convey. We should ask for clarification calmly when the message is unclear or sounds weird. In the above example, both spouses' communication had been flawed, while the wife's oversensitivity and harsh reaction had surely had their own extra negative effects for them.

3. Managing Our Tolerance Level

A major role we should play through 'alienation awareness' is to, i) set and monitor our tolerance level objectively and, ii) remain vigilant about misinterpreting both partners' tolerance levels.

i) Setting Our Tolerance Level

It is crucial to set a *level* for tolerance that feels meaningful and reasonable for us based on our relationship's specific conditions. No scientific rule exists, but two major guidelines are essential: 1) Never adjust the tolerance level (and use it) during a marital crisis. And, 2) Remember that, nowadays, couples usually have less tolerance than is normally justifiable and necessary for an average relationship. Our growing romanticism, obsession for individualism and identity, and general stress have made almost all of us less patient and more sensitive. Therefore, we begin our relationships with inadequate level of patience, compassion, and tolerance.

Having an objective tolerance level helps in several ways. First, we become immune against Ego's interference during a crisis and forcing hasty or illogical decisions. Second, we sustain a rather high standard to measure the impact of any crisis against it and assess the health of our relationship. For example, we do not allow our spouse's fierce disagreement turn into a painful crisis when, for instance, the issue is whether s/he spends too much time with his/her friends. During such arguments, partners' Egos usually get too anxious and their tolerance levels diminish. Therefore, the trick is to ensure that partners' brains do not rush in to reset their tolerance levels during a few seconds (or days) of extreme rage or disappointments. They should learn to make a judgment only after they cool down and review the whole issue against their objective *preset* tolerance criteria.

A preset tolerance level means that we have taken our time to assess and grasp our relationship's strengths and flaws rationally. It also means that we always lean towards reconciliation, unless we have decided calmly and logically that we have *well* past our wisely preset level of tolerance. Usually, our level of tolerance shows our aptitude to assess and balance our relationship's merits against its conflicts and headaches, yet measuring and balancing our relationship's evils and virtues are not always easy or wise. In fact, tolerance cannot be just a matter of balance between good and bad, but rather how much abuse we can take without hurting our health and stifling our soul.

Accordingly, finding good criteria for *presetting* a tolerance level that is logical and workable for any particular relationship depend largely on its unique atmosphere and merits in terms of partners' intelligence, flexibility, and goodwill to improve their attitude and expectations. Especially, partners must disallow daily turmoil, disagreements, and disappointments rule their general moods and tolerance level. Instead, the criteria should be adopted only after weighing their relationship's merits objectively and calmly. They should also adjust it occasionally whenever some major facts make it necessary to reassess their marital prospects.

ii) Misinterpreting Tolerance

On some occasions, our partner may misinterpret our tolerance as a sign of weakness and submission to his/her demands. Although this misunderstanding should not really affect our approach, we cannot let it linger and dominate our relationship. If our partner misses or ignores our intention for saving our relationship, s/he would never appreciate our tolerance, nor make any efforts of her/his own. At the same time, bragging about our tolerance only causes a negative reaction, because it might sound we are doing our partner a big favour. That is exactly what we are doing, in fact, of course. We are doing ourselves, our relationship, and our partner a favour; however, our partner would not appreciate our insinuation. Therefore, we must make our tolerance known to our partner in a subtle way. (Gosh, how much work and diplomacy is needed just to maintain a basic relationship, nowadays!)

At the same time, partners must not overestimate each other's tolerance level and then face a sudden, drastic situation, e.g., when one of them asks for divorce abruptly and adamantly.

As noted before, the main purpose of tolerance is to encourage an atmosphere of cooperation for gradual change of attitudes and approach. If one partner is not interested or involved in sustaining this environment, the other partner's efforts cannot help much, other than raising his/her own awareness and tolerance, of course. In addition, our partner may keep raising his/her expectations and demands, instead of adjusting them if s/he does not recognize the purpose of our tolerance. Thus, while we are working hard to mitigate the sense of alienation, our partner may be completely off the track, pushing his/her own personal agenda, or maybe even testing our limits.

Thus, we should be assertive, *tactfully,* in our communication and stating our intentions of tolerance. However, again, our hints should not sound like a threat or a sacrifice. Rather, we should portray our good intentions to make our relationship joyful for both of us, because we care about it. We should not only express our good intentions and convictions, but rather demonstrate them in our actions. We should be nice but show confidence, mainly by controlling our emotions, both positive and negative ones.

Tolerance and confidence are the prerequisites (and also the cause and effect) of each other. They reinforce each other within a person. As a confident person, we gain more tolerance against opposing views and arguments of our partner without feeling our pride demolished. And with tolerance, we learn more about our Self and our relationship in a rational way, thus gain more control of our attitude and situation. The rational control of our emotions in our relationships directly boosts our confidence even further.

If our partner seems to be taking advantage of our tolerance, or continues with his/her misinterpretations of our intentions, we must rethink our options more carefully. We make a decision that serves us best personally, i.e., to accept the situation and show more tolerance or go for separation. For the former option, we need a personal approach and setting for some type of cooperation and communication, even if it remains a rudimentary (passive) approach. We might even need to give in a little at the outset. If we can create an atmosphere to convey our initial ideas to our partner, we might eventually succeed in discussing the concepts of alienation preparedness, tolerance, and cooperation for saving our relationship. If we conclude at the end that no such possibility exists, the only thing left to do would be to project our life under present substandard circumstances and the chance of a miracle turning things around. Then decide.

At the end, we are responsible for the tolerance level that makes sense to us. The whole idea of tolerance is for our benefit only, not our partner's. All our efforts are solely for increasing our objectivity, although our partner and our relationship benefit, too, if the alienation process is slowed down. In fact, the whole 'alienation preparedness' routine must be viewed as a personal attempt to learn about life and relationships without expecting any other rewards. Well, may be the only reward is facilitating our marital relationship and raising our chances of enduring a life with a person who, in most cases, cannot think, feel, and act the same way we do. Yet, we still care for him/her!

Luckily, an opposite path to alienation is available for sincere, smart couples to not only elude alienation and separation, but also flourish their marriages to an enviable stance. We might envision and follow this sacred path just by staying alert about marriage purposes and relationships' success factors suggested in this book. Instead of letting our naiveté and high expectations put us on an alienation journey early in our marriages, we could follow a 'relationship awareness path' and stay objective and active about marriage purposes and means of accomplishing them.

Without alienation preparedness, we cannot make a conscious judgment about the state of our relationship, thus have difficulty making rational, fair decisions. We remain doubtful about many variables in our relationship and our options, until our partner forces a decision upon us, or we make a hasty, irrational decision in a moment of distress and Ego attack. Surely, these are exactly the kind of disastrous decisions that we all would like to avoid. Especially, if we are reaching the end of the alienation journey, we keep in mind that this is our last chance and the right time to **think of marriage now that it appears like the time of divorce**.

CHAPTER THIRTEEN
Marriage Salvation

Eventually, we must assess our marriage realistically in hopes of salvaging it, if possible. We have pondered our marital issues and shown our sincerity and seriousness. We have done our best to activate an 'alienation preparedness' process for reversing the deteriorating relationship conditions that are paralysing partners' minds and judgment. We have suffered the disturbing thoughts of separation, while staggering on a dire alienation path. Through this self-awareness process, we have also learned to judge and decide regarding our marital problems only when we are in full control of our minds and emotions, and not when we have lost our senses in the heat of arguments. We realize that our judgment is sound only when it is free from prejudices, heated emotions, and Ego. Thus, we are now equipped to weigh our options.

The Ultimate Options

The bottomline is that we must choose the path of our lives with utmost awareness and sincerity for our own benefit. That is the only way we can survive in society and our relationships. That is also the ultimate goal of alienation preparedness through rigorous self-awareness. Our ultimate options are to: i) stay positive and continue to play an active role in defusing the alienation process, ii) stay in the relationship passively and patiently, or iii) separate.

We try to choose one of these three options cautiously and *consciously* and then learn to live with its consequences. We must make a conscious 'decision' to mitigate our doubts and pains and we face the same options with or without a valid judgment about the state of our relationship. Yet, with an objective judgment, we are convinced, committed, and set to play our roles with minimal doubts regarding the risks of the final decision and outcome. Hopefully, we make that tough decision calmly based on a valid judgment about the state of our relationship. Option (ii) is most common in society, nowadays, as partners wish to make the best of the present situation without fussing so much any further about improving their relationship conditions. They reach this point and live in some form of suspense due to their past failures and their partners' seemingly irreversible apathy and carelessness.

All three options are viable and wise choices depending upon our relationship's conditions, our awareness of the sources and depth of problems, and our past efforts in resolving the conflicts. Each option becomes applicable and most viable at some stage of our relationship, but our options become restricted over time. That is, first we become aware and eager to resolve the problems. Next, we give up and accept problems as irresolvable, thus try to live with them without seeing or seeking any chance to boost the relationship. We choose a different relationship model that gives partners more independence within a rather passive relationship. Then, eventually, we may feel that our relationship is intolerable in spite of our efforts to correct or tolerate the situation, thus we choose to separate—the ultimate, most deplorable option, sadly. During these three long stages, we are forced involuntarily to travel fast on an alienation path toward the separation destination. All along, however, we struggle, with all our wisdom, conscious, conscience, Ego, Model, and Self, to reverse the direction of the demised journey and return to the point of departure, where our relationship was meaningful.

Everybody follows the same order of correcting, tolerating, and quitting his/her relationship *intuitively* over the length of his/her marital life. However, intuition would not help if it does not contain a high level of awareness and patience. Our efforts would be productive only when we encounter these stages with full awareness, high consciousness, and clear conscience, based on an alienation preparedness process. Only then, we might get a better chance to resolve our marital conflicts, or at least find a better means of controlling our doubts and making a valid judgment.

In all, it is unwise to jump to the second or third stages before fully exploring the opportunities that prior stages can offer. We should go through each stage patiently with full awareness and valid judgment before making a decision to move on to the next stage. Within each stage, we should not expect a sudden change and results, either, because most likely our awareness still needs expanding, while the process of self-awareness takes a long time to perfect. If our aggravated Ego or emotions put us in the third stage fast, without giving us the benefit of following an alienation preparedness routine, we are bound to make a major mistake that the whole family would suffer from and regret.

No right or wrong answer exists for the question of 'live or leave.' The only criterion is to ensure we make a *valid* judgment and a timely decision according to the ideas suggested in Part IV. The whole intention of alienation preparedness is to help us with this judgment and decision after recognizing one crucial fact: **We are all too hasty, needy, idealistic, and emotional these days when judging the state of our relationships.**

The importance of a separation decision calls for pondering many relationship issues and highlighting the implications of many crucial factors. A main point from our limited discussions is that, during a relationship crisis, we usually do not have the right mindset to judge and decide properly. Thus, we need an 'alienation preparedness' process, which goads self-appraisal and self-awareness, to study and deal with ongoing crises and then judge without letting egoism and emotions overwhelm our thoughts and senses in a stressful instance. Marriage counsellors might provide some basic advice, but nobody can help us make a good decision without our genuine involvement, self-awareness, and a profound 'alienation preparedness' mentality.

Thinking Romance and Remarriage

When the thoughts of separation and divorce overwhelm us, it is the best opportunity to awaken our mood of romanticism to put off spite and urges of retaliation that are boiling inside us. This is a difficult task—and perhaps even suggesting it appears pure silly —when partners are on the verge of breakdown psychologically and emotionally. Yet, a mix of romance and self-awareness can help us control our Egos and then notice our emotions begin to settle automatically. The question is, 'How to watch our Ego and curb it in such trying circumstances?' One way is to think of our marriage ended and our partner not being around to cause pain and frictions. Creating this image in our heads realistically would feel impossible initially due to marital tensions and the abuse we feel our partner has inflicted upon us. Actually, we probably want our partner dead or at least out of our life immediately, *right this minute,* instead of cherishing him/her again like good old days. *"What a weird solution!"* we can yell rightfully. However, with *alienation preparedness mentalit*y, we may cool down a bit and redirect our energy wasted on hostility toward positively charged self-awareness. Surely, these efforts would succeed only if some basic attraction and *reserved* respect still exist between partners.

At this point, *thinking marriage* is couple's last refuge before actually pondering the separation option. By thinking marriage, partners assume they have reached the end of the road and they are facing one last chance to enter into a new marriage contract. Except that now partners are wiser, understand each other better, and even writing a contract feels viable. This is surely possible only if partners are mature, willing to reduce their expectations, and choose a relationship model that gives them a higher level of independence without tainting the sanctity of their marriage. Nonetheless, at this stage, we do not care anymore whether it is romantic to sign a contract or not. Rather, the point is to clarify the chance and practicality of both partners' lowering their needs and expectations from their relationship. We like to gauge the chance of renegotiating a contract with our partner to address our needs and commitments before agreeing to give our marriage another chance. *Ironically, most last minute reconciliations these days entail a vulnerable partner accepting more dependence and giving more promises of loyalty! And then they often fail.*

Luckily, we might be able to overcome our anger and maybe rekindle some romantic moods, too. If so, we may think of funny experiences and delightful memories we have shared, including the birth of our children. Instead of feeling pity for ourselves and mourn our wasted lives, we can try to elevate our compassion by recalling our partner's devotions, triumphs, and hopes. We can try to generate creative thoughts about the good aspects of our relationship (past and present) to detect how inadvertently we have let our oversensitivity and quirks ruin everything. Nobody is to be blamed, because this is not the right time for it. Now, it is time to revive the moods of romanticism, if possible, to stir some positive energy in this time of crisis. We must try to reconcile our differences somehow before despair leads to a self-destructive mindset. Surely, if no sense of romance is left between partners, so little chance of reconciliation exists, considering the depth of issues that have carried partners to this level of apathy and hatred. Realistically, despite any possible attraction, we might finally get tired of struggling to save our marriage so many times and keep failing repeatedly; so it would seem quite logical to quit.

Romanticism at this sad, controversial stage implies mainly compassion driven by plenty of insight. The mere decision of stopping our spite and retaliatory attitude reflects our wisdom and compassion, which are the bases of genuine romanticism. It does not even have to be expressed or exchanged with our partner, but felt individually. One way is to recall (perhaps even sarcastically) the romantic moods and memories of yesteryears, then perhaps use Model later to share them with our partner even if it might look rather foolish under the circumstance. The idea is to elude negative moods and thoughts, at least for a while. Later, when the situation seems more stable, we might add some romantic flavour to this 'first step' by showing love, understanding, and eventually a novel plan to build a new joint life with new principles.

If we cannot elude our negative feelings about our partner, in spite of our efforts to be compassionate and understanding, we have possibly reached the last stage.

Reviving the moods of romanticism in a broken marriage sounds ridiculous and futile. However, this suggestion is based on the author's own personal experiences and positive results—although a divorce eventually became inevitable ten years later. From a logical perspective, we can note that, in the absence of any other option but divorce, following an unorthodox approach of feeling and expressing romance is our last resort to turn things around, so that partners may hopefully cool down and make a valid judgment. Unfortunately, during these trying times, when marital conflicts feel overwhelming, we usually adopt a hostile and controversial approach, which often only expand hatred and expedite separation foolishly. Only retaliation seems to make us feel good! But we are wrong. It is easy to be spiteful. However, the art of living is to finally get hold of our Self and grasp our sense of humility, which automatically also revives the romantic moments of our lives, including the ones with our inconsiderate, foolish spouse. We could change gear and reach for the more tranquilizing emotions of forgiveness and love if only we can overcome our false pride and disengage our Ego. We can activate our Model to express our raw emotions, if we have a hard time using Self to show our very deep feelings. Occasionally, we can make a good use of our Model, and this could be one of those precious occasions.

My personal experience relates to the first occasion when my wife and I decided to separate—about fifteen years ago. Despite our heated power struggles and confrontations, we agreed to visit a marriage counsellor based on our family doctor's advice (after giving us enough stress medications to no avail). The counsellor had an impressive background, with a Ph.D. in psychology and many years of experience in marriage counselling. We visited him weekly for three months and explained our backgrounds, concerns, and our relationship situation. He gave us his advice, and we covered many grounds throughout this exploratory and reconciliatory process. At the end, he bluntly announced that he did not think we had a chance. He gave up on us as well! I recall that day very well. We left his office in silence and delved into our own thoughts and emotions. We felt lonely with nobody around to help us, at least as a fair judge, and perhaps pinpoint the issues that the marriage counsellor had failed to rectify. The way he had dismissed us had felt rude and funny, too!

It became clear to me, at the end, that it did not matter what the sources of problems were, anyway. We are humans, after all, and full of flaws and foolishness. So many things entered my mind, and finally I realized that I had to change my approach, if only because that was our only hope. We were getting ready for divorce, anyway, so why not give ourselves a last chance by thinking marriage in these dying moments of our relationship.

Gradually, new ideas and options crossed my mind through deeper self-awareness and reading related books gradually. I learned a lot regarding marriage and divorce. I did not submit to whims and ways of my wife, nor did she to mine. Rather, we made a point to express a subtle, raw compassion, friendship, and some feelings of romanticism. In particular, growing the moods of romanticism was not easy for either of us, due to our recent alienation and our relatively logical minds. Often, we drew on our Model to make romantic gestures, which although did not feel or appear as sincere as we liked them to be, they still made a positive impact on our relationship.

With a very rudimentary alienation preparedness process that my wife and I built gradually, we were successful in reversing the progress of alienation and accomplished the tough task that even a specialist had assumed impossible. We achieved this only by faith and resorting to a more suitable relationship model for us—at least the one I thought might work. I cannot say whether we both came to the same conclusions simultaneously or not. But my guess is that one of us played a more active role in pondering and propagating the alienation preparedness process without even recognizing what s/he was about to do or achieve. And, of course, both of us quickly encouraged, or at least approved, the intentions of the other. Our relationship was not perfect by a long shot at this time yet. Still, it had improved a lot, from retaliation and spite to a more civilized and romantic approach with tolerance and by avoiding hasty invalid judgments, accepting that personal flaws cannot be defused quickly, giving each other more independence, separating our financial affairs, and resisting egoistic arguments.

Ten years later, we made another valid judgment and decided that it was time to quit, and we did. By then, at least our kids had grown up and left us. The main question and doubt in my mind is whether we should have separated the first time, ten years earlier. Maybe one or both of us now regret our past decision to reconcile, but then (10 years earlier) we had decided that giving ourselves another chance was a wiser decision. The problem, I believe, was that most likely we did not have enough expertise and mutual goodwill to build a proper alienation awareness process suitable for us. Yet, we, or at least I, apparently chose our options based on the order suggested at the beginning of this chapter! Another problem with life, nowadays, is that most of our crucial decisions do not prove fully satisfactory or effective at the end, for giving us a relative sense of happiness, or for helping us resolve some of our fundamental doubts about life. No real solutions seem to exist for many of our primary problems, anyway! That is life!

Like all life's major decisions, marriage and divorce might also lead to irreversible life experiences that can hurt us forever and yet have so little educational value. Such is life!

PART V
Consciousness and Awareness

About Part V

The fundamental facts reviewed in this trilogy offer the following gloomy picture about humans' life structure and future:

- Socioeconomic and political systems are quite dysfunctional globally and the situation is about to get out of hand.
- The effects of too many raw philosophies about freedom, life, and love have screwed up people's minds at the worst time—when all other aspects of social existence are threatened.
- Humanity is facing too many existential dilemmas and must make many crucial decisions fast to elude distinction, yet have no guidelines, mindsets, and spirits to do so.
- Morality and morale have plummeted drastically personally and socially in line with growing corruption and the spread of naïve ideologies driving the core of societies.
- Accordingly, we suffer a lifetime and damage our psyches and spirits, as we do not learn about our being per se or explore our innate potentialities and urges for spiritualism.
- Nevertheless, we can still attain contentment and peace within a rather self-defined, independent lifestyle according to a viable personal life philosophy if we explore our curious Self through self-awareness and develop a simpler mindset.
- More details are offered on pages 292-3.

Accordingly, the next three chapters (14-16) discuss the following concepts as additional tools and insights for self-realization:

14. **Learning Fundamentals** and mechanisms useful for raising self-awareness and personal consciousness mostly for coping with the rising social chaos, and maybe enhancing the quality of our lives, too, without relying on materialism.
15. **Living for Learning** as an ultimate human ambition per se —for living freely, and perhaps a chance for enlightenment.
16. **Rethinking Education** to reshape social structure somewhat and save humanity in line with wiser objectives.

CHAPTER FOURTEEN
Learning Fundamentals

Humans' natural urge for learning is fulfilled in various forms, mostly outside the educational process. Education is a restricted type of learning at best, although it has gained a high importance within humans' life structure due to its socioeconomic role and purposes. Real learning, however, is for *wise* social adaptation, self-improvement, and perhaps even enlightenment. This chapter explores these means of learning that have much higher value for personal and social wellbeing than formal education per se.

On the other hand, the discussions in this and the next two chapters (Part V) about humans' learning capacity and desire for self-realization and tranquility sound naively optimistic even to the author himself. Sadly, social conditioning and the effects of misleading social values and lifestyles have overwhelmed our psyches and mentalities, so we are left with little energy and time to think about our real needs and learn life's essentialities through self-awareness and conscious learning regimens discussed in the remainder of this book. Nevertheless, studying some principles about humans' inherent needs and how some keen individuals can explore them felt useful to include at the end of this trilogy. In particular, developing a new mindset about learning—to focus on humans' real needs, instead of teaching so much superficiality and self-gratification ideologies—is the only way out of the rising crisis inflicting humans in the early part of the 21st century. At least a few of us might associate with these unorthodox thoughts and build the courage and life philosophies to redefine our means of thinking and living.

The Impact (and Value) of Learning

Mainly three types of learning exist with different effects on our way of thinking and happiness:

1. **General learning (conditioning)**, which mostly results from rearing, religions, general information, chitchat, and debates. This mundane learning is mostly automatic, subconscious at best, and common among people. It does not help our mental growth or happiness directly and enough, but actually raises our naivety and the overall ignorance in society. Through this process, we learn to cope socially and become like others—mostly obnoxious and pretentious—in order to receive their respect and approval and be accepted in their midst. What people learn from one another in this manner only distorts their sense of identity and integrity. No real happiness results from these types of learning, either. Not even all their social knowledge or hot debates can bring them happiness, except for those rare occasions when people's *thinking, feeling,* and *dialogues* raise their urge for self-awareness.

2. **Learning for career purposes,** which entail education, skill development, and the learning to fit within social structure and norms. The impact of these types of learning is **indirect**, as we use our income to buy things that boost our Ego and make us *feel* happy (an illusion of happiness mostly). On rare occasions, people learn to build a balanced path of life in line with a basic life philosophy to guide them in society without losing their identity totally or being rejected fully. They learn to adapt themselves to basic rules and get along with people without seeking their acceptance actively or imitating them.

They learn to practise their own values with a certain level of integrity in society without getting absorbed in organizations and the mainstream values and ways. They learn to endure hardships better and possibly reach a relative peace of mind. Yet, they do not pursue any special means of learning as a device for psychological growth.

3. **Learning that raises our self-awareness and pinpoints our authentic life purposes.** Only this type of learning helps us find real happiness **directly**. It evolves as we explore our vulnerabilities, become selfless, and let go of our debilitating ambitions. Only a small group pursues this kind of learning consciously, due to not merely the demands of this type of life path, but also the difficulty of ignoring social norms and the public's apprehension of their odd lifestyles and opinions.

For any likelihood of capturing even a semblance of freedom, happiness, and tranquility, we need a lot more learning of the third kind. Other learnings are useful, too, if we maintain at least a sense of our integrity. Yet, mundane learning merely for social adaptation and job opportunities consumes lots of our time and energy, muddles our psyches, and hardly gives us self-fulfilment. It mostly goads habits and values that inhibit our search for life essentialities and tranquility. Most learnings these days for career or adaptation purposes confuse and consume our life path and waste our valuable lives. They suppress our innate potentialities and stir distress, stress, and psychological defects by encouraging greed, jealousy, rivalry, or narcissism.

For building a healthy mentality and path of life, we must first learn to become quite conscious of our learning habits, overcome (unlearn) our idiosyncrasies and narcissism, and revamp our life outlooks and personalities. This is a major challenge for most of us, since it is hard to modify our old learning habits and channels that we have subconsciously followed all our lives. We should try to become conscious of all involuntary learning, which are often imposed on us, including social values and upbringing lessons.

The goal is to detect and reverse the effect of universal learning, conscious or unconscious ones, ongoing or old sources, especially the rearing and social learning (conditioning) noted above under learning type # 1.

We can distinguish the sources of conscious learning (such as reading, meditation, research, etc.) from unconscious training and culture (e.g., television, social trends, friends and family, etc.) Naturally, it is hard to resist the influence and force of everything we have already learnt, abandon our habits, or break away from people we are attached to despite their odd mindsets. However, we can begin to observe our actions, reactions, and relationships more consciously. We may ultimately unlearn some defective aspects of our lifelong unconscious learning after acknowledging their debilitating effects. We could stay vigilant about the type of learning that our phony lifestyles impose on everybody. Then, we could stress on the kind of learning that supports self-awareness, instead of the kind that gives us only an illusion of success and a viable existence.

Conscious learning evokes our innate potentialities, drives our psychological growth, and nurtures our sense of spirituality. The mere significance of these types of learning for one's psyche and spirit reveals the triviality of all other learning, and the futility of all our efforts related to them. For example, we learn how foolish our greed and egoistic power struggles are, and how ignorantly we are driven by such enormous amount of worthless teachings of our modern societies to satiate our Model and Ego.

Part III in Volume II discusses the importance of learning about our potentialities and limitations for raising self-awareness and nurturing our spiritual urges. Discovering our potentialities and spirituality is actually a major life mission (decision.) In this regard, we want to learn about our purposes of living in line with humans' innate needs, instead of all the superficial ones created in society as symbols of civilization. Of course, we cannot ignore mundane types of learning needed for our survival and careers. Yet, we can balance our learning efforts more wisely according to their importance for personal happiness and our psychological health. We have both a divine urge and a personal responsibility to grasp the essence of our being through conscious learning.

Learning Processes

Most of our learning is *unconscious* through many *involuntary* processes. We are normally not much keen about learning or its nature, anyway, in spite of our natural deep curiosity (which is general and random for no specific purpose). In fact, our random motives or plans to learn are also usually superficial and transient, though they could lead to equally deep, irreversible conditioning traits and nasty habits. Real learning, on the other hand, manifests as a *conscious* process of awareness with an intention to learn. As a lifelong, rigorous discipline, conscious learning needs a specific objective and process driven by our curiosity and commitment usually for boosting our lives' quality or humanity, for example, by exploring our life philosophy. Moreover, conscious learning is for offsetting or eluding the alluring effects of our subconscious learnings, which are too deep, severe, and often in conflict with our ultimate goal of finding 'self' and tranquility.

Actually, a major role of conscious learning (self-awareness) is to monitor the type and process of our unconscious learning, which either funnels through daily interactions or results from our random curiosities. Of course, natural curiosity, as distinguished from prying, triggers a healthy learning process depending on the quality of our thoughts and ensuing creativity. As an extension of personal intuition to explore and learn, curiosity might evoke our conscious learning, especially about the universe and essence of life. However, human curiosity is often general and random with no specific goal attached to it, or is merely wasted on snooping habits. Wasting time and effort on random, raw curiosities has no value or objective for conscious learning. Sometimes, curiosity may also misguide the process of exploring our true potentialities. Random learning and curiosity might raise our intelligence, but they do not help our psychological growth and happiness if we cannot bring them into focus and find their purposes in line with our potentialities and needs.

For conscious learning, we have a set objective and follow a rigorous process, similar to a methodical research to find cure for cancer. Consequently, we penetrate and activate our potentialities with sharper scrutiny, and solutions evolve more fluently during those periods of mental focus. All along, we stay aware and wary of unconscious learning (prejudices and conditioning) hindering our conscious learning efforts. Discovering our idiosyncrasies and defeating their sources are main goals and challenges of conscious learning. The highest level of conscious learning happens like a divine curiosity, however, as will be reviewed in the next chapter.

Naturally, general knowledge helps us analyse life situations and options, in spite of its lack of immediate purpose or effect on our wellbeing or happiness. It might strengthen our cognition for possible use in some conscious learning efforts or situational analyses. However, unless general knowledge goads a conscious learning regimen for specific objectives, it remains useless, if not a major hindrance for proper reflections and self-analyses.

Overall, our knowledge (and perception) of the world and life outlook evolve through a mix of learning processes that are partly conscious but mostly involuntary. The question is how (and how much) we are helping or hurting ourselves by allowing particular learning processes affect our lives. In other words, how should we judge the value of our 'learning?' And how might conscious learning affect our lives' direction by mitigating the repercussions of involuntary (conditioning) information that is bombarding our minds constantly. In particular, eluding and reversing the ruinous effects of social teachings and economic pressures would be a big challenge for any person wishing to rethink his/her existence.

Monitoring the sources and factors of learning, as explained in the next section, is a crucial part of the conscious learning process in itself, especially for raising our consciousness about our idiosyncrasies and revamping them.

Learning Sources and Factors

We learn through six main *sources*:
1. Natural growth—instinctual urges, curiosity, intuition, and emerging potentialities
2. Other individuals, mainly parents and teachers
3. Culture and society, including television, publications
4. Personal experiences
5. Universal experiences
6. Objective thinking and awareness

The extent and depth of learning from any of the above sources, however, depend on the strengths of the following three main *factors*:

i) Personal potentialities (including learning ability).
ii) Exposure to educational environments.
iii) Conscious efforts to learn.

Obviously, the above sources and factors of learning are all interrelated. The purpose of distinguishing them is only to grasp the overall mechanism of learning and raising our consciousness. Overall, personal potentialities (the first factor noted above) goad our *natural growth* as the main source of learning. Environmental conditions (the 2nd factor) mainly facilitate the next four sources of learning, *which include learning from other people, society, personal experiences, and universal wisdom*. Finally, conscious effort (the 3rd factor) is crucial for driving our *objective thinking and awareness*, which is indeed the main source of learning about life, but also about our limitations and potentialities.

Nonetheless, despite these academic distinctions, usually a multiple of *factors* and *sources* of learning cross and combine all the time. For example, we learn through interactions with people who stimulate our curiosity and learning capacity. This becomes a 'personal or universal experience' or a 'learning from another individual' depending on how it happens and how we interpret it. Still, this unique learning might have been invoked automatically, anyway, perhaps through natural growth. As another example, a personal experience might make us think deeply about a new topic, which then results in another kind of learning. Therefore, both our initial experience and subsequent reflections present different *sources* of learning depending on the strength of one or more *factors* of learning stirring the process.

In the final analysis, what and how much we learn depend on our personal potentialities and limitations, including logic, mental capacity, personality, emotional stability, commitment, aptitude, education, personal experiences, and life outlook. However, our learning efforts would not become focused and productive until we exploit our opportunities for exploring our potentialities for specific purposes, especially for fulfilling our spirituality needs. This type of divine learning demands lengthy conscious efforts, sacrifice, and a favourable learning environment, of course. This is a big challenge for most of us to pursue on a highly disciplined process. Thus, our learning often remains shallow and aimless, too, while our potentialities stay neglected and our idiosyncrasies besiege our lives in line with all our involuntary learning.

A detail study of the above six sources and three factors of learning (plus their interworking) would be interesting to pursue in another book. For this book's purpose, however, only a brief review of the special features of each source of learning follows.

Learning through Natural Growth

We learn instinctually from birth, as an infant learns to walk, talk, reason, and react. Then, the process expands fast, but in a lesser noticeable pattern throughout our lives. Little conscious efforts is made for learning essential facts about our being, nor do we learn much from our life experiences. We simply think and perceive things and situations and build our cognition as we mature rather randomly with little guided efforts. Alas, even this basic natural knack for thinking and learning is soon sabotaged by other means of learning regularly, especially family and societal conditioning forces. Environment hinders or deforms our natural growth and the use of our instincts and brains.

We each ponder and perceive life differently as time goes by, which is a symptom of natural growth under the influence of the environment. Our thoughts and perceptions stabilize somewhat as our interpretations about life and our place in it change (often improve *within its warped format*) with maturity, e.g., when we acquire some flexibility to improve our daily lives. Remembering this crucial fact per se can prevent us from becoming dogmatic, overanxious, or prejudiced about some ideas, decisions, or ideals that would prove to be much less significant or consequential than we had imagined in an earlier stage of our lives, especially during adolescence. We often regret our past decisions a few years or so later. We wonder about our flimsy logic and criteria for making those poor choices when we had actually bragged about our wisdom and trusted the validity of our thoughts with absolute certainty. How sure we had been about our choices and everything else!

Learning from Other Individuals

Some people are more open to other individuals' ideas without being influenced illogically. We call them open-minded! They test and apply those seemingly useful ideas for strengthening the foundation of their thoughts (discussed in Volume I). This group is naturally less dogmatic and egotistical about their ideologies and keep a higher level of doubts about many issues that self-centred people insist on as ultimate facts. Consequently, this group builds a stronger base for developing resourceful and creative solutions for life issues. They learn and live better than average population. With a positive attitude toward learning, they partake in various social situations and interactions with different groups without judging their thoughts and attitude. Therefore, they learn to expand their decision-making platform and wisdom to offset their chronic belief regarding humans' innate impurity. They just widen their horizons by absorbing people's thoughtful views without being unduly influenced by them.

In contrast, most of us become too rigid with narrow mindsets and show no flexibility towards other life options, not even for learning from our own mistakes. We resist any kind of learning, as it appears like a demand on us to change, thus a threat to our identity and perceptions of life. We get frustrated and defensive when alternatives are proposed. Thus, we simply shut off our ears and learning mechanisms. Ironically, this group is also susceptive to some naïve ideologies and get dogmatic about them as well.

Most of the communication problems in our society relate to our defensiveness and other people's reactions to the threatening implications of our messages. We are highly protective of our crude perceptions of life. Yet, learning depends highly on how receptive and flexible someone is. One's interest and talent for pondering new ideas show his/her maturity, innate curiosity, and learning drive for his/her own benefit at least.

Learning from Other Sources

Many kinds of information are disseminated through media for various purposes. They may contain helpful opinions to improve our physical and psychological health, but they are often biased and solely used for general information, propaganda, marketing, etc. It is getting harder for most of us to anticipate the purpose and impact of this information and avoid their negative impacts, especially when we prefer to trust the socioeconomic systems that support or produce that information quite a bit. Thus, lots of efforts are needed to assess and resist the subconscious learning that results from social living and hinders our mental growth.

Learning from Personal Experiences

Ironically, most people resist learning even from their firsthand experiences and the repercussions of their previous decisions and actions. They seem eager to repeat the same mistakes, as though enjoying self-destruction and self-pity. They act like gamblers who keep going back to casinos to lose more every night.

The value of personal experiences is low for other reasons as well, aside from a person's dogmatism and addiction to failure. For one thing, it takes us a long time to sense the consequences of our actions and decisions, and then in many instances we may no longer have a chance to make use of this learning and make up for our past mistakes. One point we may learn eventually, though, is that many lessons we may learn in the future cannot help us correct a sloppy decision we are going to make today. The other point we learn too late is that we most likely change our way of thinking when we mature in our upcoming life stages. In fact, many rather open-minded people usually realize the stupidity of their past mindsets and decisions regularly during every life stage.

Life experiences are usually specific and unique, thus useful only for a similar situation, if at all. For example, our experience from our first marriage is extremely shocking and informative. Yet, this critical information has limited value for improving our relationships, especially for replacing our partner or making her/him change her/his attitude. The information may be partly useful for our second marriage, if we still desire or can marry again. The fact is that, by then, we have usually become too apprehensive and cynical about marriage, anyway, and biased in different ways. Life experiences ruin our objectivity and impartiality in their own ways. Nevertheless, we often make the same or similar mistakes and often marry another jerk soon enough.

An important lesson we can possibly try to remember is that: Considering the low chance of getting second chances in life, and the limited value of learning from our experiences, if at all, we must try to assess all feasible options and possible consequences of every decision open-mindedly and diligently without allowing our emotions get in the way. This unseemly procrastination and indecision often helps us manage our deep emotions, prejudices, predispositions, and stubborn attitudes towards things and others.

We can use the wisdom that 'our views of things and their values change as we mature (forward thinking principle).' This mindset might make us think twice before committing to an action or plan. It gives us the incentive to spend more time and efforts to assess our other options, too. We may pause to listen to others, assess our doubts, read some books, and definitely think a little deeper. The decision to get married at a young age is a good example. When we are young and passionately in love, we do not stop to ask ourselves how long we would expect to be married to this person. If the answer is forever, the smart thing to do is to explore the manner we lovers are going to make this marriage actually work. The factors for making a relationship successful are vastly complex these days and love can at best play a small role for this crucial decision. A hasty decision would most likely lead to big disappointments and problems, if not misery. A passionate love today could lead to a deep hatred after a few years when several kids are born, careers are not developed, financial resources are wasted, and partners start to regret their decisions. A decision that seemed fully justified in the lovers' minds a few years earlier turns into a nightmare. How do we ever *learn* our lessons! Often in a very harsh manner and when it is too late.

Learning from Universal Experiences

People's life experiences are often private and unique, but they gradually evolve into a universal set of thoughts and conclusions. In our search for the truth and the meaning of life, most of us reach the same results, most often when we have passed through all the stages of our lives and tasted happiness, sufferings, and disappointments, tested our optimism and hopes, and dealt with our doubts and pessimism about many things, mostly the nature of human beings. This collection of universal experiences is the kind of knowledge or wisdom that we can all share.

Two points are interesting to remember about these universal experiences. **First,** over the long history of intelligent humans' life, we have not yet put these thoughts and findings in a simple, comprehensive, and authoritative document for people, especially young people, to rely on for mapping their lives constructively. Many philosophers have tried to achieve something like that, but we still do not have a mechanism and the will to let people learn the relevant stuff of life in a simple language. Instead, we have deliberately propagated ignorance and greed through religions and capitalism so that a small group can benefit from the corrupt situation. **Second,** we all resist learning from the vast amount of universal knowledge that has passed the test of time and proven valid over and over, e.g., the fact that we are going to pay dearly for the damage we are inflicting on environment so carelessly. Our greed, naivety, and arrogance stand in our way of learning anything from these clear and proven universal experiences and knowledge. Or conversely, we abuse some of our learning from these universal experiences only to justify our crooked desires, e.g., abusing the fact that 'life is short,' for seeking more pleasure at all cost with little regard for morality or integrity.

The amount of universal experiences that we can benefit from personally, and collectively as human beings, is enormous, which makes our indifference quite amazing. We deliberately ignore all the basic facts that can help humans live a more peaceful life, and instead we chose the stupidest, toughest options that create more stress and confusion for all. The few universal experiences listed below are only some examples of millions of lessons out there that could be used for improving humans' lives and relationships if only we can overcome our greed, dogmatism, and arrogance.

A comprehensive collection of life realities in the 21st century is needed to give the world at least a basic exposure to obstacles humans are imposing upon themselves. For now, we can at least ponder the following short list of human ignorance and follies:

- Capitalism and materialism cannot fulfil humans' real needs.
- Humans are greedy, naïve, and arrogant naturally, but rearing and social conditioning worsen their characters vastly. Thus,

expecting them to be pure and decent merely shows people and governments' tenacity to deny reality, e.g., about the possible role of freedom and democracy in society.
- The mix of capitalism and human greed has created the biggest hurdle for any sense of humanity ever emerging. We wonder if we can ever escape this immense trap as long as self-serving academicians and authorities insist, so foolishly and arrogantly, that capitalism and materialism serve humans best!
- Only through compassion, tolerance, and caution we can relate and cause one another and society less damage. Yet, we have no means or plans to make this a universal objective.
- The harm we are inflicting on environment is going to abolish humanity all by itself, yet we just remain paralyzed about this immense obstacle within the current world economic structure.
- Religions have caused only more animosity across nations and groups, and made people more ignorant about themselves and life in general, including the need to explore their own sense of spirituality and finding tranquility.
- Wasting our short lives to merely serve our Egos and greed or pursue shallow pleasures is idiotic.
- We are alone on this planet, despite all the friends and family surrounding us.
- We have not still grasped the meaning of individualism as a personal challenge for self-growth, however societies insists on pushing a demented interpretation of it and confusing people even further.
- Spoiling our children and the youths in families, society, and media (including movies), about extravagance, sexuality, love, individualism, freedom, happiness is abolishing their abilities to relate, sustain a decent means of living, run their marriages, or show initiatives for salvaging humanity.
- Marital relationships are fully undefined and unreliable now in the present format.

- Our obsessions for sexuality, corruption, and immorality have hindered the possibility of grasping our true self and growing our spirits.
- The option of finding productive jobs to match and nurture our potentialities is becoming less viable.
- Organizations (both private and public) are largely corrupt and inefficient due to demented human nature and socioeconomic structure. In return, they have become a major source of stress for their employees, customers, and society, with little capacity to serve their social responsibilities.
- Personal and family debts are growing at alarming rates and stirring widespread social distress. We simply like to ignore that spending beyond our means has become a social disease.
- The bigger problem is that we do not learn the vanity of our needs for luxury and extravagance to build a pleasant, peaceful life and become a better human. To the contrary, we are only causing our own pain and indignity, not to mention the loss of individualism and spirit, due to our phony, materialistic habits and hoping to prove our worth through arrogance and wealth.
- Governments' overspending and national debts are going to haunt the future generations and humanity with lesser options available to remedy these rising concerns.
- Etc.

Ironically, nowadays, everybody likes to figure out the meaning *of life* based on his/her raw personal experiences and superficial social values, which merely advocate materialism, sexuality, and pomposity. Such an ambitious, bizarre task!

The mere fact that we are so eager to find the meaning of life clearly indicates our dissatisfaction with our routine existence and our desperation to make a better sense of our lives. For cracking the mystery of life and happiness, however, we should first gauge the meaning of our lifestyles and the validity of the current social structure that contains our living. We should first understand the components of our relationships, social systems, and major life decisions within this perplexing environment. It is crucial to learn about, and make, our life decisions carefully to avoid perpetual disappointments, stress, and depression. We might eventually realize that merely our dogmatism and devotion to our peculiar mentalities and lifestyles is making living so difficult. Merely our reluctance to test the simpler—yet more gratifying—options of living is to blame for humanity's failures and looming demise. In all, our resistance to learn about ourselves and adjust our attitudes hinders our chances of even understanding the basic purposes of existence, let alone grasping the mystery or meaning of life.

Nevertheless, our intention to learn something from our own, as well as 'universal,' experiences gives us a chance to see life in a keener and more compassionate way if we consciously plan to do so. Such joyful and dismal experiences can help us learn about life and ourselves, though using them for future decisions is often unlikely. We can learn a lot at least about human nature and our dwindling socioeconomic mechanisms without dwelling on our personal failures too much.

Learning through Objective (Focused) Thinking

Objective (Focused) Thinking is the most intimate and potent way of learning if we know how to do it. It needs lots of patience, perseverance, and focus, which is hard for many of us to achieve. The process is tough and our findings are often vague and slow. Even when we believe we have found a solution or established a fact, we usually face many doubts about its validity and value. Thus, we often undermine the power of 'thinking.' However, we humans have learned a lot from other individuals' successful visualization and contemplation, when they have mixed pieces of information with divine personal intuitions to build fundamental principles or valid concepts. Einstein developed his complex theories of relativity and gravity mainly through visualization and focused thoughts. Equally, every simple matter can be viewed within a focused state of mind (awareness) in accordance with one's general intelligence level.

Meditation and focused thinking have parallel objectives, but the latter places a higher emphasis on the learning aspect of this process, while meditation is valued more for creating inner peace. With meditation, we intend to stop our erratic thoughts and with 'focused thinking,' we wish to focus our thoughts and delve into the depth of a phenomenon. We can benefit from both of these rather complementary methods of learning.

Learning happens naturally when we experience an event or feeling. However, this learning can be boosted through conscious efforts to understand why and how an event happened. Wisdom is simply the product of knowing the right issues to choose for learning, how to go about it, and the depth of details that need working out. Only then, we feel the process of maturity and our psychological growth accelerating. Only then, our decisions and actions appear sound and profound. We learn about self, Nature, philosophers' envision of life, our relationships with others, and the essentialities of life. The most important learning experience is to *learn* what those life essentialities are. That is, *to learn what to learn*. Surely, everybody believes strongly in his/her lifestyle and value systems. Accordingly, the definition and meaning of essentialities differ for each person. So, who is to judge which issues are essential? This is a matter of opinion and controversy. However, in the final analysis, there is no need for judgment as life essentialities become obvious only in the minds of those who find the wisdom to separate purities from pollution. And this, in fact, is the general purpose of learning: to distinguish right from wrong and purities from pollutions.

Overall, we learn much more by thinking per se than relying on accidental, unconscious learning through life and personal experiences. Sometimes, we combine the effects of these two means of learning by thinking very deeply about our experiences and consciously analysing our past evaluations and judgments. We look for the motives behind our deeds and needs, too. The synergy that results from analysing the gist of our experiences through active thinking (conscious learning) would be massive. Our ability to learn would improve substantially compared with the cases where experiences are left in our subconscious only with their subliminal effects without analysis and focus on valid thoughts.

In all, our life experiences often reveal the foolishness of many of our previously *deemed* correct decisions and actions. Learning thru 'objective thinking' about past events and situations gives us a fresh perspective of life and we feel more in harmony with the universe. This is a sign of maturity and the value of learning from our mistakes through conscious, objective thinking. Another big irony about life is that we usually understand its real meaning too late to enjoy it. Worst of all, what we learn today most likely would not have the ultimate value that it could have had when we were younger and had more opportunities to explore and exploit. Sadly, we mature and learn a bit about the meaning of life when our options are restricted and our wisdom is hardly applicable to our future life. This is a major lesson to remember, especially by new generations and for parents to propagate in their families. It says something about the mystery of life and God's wisdom for creating such helpless humans!

The main depressing fact is that what families, educational systems, societies, and religions have been teaching us, especially to the youths, has been too detrimental for humans' personal and social welfare. They have merely ruined their opportunities for conscious learning and building at least the basic wisdom needed for a simple existence, let alone humanity's long-term survival.

The 'Focused Thinking,' as a source of learning, is in itself the tool for raising the levels of our consciousness and awareness. It is a conscious learning process, which constitutes a long-term commitment for self-improvement and exploring a wide scope of life and 'self' experiences towards enlightenment.

CHAPTER FIFTEEN
Living for Learning

Most of us have lost our knack for learning, although this *natural* urge drives our needs for creativity, achievement, and spirituality. Still, many people feel and act upon their learning urge, and some are actually obsessed with it. They are living mostly for the sake of learning, although they might not realize it readily or consider it the finest aspect of their existence. Most scientists and scholars throughout the history have been perfect proofs of this precious human obsession.

Sadly, however, most of us do not see learning, reflection, and contribution as vital facets of social living or our being, since we have let lust and materialism besiege our senses. Despite all the education we get, we still do not even know how and what to learn in order to help ourselves and society. Our natural instincts about learning have been subdued throughout the history, but much more in recent decades due to growing social pressures for vanity in modern world, as noted in this trilogy. Thus, now only a small fraction of humans feels the urge and urgency to pursue learning as a crucial virtue of their existence—as though living for learning per se. Strangely, the public sees this tiny group as eccentric, and maybe even mad, boring, and abnormal, although they also consider them respectful and geniuses.

Anyway, this chapter's discussion of 'living for learning' per se offers the opposite side of the coin to 'learning for living' that was highlighted in Chapter Two. The goal is to study the means and objectives of reflection and learning merely for growing our consciousness and self-awareness to help us with our life's major decisions, e.g., about education, work, marriage, alienation and divorce. For example, two points about 'work' on Page 59 are reprinted below:

"Working is an obligation to 'self' for building our identity."

"Our individuality is highly represented by the two opposing (but inherent) purposes of work, i.e., for 1) fulfilling ourselves (to satisfy our 'self'), and 2) validating our existence (to satisfy our 'ego'). These dual purposes of work are ingrained in our psyches as reflections of human nature and instinctual needs."

Work, as a major life decision and routine, occupies us all our lives and demands our high consciousnesses and self-awareness, especially if we intend to find our 'self' and a more meaningful means of living. High consciousness and self-awareness are, in fact, the main requirements for all life decisions emphasized in this book—for understanding and improving our relationships, for social and organizational adaptations with minimal pains, for handling our strenuous marriage and divorce dilemmas, for grasping our potentialities and spirituality urges, and for making many crucial life decisions.

Learning and education have been noted already as two major life decisions themselves. Yet, raising our level of consciousness and self-awareness for salvaging our souls, besides handling our major life decisions, needs lots of conscious learning by itself. The truth is that if we spend only half of the intelligence, efforts, and time we currently waste on formal education or for satiating our sexual urges to strengthen our 'self' and spirits, we would all become prominent gurus living peacefully in caring, productive societies. Thus, consciousness and awareness, especially for the purpose of learning, are addressed in more depth in this chapter.

The learning fundamentals noted in the last chapter might also help us achieve a higher level of consciousness. Accordingly, the next chapter offers a guideline for making our decisions regarding learning and education more objectively along with more hints about the shortfalls of education.

Rooted Learning Disability

A main obstacle to learning is that we trust the adequacy of our educational systems and cultural values for planning our lives. We hardly draw on our intuition and intelligence to question the validity of some of the basic teachings (but also the alleged life essentialities) we have eagerly adopted. We depend on others and a sadly doomed society to tell us 'what is right' and 'how to live.' When someone talks about discovering our potentialities, many of us ask, "How should I go about this?" When somebody says we must become more self-aware, we ask, "How?"! *Judging by the way modern society is progressing,* maybe soon, if we tell somebody to use his/her intelligence or logic, s/he would ask, "How?"!

We humans have an immense capacity and enthusiasm for education, which involves only impersonal subjects, but we have almost no interest and capacity to learn about life and Self, which are delicate and essential for personal growth, better relationships, and maybe even enlightenment. We do not learn even from our own personal mistakes to improve our lives, as if we were born to be self-destructive. We seem to be in denial of the gloomy reality we have developed around ourselves with our crude perceptions and ideologies.

Nowadays, kids take custom-made lessons in swimming, drawing, ice-skating and everything else that so many of us used to learn just by trial and error and watching our parents or friends who knew it. Having an instructor seems necessary, nowadays, because we want to teach our kids to become perfect swimmers, ice-skaters, drawers, etc., as rapidly as possible. This is a worthy objective and has some merits. However, it cultivates the habit of relying on others to tell us how to think and do things, step-by-step, instead of taking our time to figure out most of those things on our own. As we grow up, we get into the habit of doubting our inner abilities and intuitions to think and learn independently. Worst, we are losing our confidence to depend on our intuition to observe, think, imagine, analyse, and learn outside the box.

Surely, it often makes sense to use the specialized knowledge to do things more effectively rather than trying to reinvent the wheel every time. However, there is also need for trusting our intelligence and intuition to do so many things that we thought only specialists could achieve. We should train ourselves to make better use of our brains and discover the vast level of intelligence and potentialities that can help us with our doubts and decisions. The way we are training ourselves, soon not even one percent of our brain's capacity would be utilized, compared with 3 to 5% nowadays. Instead of developing our brains for essential learning, we are letting it go to waste. As noted before, learning entails a lot of feelings and imaginations. We can train ourselves to draw upon our intuition and creativity to unlock the secrets of life or at least handle our own lives better. We can discover certain options that are normally not obvious to us, because we are spoiled or conditioned to perceive things only in some standardized and conventional forms. In his book, *The 90 Second Therapist*, Summerhill Press Ltd. 1988, Timothy Bentley states:

"But in this world where we leave so much up to experts, it is a tempting fallacy to believe that the real therapists are the professionals. In fact, nothing could be less true. As intelligent human beings, we are called by nature to be the primary therapists for our lives." Ibid., page 194.

Therefore, as a first step, we should revamp our mentality and begin learning things mostly through higher consciousness and self-awareness. This way, we can discover the depth and scope of things rather than expecting others to show it to us, which in most cases would not be right or helpful, anyway. Unlearning some of our habits, thoughts, and defects is extremely difficult, though, like asking a swimmer or skater to unlearn their skills. Awareness includes this knowledge about the difficulty of unlearning our habits or finding the means of offsetting our rooted shortfalls. As noted in Volume I, adjustment is necessary in at least one of the three areas of our *thoughts*, *attitude*, or *situation* in order to cope with external demands and other people's needs without losing our integrity or the control of our lives totally. We need a similar type of mental adjustment about the means of learning both the basics and essentialities of life on our own. This is the way of learning through self-awareness and high consciousness.

Our ability to learn depends on the strength of our thoughts and feelings and at least a basic desire for self-awareness. Yet, we initially need a high personal incentive and commitment to even care about self-awareness. We must pass these initial stages of reflection and make a decision to adopt a fresh path of life in search of the truth. Then, we can focus on actual work. Through self-awareness, we learn from our 'observations of things,' and from our feelings and thoughts. We learn about the facts of life directly when we see some value and application for them in some aspects of our lives. For example, we usually learn that some activities are pleasant but meaningless (like sex) and some are laborious but fulfilling (like hiking). We might even learn something new every day from the obvious fact that sun rises from the east and sets in the west. We grasp the new meanings of facts we have simply accepted as fixed fixtures surrounding us, like the obvious fact that we must breathe *constantly* to survive. Then, we decide how to apply these intricate facts of existence to our unique situations and thoughts. With awareness, we learn not only facts (or myths) that exist as some apparent reality of the universe, but also how they affect us, how we relate to them, and how we can possibly enrich our lives through these relationships according to our dynamic knowledge of existence.

With awareness, we also learn 'from things' through our imaginations and visions. Our intuition and ingenuity can help us see behind and beyond the obvious. We assess an event or thing to learn about its essence and motives way beyond its superficial and observable facets. When we see the moon, we conclude that it shines, but many other facts lie beyond this seemingly obvious conclusion. We learn *from* our observations; not merely what we see, but rather what makes it real or radiant. With awareness, we seek to find the hidden facts and learn from them. For example, in our relationships, we are confused or fooled by what we say to one another, since we simply judge others based on what people say or what we choose to hear. Yet, neither what they say nor what we hear (understand) reflects both persons' true intentions. With awareness, we always remember this fact and honour it, but also we find the urge to seek and learn—more objectively—about the motives behind people's and our words. More importantly, we become more careful in our ways of talking with others.

Then, learning about myths opens up even a larger sphere of insight about the universe and human existence. The principles and process of awareness apply to all aspects of our existence and constitute the finest platform for our judgments, interpretations, and learning about the world and life.

With awareness, we begin also to 'learn from' coincidences that influence our lives in unforeseeable ways. We learn from our experiences as they provide clues about the existence of some superpower, maybe Allah, directing and watching over our lives. We 'learn from' our experiences when miracles occur and when our sincere prayers are answered, maybe not necessarily in the way we desired, but in the way that proves to be the right option for our *peculiar, personally designed* existence. We 'learn from' spiritual experiences when our souls float outside of our bodies and we feel unearthly sensations and attachments.

Awareness is the insight that directs what we 'learn' and what we 'learn from.' However, it is also the mechanism for 'learning to use,' including *how*, *when*, and *why* to rely on, the secrets and principles that are essential for our lives, and anything that may affect our major decisions and actions of life. This regimen and discipline for self-awareness entails extensive learning, then a lot of practice and patience. We should go through many stages of learning before approaching the summit and gaining self-control. Even then, awareness is not an absolute state to be attained and enjoyed automatically forever and equally by everybody. It only evolves gradually according to the individual's basic personality, intelligence, conscious efforts, and full-time consciousness for the rest of his/her life. Still, even an initial awareness enables us to see and learn more openly and directly.

Learning 'awareness,' stepping on a wisdom path, and stirring serious thoughts about life, mean the same thing. They all feel like a coincidental and radical revolution that manifests the 'truth' of our existence slowly. This inner transformation and revolution is often induced by a shocking incident (a near-death experience maybe) or even reading (or hearing) about alternative paths of living. That is how the true learning process begins; with a basic notion inciting our curiosity. It feels like a moment of awakening, as we begin to see things deeper and more profoundly. That is how and when we learn about the process of learning, learn what to learn, learn how to use what we learn, etc. We also learn about our passion and compassion that are endogenous attributes of learning. The process of learning involves a feeling of passion for what we learn, but more importantly for a divine reality entailing all those facts or principles that we learn. For example, when we learn about atoms and particles, we could feel the passion that stems from learning such seemingly intangible, inconsequential facts. More importantly, however, we appreciate the intricacies and delicacies that contain these facts deeply and feel a special connection to what is happening constantly around us, in every single atom and particle at every single fraction of a moment. We might even feel, and learn from, our sense of nothingness in the midst of this limitless realm. The same feeling of passion can be induced in all of our learning, e.g., when we learn about our 'self,' our relationships, etc.

Learning also requires deep patience. Awareness, learning, and exploring our potentialities, need concentration and attention to details. We are usually very selective and discriminating in our span of attention. When we read an article, we often grasp some aspects of it, which appear to us as the main theme, and ignore or forget all the other meanings that often hide behind many delicate details we bypass. Like reading a novel so fast, we lose its real, deep highlights that the author has painstakingly tried to convey. We are merely eager to follow the story and get to the ending, ignoring that the significance of a good novel is not in its ending, and it hardly has a definite, clear ending, anyway. We have no time or patience to absorb the essence of a book. Or when we listen to a piece of music, we understand and select the melodies and ignore or forget all the rest of it that connect those melodies. We all seem to be in a hurry to learn the superficial aspects and obvious parts of things and dispense with the rest of it. In real learning, however, the essence of things is usually found in the details. For example, those parts of the classical music that many of us do not seem to hear or show much interest in are often full of innate beauty and value. A trained mind has learned how to seek and enjoy those details that boost his/her delight many folds.

In all aspects of our learning, we have a tendency to show this low patience and subvert experiences that find their significance in sacred enduring moments had we realized and nurtured them. Thus, our learning is limited and meaningless. We have no time to learn how to live, as we devote ourselves to pleasures and phoniness under the guise of living. We really cannot grasp and feel the beauty and values of Nature unless we learn to go into its details patiently and passionately. For the same reasons, many of us do not get the opportunity to excavate and enrich our hidden potentialities that might be invoked mainly through our contacts with Nature within and outside us. We are usually too superficial and impatient to envision the underlying properties of things.

Sadly, modern lifestyles have ruined our chances for learning the right stuff for living. Especially, our obsessions with sexuality and materialism have abolished our capacity for self-awareness and finding the right path for a dignified existence and salvation. Naturally, lust is a huge debilitating urge, but letting ourselves become slaves to it all our lives is simply too disgraceful. Then, ignoring these basic facts and staying the course is a sad reality that makes us much more concerned about human intelligence and the chance of ever finding the urge and wisdom to redefine the purpose of human existence, which often feels quite different from what we have fathomed so far!

Besides 'learning' per se, our ability to stay on an awareness path and apply our new wisdom in our lives and relationships on a consistent basis is more important. Often, we learn something and start to believe in it. Then, gradually we ignore or forget what we had learned—our new convictions—as social pressures grow, or as circumstances in our families and relationships change. We have a tendency (as a rooted psychological barrier) to ignore our novel thoughts and ways of life rather fast even after we believe we have learned a lesson. This is another sad symptom of human beings' pathetic nature with little zeal for conscious learning.

Conscious Learning Endeavour

The main objective of conscious learning is to offset our growing apathy or frailty to learn some important stuff about humans' real needs and being. A big reason, of course, is that everybody in new societies spends so many years in colleges to educate themselves in line with all kinds of materialistic goals and lame ideologies about happiness and positive thinking. We are simply too busy with our obligations and ambitions to reflect properly. Thus, we trust the alleged words of wisdoms that some presumed scholars and society propagate and feel appealing to us. Accordingly, the accelerating amounts of naiveté and crude slogans in societies are threatening humans' sanity and survival.

Besides its main purpose to keep our efforts and time focused on learning per se, conscious learning also stresses on the topics vital for humans' salvation, especially about our health and spirits thru novel ways of thinking, feeling, and acting. By cleansing our minds, we try to discard our idiosyncrasies, develop a simple life philosophy to grasp life's essentialities, nurture our natural needs, discard our superficial needs and lame habits, and cope with the growing social mayhem, all in hopes of minimizing life's routine agonies. Conversely, our zeal for self-awareness towards a serene existence requires our lasting commitment to conscious learning. This is a huge task, however, mostly for adjusting our mentalities and lifestyles by resisting the tempting, conditioning forces in society. It needs sacred visions, principles, goals, and ideals as a compassionate, humble human before setting out to explore the details and means of becoming such a person for our own good and perhaps serving others as well. It requires finding a rather independent means of living by curbing our phony personalities.

Through conscious learning, we also aim to resolve our inner conflicts and lifelong doubts about our identity. Accordingly, our first challenge is to 'learn what to learn.' We should figure out our divine potentialities and draw on our sacred experiences that normally ensue our conscious learning. Yet, even our first step— our mere conscious efforts to step on the path of wisdom—would be a big accomplishment all by itself. The formidable mountain of wisdom stands too high above our eager heads and climbing to its summit looks absurd. And, of course, learning about ourselves is not the only thing we want (or are allowed) to do in our lives. Therefore, another challenge is to balance our conscious learning efforts with our social and family obligations, as we remember that the ultimate purpose of our onerous conscious learning is to face life responsibilities that make living difficult, interesting, and joyful randomly. We need basic wisdom and mental stability at least to detect, and do, the essential things of life, while cope with our crooked society, too, without ruining our psychological and physical health with senseless pleasures, relationships, work, etc.

Naturally, our sense of commitment evolves gradually after a deep personal conviction to overhaul our mindsets by studying our life aspirations, thoughts, and behaviour perpetually. We let (and sometimes force) our egoless, objective observations and honest feelings drench into our conscious mind smoothly. At the end of our meditations and contemplations, we discover the new meanings of things along with firmer beliefs. We ensure not to leave the learning process to the natural course of life, random experiences, or short-lived feelings. We do not wish to merely go through life, do a lot of education, and maybe learn from some life experiences, too, without ever finding at least a tentative meaning for life and a purpose for our existence. We remember that we are on a sacred mission on an exotic path with its various challenges, disappointments, and hopefully enlightenment at the end. Through this divine self-awareness mission, we also learn about, and from, our daily mistakes, as we see life's essentialities realistically outside the social norms imposed upon us. These efforts entail an eternal, proactive process of learning, at a high level of consciousness, compared to education and routine life experiences that are mostly subconscious and merely for satiating our ambitions without any 'self'-realization goals.

We all like to define the meaning and criteria of 'life quality' and the means of achieving it. A conscious learning process is for achieving these goals by exploring the contents and structure of one's life, because 'how to live' is a major life decision in itself—to set our life outlook and path. *We must learn what to learn in order to know how to live.* We need a personal plan rather than merely imitating social trends or leaving everything to fate with no defined path of life to follow actively. Conscious learning is not for just making temporary adjustments to our lifestyles or life expectations in response to circumstantial situations and moods. Rather, our efforts should reflect a lasting commitment and belief to redefine our being on a divine path. The first step is to resolve the rooted learning disability in humans noted in the last section.

Awareness Domain and Power

Despite all these fine ideas about the role of conscious learning, we might still doubt the value of so much personal efforts for gaining higher consciousness and self-awareness, on top of the risks of social abandonment, all for some abstract objectives and potential sensations about our being. We might still ask, 'What is awareness, really?' and 'What is it good for, anyway?'

Well, awareness is simply a distilled knowledge of reality. It evolves through 'conscious learning' when we synthesize our needs and life experiences by focused thinking and creating our new beliefs and natural needs at various levels of significance.

And, awareness is mainly for keeping ourselves on a steady, thoughtful life path. We simply try to stay conscious of who we are and why, in order to maintain a peaceful relationship with our surroundings and ourselves. Aside from ensuring our stability in thoughts and actions, awareness helps us improve our thinking and living habits. Furthermore, awareness becomes an important source for deciphering our routines and experiences consciously and objectively to make good decisions. It is valuable also for gauging our past decisions and actions, noticing our mistakes, and polishing our life philosophy. We may even be able to correct our past erroneous decisions, although most critical life decisions are only once in a lifetime opportunities.

Unfortunately, we hardly learn anything from our stressful routine experiences, as we are conditioned to accept social trends as inevitable facts of life. Although we doubt the purpose of our struggles to survive another day, we usually feel helpless resisting the norms and temptations within this rigid social structure. For example, our jobs and relationships are the main sources of our stress and depression, nowadays, yet we suspect the viability of other options for living, or the validity of our raw observations (conclusions) about our boring, painful jobs and relationships. Then, we rebel suddenly or merely despair without analysing the causes of our tensions calmly and changing our lifestyles slowly and objectively. Only through conscious learning, we might elude these radical reactions to our surroundings and mental pressures that ensue. Only through conscious learning, we might grasp life essentialities, stay focused, and change our debilitating habits gradually. This is an essential purpose of self-awareness, too.

We might learn something from our experiences (and raise our awareness) if we consciously analyse their consequences and details to make objective assessments. Of course, the value of the lessons we learn from our experiences or meditations depends mainly on its perceived application to future decisions (according to our personality, too, of course). For example, subsequent to a car accident, a rational person becomes more aware (conscious) of his/her driving habits for a long while and often abandon his/her bad habits, too. On the other hand, the death of a dear family member usually finds limited application for future decisions in spite of its deep impact. We may remember more consciously for a while that our expectations from life are absurd and our habitual worries are senseless, since life is too erratic and short, anyway. We might even learn to bear the death of another family member slightly better next time. However, we usually do not learn much from such a sad, uncontrollable event if it does not have a direct application. Sadly, most of us have little imagination or foresight about life and future to contemplate our experiences thoughtfully and dig out the secrets within them. Surely, if we cannot imagine an immediate purpose for a particular experience, its learning value seems limited and quickly erased from our memories.

The main obstacle for raising our awareness is that we must remain objective and patient to find the roots of our idiosyncrasies thru a long process of conscious learning. Our resistance to learn from our mistakes, or even study our experiences, is normally too deep. Therefore, our growing, unresolved inner conflicts turn into complex, deep delusions that guide the structure of our lives and routines permanently. We keep making the same mistakes, while trusting our rationality fully and foolishly. Without adequate care and awareness, we always do a sloppy, selfish assessment of our thoughts and deeds merely to justify our crooked mentality. Without an ongoing regimen of conscious learning regarding our being, needs, and plans we never gain control over our destiny, although the impacts of fate and random events for social living can never be avoided or underestimated, either.

We resist change, as we love our personalities, attitudes, and rigid beliefs. Change is difficult, anyway, because it might occur only through a deep process of self-awareness and growth, which is mostly gradual and slow. It occurs only when we have a strong incentive to change—to follow such a rigid ritual at our own pace based on our intelligence. That incentive often comes from our desire for a simpler, more peaceful life through personal growth and wisdom. This trilogy's main objective has been to raise some fundamental questions and thoughts for those who have enough motivation to learn about life essentialities, expedite their mental growth towards tranquility, and use their new wisdom to revamp their personalities, attitudes, and beliefs.

In addition to patience and objectivity required for analysing our experiences, we must retain all that information, like building a database on computer. Except that the complex nature of life experiences, combined with all kinds of emotions and cherished beliefs, makes managing (storing and retrieving) that information cumbersome. It is too difficult to interpret our emotions, and it is even harder to rekindle them. People can benefit from recalling their exact emotions in the past, e.g., the love a couple had shared before their relationship problems had begun contaminating their judgments. Yet, hardly anybody can retain those old emotions, no matter how sentimental or agonizing they had felt at the time. That is why the idea of 'thinking marriage at the time of divorce' sounds rather absurd, though still possible as explained in Part IV. It becomes especially hard to recall the essence of our memories when some new emotions overwhelm us, maybe even in similar circumstances, e.g., when we fall in love again, despite the agony of a previous experience. We do not learn our lessons in time! Still, remembering all these facts raises our level of consciousness.

On the other hand, as we change with maturity, both the logic behind, and the meaning of, an old emotion feel absurd, which could be considered a learning experience in itself. With age, our emotions settle, while we control our naive beliefs and passion a bit better. In fact, we wonder about the absurdity of those old raw emotions, how they were created or felt, and why. Sometimes, our reminiscences of those old feelings make them appear silly and amusing, in fact. Such embarrassing observations reveal the flimsiness of human emotions, as an innate source of their severe vulnerability. It feels pure silly, because we know the extreme value of healthy and stable emotions for finding happiness. This is an important source of self-awareness, if we learn a lesson, remember the futility of our youthful infatuations, and instead apply those raw sentiments to grasp life and Nature. These self-awareness virtues make us mature faster and gauge our emotions better without allowing any quick influences in our thoughts and beliefs. This is what self-awareness is all about.

Obviously, full awareness and remaining objective about our experiences is a rather optimistic expectation. Sometimes, we can bounce our thoughts off an 'impartial, wise mediator,' or maybe even let him/her challenge our way of seeing and feeling things. Anyone who can stir our conscience and objectivity would do, such as a counsellor, a confidant, or even ourselves when we grow the power and personality to pursue a rigid self-questioning, 'self' awareness regimen. Often our oversensitivity and wishful interpretations of our experiences become additional obstacles for learning a useful lesson. Our boss or spouse's communications feel hostile and spiteful sometimes, whereas our bad judgments or insecurities cause misperceptions and misinterpretations often. Our false pride also prevents us from thinking objectively and honestly. Most of our conflicts with people relate to our Egos and ways of judging them and the events around us hastily.

All these facts about the purposes of awareness reiterate two important points: 1) We are vulnerable all our lives, especially during adolescence, when we have no substantive experiences or enough self-awareness to rely on and we have little capacity for objective thinking. 2) A mistake we make today may ruin the rest of our lives. If only we were as mature as we would be in a few years, especially when the consequences of our decisions and actions become obvious, our lives would probably be less hectic and miserable. However, since we have no such wisdom and opportunity, we should do the second best thing available to us. That is, we should strive to learn about the nature of life's major decisions, their underlying factors, and their potential risks, as much as possible beforehand. We can learn consciously about the decisions and situations that can directly influence our lifestyles and outlooks on life. If we learn to do this exercise consciously and objectively, our upcoming life experiences would match our expectations better, although we can never escape our fate, life's randomness, and humans' crooked nature ruining our plans and spirits. Still, the best way to survive in our crises-ridden societies is to adhere to a solidified life philosophy that supports a simple, independent living, and then hope for the best.

Yet, most importantly, remember: Learning is imagination; learning is feeling; learning is awareness; learning is patience; learning is compassion. Learning requires conscious efforts to grasp our neglected 'self' and identity mostly by raising the level of our consciousness in our thinking, feeling, and acting.

This chapter has stressed mostly on the value and power of conscious learning, as well as the idea of 'living for learning' as a divine lifestyle. With these general principles in mind, it is useful to revisit the topic of education in the next chapter for answering some questions: Can we ever overhaul our educational system, as an essential part of social structure, for serving people better and saving humanity? Can education ever teach us some of the vital facts about the objectives and value of humanity, or we must find some semblance of peace and happiness only through personal efforts and conscious learning?

CHAPTER SIXTEEN
Rethinking Education

For achieving this trilogy's objectives noted in the Introduction —even for the simplest one about learning to cope with social dramas and chaos—we must reassess the goals of our education efforts and systems. Both governments and individuals must play active roles through this rethinking process and adjusting their mindsets substantially. This chapter's criticisms would hopefully help in this process in addition to the discussions in Part I about humans' needs for education versus learning.

Education-Related Social Inefficiencies

Education is still a major life decision, but not because of the conventional rationale about college degree bringing us a high social status or increasing our chances of finding lucrative jobs. Rather, a decision about education (what kind and how much) is crucial due to big social inefficiencies and concerns it causes. So much of our lives' setbacks are outcomes of our earlier decisions, especially those made during youth. The matter feels particularly too depressing when these shortfalls relate to 'education.'

1. **Education Contents:** It has been emphasized throughout this book that we are not teaching our children and youths the right

stuff about life, not even for handling their basic needs, such as marital relationships, the meanings of success and happiness, or the reasons and means of being better human beings. Thus, Education Contents are not stressed too much in this chapter. We simply do not teach our kids what to learn, how, and why.

2. **Time Spent:** Basic education is required for activating our thinking, analytical, and social abilities. Yet, pursuing higher education is an absolute waste of time if it does not guarantee at least a job, or is not justified for a self-fulfilling career. In addition, unless a person is sure about the nature of a career matching his/her personality, wasting so much time on formal education would be a risky strategy for an intelligent person. Education should not be treated as a means of procrastinating, either. Especially, youths' common tendency to use education as an excuse to postpone their responsibility of finding work and facing the harsh realities of life is an absolute waste of their precious time and talent.

   Overall, we should think carefully about any education that may not relate to a specific, long-term career in line with our temperament and a solid life path. Unless the outcome is rather foreseeable and guaranteed at the outset, the risks of spending so many years on some perfunctory education solely in hopes of getting a job is a huge mistake. It is getting more illogical to gamble on our chances of finding a job just because we spend four or more years in college.

3. **Obsolete Incentives:** Traditionally, higher education has been associated with financial rewards and social status. These days, however, these expectations are both unrealistic and unseemly for an intelligent person stressing on life's innate values rather than money and status per se, especially if higher education does not guarantee a job even for a moderate subsistence. Even specialized engineers get laid off in depressed economies and remain unemployed for years. The notion of high rewards is invalid in economies where jobs are becoming scarcer every

year and more university graduates have less direct, applicable expertise. So many people working in jobs unrelated to their initial educations shows that many of us have miscalculated market potentials or our own temperament. Furthermore, so much politicking, personal power struggles, and egotism, even in hiring practices and promotions, render financial rewards for higher education quite unworthy. In fact, knowing how to cope with organizations' crooked norms and politics is more useful than education and even work experience for sustaining those presumed higher financial rewards. The trite expression that, 'It is not how much you know, but rather who you know,' is becoming a bigger reality now. And this travesty will become even more common in the future with rising job insecurities and corporate corruptions. Therefore, unless a definite market demand justifies pursuing highly specialized fields, such as medicine, we should fight this misleading perception about the customary rewards of higher education or ensuing status.

4. **Job Contents and Market Structure:** If the main purpose of higher education is finding a job, its format, content, and depth must fit the requirements of future jobs. However, this direct matching is becoming too hard. In fact, in our vastly dynamic and volatile societies, both job contents and the structure of job markets will change drastically in the immediate future. The advent of computers and technology is changing the nature and format of jobs vastly, including educational requirements to perform those jobs. At one level, it would become harder and less necessary to establish a link between general fields of education and jobs. Other than highly technical jobs, such as medicine and research, most other jobs would have formats that can be performed based on certain intelligence level and fuller on-the-job training. At the same time, very focused and specialized education would be required for limited, particular jobs. Still, the competition would get even fiercer for those limited jobs that organizations offer, with college education

playing a lesser importance for getting one of them. We must become innovative and present our services independently and directly. Now, what kind of background and flexibility would support personalized jobs or services depends on the economy and personal ingenuity, not education per se.

5. **Work Experience:** At the same time, the format of future jobs would value work experience and proven success more than education. Accordingly, intra-organizational promotions will become more prevalent, which makes the chances of getting higher echelon positions based on education e.g., a master's degree, less likely. It may over-qualify individuals, as most of the hiring would be for entry-level jobs with basic education requirements. Starting at an entry-level job in an organization would be easier and faster for getting the desired on-the-job training and acquiring the valuable work experience.

6. **Human Relations:** As a criterion of success in securing a job and advancement, 'who you know' and 'how you adapt' need special efforts and expertise. Learning and practising special work relationships would be more valued than specialized knowledge. We should do a lot more than adapt and cope in order to keep our boss, staff, and colleagues on our side and become a popular manager. We should learn a great deal of unorthodox human relations and much beyond that—perhaps to the point of becoming a total hypocrite or a psychopath. Even if some useful theories of human relations existed in some organizations, employees' personalities and egos always taint those good intentions. In fact, everybody should surpass even the expectations of a normal behavioural environment to communicate with demanding, oversensitive people. We are working for and managing organizations whose employees bring bizarre personality profiles to work place and are under all kinds of stress. Their aspirations and needs are unique and a successful manager must fashion his 'human relations' efforts around each of those employees' needs and personalities. We

should motivate one another to do our jobs efficiently, but also grasp and sympathize with personal shortfalls and needs of one another as well as work environments' demented demands. Yet, we are not equipped to do any of these, while our knack for rivalry and hypocrisy is growing fast. We should also be good with positive thinking and positive psychology to get our bosses' approval, while using a pushy mentality for the good of organizations. Managers, in particular, need specialized Model personality and patience to show (pretend) sympathy, which in turn spreads the level of hypocrisy in organizations.

With such an immense requirement for human relations to survive in organizations, still our educational systems teach the youths nothing about this crooked aspect of organization jobs —the horrible rooted truth—to be at least partially prepared for the harsh reality they must face. They just prepare them for an ideal organization setting so carelessly. No wonder the stress levels in societies are rising so fast so much.

7. **Unfitted Job:** Even if we are lucky and find a job related to our education, if it does not exploit our potentialities or fit our temperament, we have wasted not only the years educating ourselves, but also all the years we suffer in the jobs we hardly enjoy doing or care for. Often, we must tolerate the mismatch and strive for subsistence. Yet, the effects of non-motivating jobs on our spirits are quite substantial and lasting.

8. **Life Direction:** Our education and work experiences impose a certain label (identity) on us. Soon, we also get mentally stuck to what we are doing, e.g., as an accountant, so hardly find the courage, motivation, and stamina to move on to another job, although we are not happy with our occupations and labels. For most of us, higher education leads to lasting commitments in the areas of our presumed expertise. We accept and set our life directions based on our career and education. In a way, higher education fixes our (often-phony) identities for the rest of our lives. Worse, all our education, plus so much personal

and governmental resources devoted to it, goes to waste when we pursue some unrelated occupations a lifetime!

9. **Dire Neglect of Our Potentialities:** Education is perhaps a good measure of individuals' level of perseverance, discipline, and general intelligence. It also shows personal initiative and some level of aptitude in academic endeavour. Thus, degrees are associated with intelligence and abilities, especially since society lacks a better way of measuring and labelling peoples' aptitude. Degrees help employers rate candidates, classify their qualifications, and match them against job requirements to some extent. Yet, besides the need for gauging a person's basic qualifications, degrees do not usually demonstrate a person's potentialities or even his/her depth of intelligence (wisdom).

In fact, academic intelligence is hardly useful for coping with social demands and daily activities, within and outside work environments. Most educational degrees only provide the minimum level of support for the related jobs, especially when some of us learn to pass the exams without knowing the depth or practical implications of the material. Moreover, we lose our expertise if not applied routinely, and it often becomes obsolete within five to ten years, anyway, if not kept current.

Many of us never get a chance to explore or develop our hidden potentialities despite (or because of) our degrees. On the other hand, many people do not get a chance to acquire a formal education, yet figure out and utilize their potentialities rather effectively. Most of the renowned geniuses have not had formal education, yet created precious scientific theories and artistic masterpieces. Surely, systematic research and education have enormous values, but they do not necessarily activate our potentialities, especially if we choose an unrelated education based on economic forces and job market demands. Actually, higher education often distracts us from exploring and using our potentialities, since it keeps our focus and efforts within a narrow boundary for the sake of staying practical. Thanks to the superficiality of the new world basking in useless science, music, and arts, no longer even useful philosophical thoughts and masterpieces, like those offered by Socrates, Beethoven, and Monet, are generated by our egotistical, exhausted minds.

Naturally, individuals' true values and contributions stem from their potentialities arousing their ingenuity rather than just performing some tasks and functions rather robotically.

10. **Learning Hindrance:** Education in the present format hinders real learning in life enormously, as it consumes people's time, energy, and focus. This topic was stressed in Part I.

11. **Increased Expectations:** Our expectations from life rise in line with our education unrealistically. We also expect people's validation and respect for our efforts of educating ourselves. Although the chances of employment and recognition often rise with higher education in some fields, no such guarantee exists for most educational fields. In fact, we would be taking a high risk of facing frustration and humiliation when we do not get any recognition (genuine or fake) in line with the expectations we develop and the hardships we should endure for getting a degree. We get more disappointed, discouraged, and perhaps confused when our education does not appear to produce any tangible results, nor keep us particularly content with our lives.

12. **Education Standards:** National educational standards are set to accommodate the majority of population. School programs are developed to engage the average and lower motivated kids. Thus, many students with higher intelligence and motivation are kept back, and their potentialities are routinely suppressed. Even at colleges and universities, students find little chance or motivation to go beyond their routine curriculum and explore their true potentialities unless they get into a research-oriented occupation. Instead, they are subjected to a narrow vision of how things work in a capitalistic economy, how our specific technologies or sciences operate, etc. Formal education is like

an assembly line with no attention to students' unique needs and potentialities or showing them how to explore their own intuitions and purposes in life. The overall quality of education has declined rapidly over the years due to laxer educational and graduation norms somewhat in line with people's growing general naivety and the fad for printing useless degrees. Now, education is at best meant to serve the needs of industries and economies and not people's social and psychological needs.

13. **Cost of Education:** The direct costs of education are getting out of control, while the burden of our inefficient educational systems on the public and taxpayers is also growing too fast. Students are expected to borrow substantial amounts of money from greedy financial institutions to pay their high tuitions at ineffective universities and then work for many years in the exploiting organizations that are supported by incompetent and corrupt governments that are controlled by greedy elite groups in society. That is a good deal for organizations, governments, financial institutions, universities, and the elites, but not the youths who should bear all these hardships and humiliations just for the chance of making a torturous living. And that is only if they are lucky to find a job in the first place. Otherwise, only god knows how these people can pay out their rising debts, while the interest is accumulating fast. Is not this useless system of education a modern type of forcing slavery? Is not it an excellent reflection of social dysfunction and the cause of the youths' ultimate desperation and humiliation?

Luckily, free online courses will soon outdo the expensive, torturous method of university education in at least seventy percent of subjects. Teaching jobs will soon become redundant when a few best professors can make course videos and offer all required teachings over the internet to millions of people at a time. A large amount of knowledge becomes easily available to the public regardless of their financial means, and people's overall intelligence would increase drastically, too. All these professors in thousands of universities will be freed up to apply their talents on more useful stuff, instead of repeating the same lectures over and over for thirty or forty years and wasting a lot of public's financial resources on running ineffective, costly universities. In fact, the focus will change from education and educating (as students and professors respectively) to personal learning for better living and more useful research, especially for developing more effective family relationships.

14. **Education Decisions:** Overall, many fundamental decisions about education are necessary by people, scholars, schools, and governments. Soon, societies are forced to see the 'education shortfalls' and how our teachings have become rather harmful for people and society, e.g., when someone ends up working as a waiter or clerk with his/her college degree hanging on his/her room's wall in his/her parents' house, because s/he never finds a related job and cannot afford to live independently. Current educational inefficiencies lead to loss of human talents and life. They ruin our self-image, courage, and ambitions. We become cynical about the whole world and the purpose of living.

Getting stuck in a dead-end job, due to our education, and facing an everlasting inefficient life cause a parallel dilemma. We perform our responsibilities with minimum conviction just to keep our jobs and make a living. We might not even feel anything wrong with our lives or underutilizing our energies and brains. We merely multiply our life inefficiencies by doing some lousy jobs unfitted to our personalities and undermining our talents. Then, organizations, societies, and humanity also suffer the outcomes of our half-hearted, lousy performances.

The educational inefficiencies become even more obvious and dreadful when many people choose to pursue unrelated businesses or professions intentionally, e.g., when a physician devotes plenty of his/her time and energy to business ventures with little attention to his/her real responsibility that s/he was trained for. Inefficiencies are rising also due to the capitalistic priorities ruining overall social morality and people's sense of professionalism. This atmosphere, where greed dictates our life decisions, shows how little education assists even a person's basic integrity or life path. Especially, for people with higher education, mainly physicians, dentists, and lawyers, we expect a kind of moral core and responsibility to raise the welfare and health of other fellow beings. Instead, even these professionals have now become terrible role models for the rest of us. Who is most responsible for this travesty and inhumanity other than our capitalistic mentalities and educational systems?

The resultant rising immorality in society is disheartening when the basic responsibility attached to education (especially in highly specialized fields) is abused or not discharged. Now, everybody believes that his/her education and expertise entitle them to vast financial rewards at the cost of the patients and public's welfare. Some doctors' zeal to make rash diagnosis to maximize the number of patients they visit in a day or opt for unnecessary procedures is just embarrassing. In particular, this mentality defies (disdains) modern humans' tendency to brag about civilization. We just get sicker when we witness these greedy gimmicks to overcharge the system and people for some lousy services, rather than focusing on professional duties and showing empathy. Sadly, capitalism encourages hypocrisy and greed in all aspects of modern lifestyles and professions as a reasonable expectation—*like a basic human right!*

For example, in Vancouver, Canada, physicians expect you to complain about only one ailment, e.g., your stomach or foot, in the same visit. You must make another appointment for the second problem. Then you should wait a few weeks or months to visit a specialist before going for ultrasound or x-rays, etc. Then, you must go for another visit to get the results, which are often negative and the start of another round of long visitations and tests. These services are free for patients, so repeated visits is only raising the overall inefficiency and cynicism in society. This whole shenanigan is for charging the province more for separate visits, while both doctors and patients waste their lives on these administrative trivia, on top of all the extra burdens on the medical services and economy. What a deplorable society!

Sometimes, it actually feels as though doctors do not mind keeping us ill longer or making us sicker in some kind of a messy limbo—a lucrative game! For a modern society like Canada, still allowing these inefficiencies is appalling. Yet, it appears like a legitimate, normal practice, simply since even the supposedly compassionate professionals around the world are now fully infected with the social greed pandemic.

A funny mess is that we often feel anxious about visiting a doctor in fears of mentioning a few symptoms that might be related or not! If not related, the physician might get upset for our sneaky attempt to solve two ailments in one visit. Yet, if related, we fear that not mentioning all the symptoms could jeopardize the good doctor's diagnosis. Besides, we are quite nervous all along, worrying about our visit lasting more than ten minutes, which is the allotted time posted in large letters on the walls in the waiting rooms of some clinics. Sometimes, we rehearse our dialogue with the doctor at home before the visit to avoid a disaster! What a mess!

All thanks to capitalism, NOW the priority should be given ten folds more to money than curing patients. This is the rule and norm now. This awful mentality is rather prevalent in most capitalistic countries in all professions, but is most noticeable and despicable amongst pharmaceutical firms, physicians, and dentists that stress on their wealth, instead of patients. They do not have time or incentive to diagnose and treat our illness fast, while we must pay more taxes every year to maintain this vile, wasteful system within this corrupt socioeconomic structure—and often suffer our illness more and longer, too. What humans!

All these individual 'micro' inefficiencies by all of us in all professions have been adding up and contributing largely to the growth of lazy and inefficient economies around the world. Somehow, the 'macro' inefficiencies and wastes in society are the results of its citizens doing the wrong education, driven merely by greed, or occupying jobs that do not motivate them to produce adequately. People's low conscience or motivation to serve the public is embarrassing, yet governments and people bear the high cost of education that produces these brains and mindsets, while the real return to the economy remains dismal at best. The national productivity (per capita) of most nations is declining due to its workers' inefficiencies, which are evident partly in terms of their productive years wasted in educational systems, inefficient jobs, corrupt organizations, etc. Our basic and innocent personal decisions about education damage both our personal lives and society as a whole when most of us do not get a chance to use our talents and potentials, since we are simply stuck within an outmoded social structure—trapped by economic needs, greed, and lack of guidance. Furthermore, our frustrations affect our social lives and stir more stress, personal clashes, apathy, and social inefficiencies.

Both the sheer number of wasted degrees and the depth of unethical attitude of our professionals demonstrate the growing deficiencies in the educational systems of modern societies. However, nobody seems to have a solution or the courage to challenge the current social structure's inefficiencies related to educational mechanisms. To be fair, developing enough social conscious to overhaul the existing social mechanisms would be a huge job even if we grew the intelligence and motivation to invent more efficient systems.

Nonetheless, most of us feel the deep burdens of our present mentalities, while we strive for wealth at all cost to society and our sense of being, anyway. Our obsession for materialism has now been rooted in our psyches. It has now turned into a sense of entitlement and a normal attitude by almost all allegedly educated people. Less educated are copying us rapidly, too.

The above discussion of education shortfalls is not to undermine its value if its contents can be directly applied to an available job and build one's career. They are only for showing the public's horrendous misperceptions about the importance and relevance of education. In fact, the current format of formal education is doomed and also a direct cause of social unrest and gloom.

A Guideline for the Type and Level of Education

Despite the above negative points about the limited purposes of education, we must plan our careers and do some kind of work for living based on some type of training. Yet, the education type and amount must be coordinated carefully in line with people's personalities and potentialities for a specific career. Accordingly, developing a *rather commonsense* general guideline, like the one suggested below, might prove helpful and raise our scrutiny:

- Our intentions and the risks of doing higher education or not must be clear and justified. Mainly, we should know whether we are just following the social norms and trusting the obsolete purposes of education too much, or whether we have sound, legitimate plans for doing it. Blindly hoping that any kind of education automatically increases our chances of employment or success is unwise and a major source of disappointment.
- We should consider higher education mainly a tool for career planning, and not learning per se. Learning, as a more essential tool for living, requires a different mindset and mechanism, as stressed in previous chapters. Thus, we should push ourselves (and our children) to fully justify our choice of a certain field of education. Is it a genuine personal interest that is guiding our decision and if yes, how does it relate to job markets? Or the decision is due to some unknown (or known) external forces or needs? We should test and justify the validity of the objectives we want to set for an education decision.
- We may not be happy in the end if our career-related education does not fit our passion and mentality. On the other hand, not planning for a career opportunity in job markets can jeopardize

our social standing and life. We should understand, compare, and accept these risks along with the long-term benefits and possible drawbacks of a decision made sloppily today.
- Spending too much of our valuable lives on higher education only for satisfying our basic needs or just for prestige is absurd. Technical training and skill courses would be more productive in the long run than college education, especially if it does not relate to the jobs available. Even for satisfying our higher-level personal needs, education is only a tool for building a specific career that can provide some level of self-actualization or fulfil our legitimate aspirations. In general, *basic schooling* can fulfil our *basic needs*, especially if it is revised wisely soon.
- Our work motivations, higher aspirations, and passion must be clear to us and make sense according to some reliable criteria. Besides the risk (and incentives) for success and welfare, high financial rewards is neither a realistic objective, nor a proper criterion for selecting a field of education.
- In particular, higher education should not be perceived as a means of wealth gathering. Greed is neither a natural personal need, nor a legitimate purpose for education, especially as a physician or scientist. Greed is merely a debilitating condition (or naïve imitation) grown mostly according to parental and social influence leading to a lager useless population globally.
- At least philosophically, higher education seems impotent for satisfying either our basic needs or greed per se. Therefore, its main goal should be to fulfil our higher needs, including social contribution, self-actualization, or possibly for membership in professional groups with humanitarian interests, objectives, and responsibilities. Accordingly, higher education must be only in a field that a person has real interest and talent, with an open mind about its practicality for earning a living as well.
- The likelihood of our education supporting the option of self-employment should also be assessed. We must recognize the implications of working for organizations and relying on them for survival and security, as explained in Part II.

Epilogue

Many topics in this trilogy have aimed to explore, i) humans' fundamental thoughts about existence and society, ii) our spirits and spirituality, and iii) the features of the modern life structure—all for the purpose of making a better use of our brains and lives. Yet, at the end of this final volume, we are probably still very much doubtful about the prospect of ever overcoming the barriers of living peacefully and cordially amongst such conceited, greedy humans. In particular, witnessing so many illiterate people so full of themselves is both amazing and embarrassing. Many of us, especially in poorer nations, often have doubts even about our chances of survival and making a decent living in this chaotic, fast-declining world of politics, economy, and job markets.

Meanwhile, even people in modern societies hardly get the incentive and intuition to ponder their other options of living. We miss the opportunity of exploring the purposes of our existence, finding the true essence of our 'self,' or grasping the real joys of Nature. We merely pamper our habits, Egos, and values that only keep us floating in a haze a lifetime within a time-space spectacle (instead of a divine spectrum). We spend so much energy and time on manipulating and exploiting one another for power and greed, we barely find a chance to reflect on the basic questions of, 'Who we are,' and 'What we are really doing with our lives and to one another,' and 'Why.' When we look around, we only see a phony world filled with weird illusions. Hardly do any signs of personal intuitions or spirits lift us beyond our meagre existence towards a deeper sense of being, while we merely cherish our physical forms and assets.

At the end of this trilogy, our busy minds are probably still cluttered by enormous doubts about so many things, including:

- the severe limitations of our logic and science,
- our sense of any other reality beyond our perceived world,
- our ability to choose and follow a path of wisdom,
- the existence of an eternal spirit deep within us,
- the value and outcome of our worldly struggles,
- our fleeting passion and compassion and the chance of using them for the welfare of 'self' and humanity,
- the role we could play as a carefree *nonconformist* to make an impression on this monstrous superstructure of human egoism and faltering socioeconomic systems,
- the possibility of ever solving our urgent problems of violence and crimes, especially in modern societies,
- the future of human race with all the turmoil that we have caused and are responsible for, including the climate crisis,
- the value (and damages) of so many infantile religions around the globe still keep people in such state of ignorance,
- the complexity and prospects of family lives,
- the possibility of humans' ever maturing and learning to relate to one another more effectively and compassionately,
- the polarity of people within each nation and across the world, and,
- all the rising dilemmas regarding humans' chances for social and global coexistences!

In all, we wonder whether humanity is doomed and we have reached a point of no return. We wonder if we can eventually make our lives simpler and thus more bearable.

Nevertheless, while our doubts and decisions for living seem endless, they are totally valid and warranted. At the same time, we may now have some means of dealing with these doubts in a more effective manner, if we ponder the ideas suggested in this trilogy seriously. Surely, we cannot eliminate our dilemmas and doubts, but can possibly let our positive doubts sow the seeds of personal beliefs and cultivate a *sense of being* in our thoughts and routines slowly. We can think of our 'self' as a lost soul within a ludicrously chaotic life structure. Our convictions can surpass any religious teachings, so that we can develop our own sensible and spiritual rituals. With our life philosophy, we can put our trust in both the eventuality of destiny and a valid sense of individuality deep within us—the 'self'—that we might rely on for guidance. No one else can guide us properly, after all!

If we had any doubts about the role of philosophy in our daily lives, they must have become somewhat clearer at this point. The whole idea of philosophy is to help us explore a decent way of living, without being dogmatic, gullible, or egotistical—if there is a right way of living! We are hoping for a society where people set their priorities according to some sacred criteria and thoughts, which are moral, 'self'-actualizing, and unselfish all at the same time. That is, while one seeks inner satisfaction by utilizing one's potentials (for a soulful self-realization), one also contemplates humanity's opportunities for salvation, feels the global sufferings, and shows compassion (as a selfless, 'self' oriented person). One feels the intricate reality of the universe and one's relation with Nature, rather than being merely driven by the evil forces of the perceived world to exploit Nature and others, and to satisfy merely one's greed, lust, and egoism.

Thus, while philosophy is not an exercise in spirituality per se, it reinforces the need for some norms of morality and humanity for our actions, emotions, and thoughts. Philosophy tells us where our main detachments and attachments should be in line with the characteristics of the *real* and *perceived worlds*. In the perceived world, we get attached to material things, appearances, approvals, imitations, and deceits. In the real world, we do the opposite: We devote our time and energy to the growth of our characters by becoming more united and harmonious with Nature, 'self,' and humanity. Maybe philosophy can even help us create a *truthful* religion, too, just for satiating our spirituality need without trying to dwell so much on the existence or nature of God and eternity. Our basic life philosophy is merely meant to give us a practical way of living, while addressing our spiritualism without needing any external advice or promises, e.g., regarding afterlife or any religious ritual to get there.

Naturally, our narrow perspectives in the perceived world raise our doubts regarding the role of any kind of philosophy that rejects or distorts the naïve picture we have so elaborately painted in our vainly overworked brains of this alluring world, including our religions. It is hard for us to take our eyes off the spectacle we are addicted to and adore so much, simply because 'philosophy' tells us that our senses of, and addictions to, this perceived world is illusive and we are too naive. Still, at least our subconscious mind is now exposed to some philosophical interpretations of who we humans are and who we could, or truly need to, become. These ideas might help us somewhat in our actions, decisions, and choices of lifestyles; and in fact, perhaps even find a new wisdom path to live more peacefully.

Ironically, the need for philosophical principles and thoughts often emerge through depression regularly, too. Once the futility, pressures, and stress of living in the perceived world overwhelm us, we question our way (philosophy) of life. It happens a lot, especially to people who spend most precious years of their lives doing things that would only later prove a total waste of time and energy to them.

Sharing some basic philosophical principles with the youths might help their eager, restless brains address life dilemmas they should endure all their lives in vain. Obviously, influencing the youths' radical personalities would be impossible without the aid of essential supporting systems to encourage and guide them constantly through simpler means of living. These supporting systems should start at high schools and colleges, but also be integrated in our cultures and social reward systems driven by our governments, families, and social systems. They should explain their main decisions and doubts for living. These techniques can enhance the youths' incentives and curiosities to reflect on some fundamental thoughts rather systematically at an earlier stage of their lives. This type of early exposure to life's realities would be more useful, and less stressful, for them than letting them struggle a lifetime to find the right answers on their own, even if the youths ever looked for facts actively or learned useful stuff from their life experiences in such a confusing world.

Is it too late now for humans to start building a real culture that might eventually help new generations at least? Is it too late for humans to learn some humility in order to survive?

Often, we get frustrated and furious about the life we have made for ourselves and the kind of life others impose upon us. Yet, we do not find the courage to think and behave differently. The youths, in particular, must make tough decisions about many life dilemmas and struggle with their painful doubts. In addition, if they ever arrive at the intersection of wisdom paths, they must still decide whether they are ready to change their mentality and lifestyle for possible transcendence to the real world. It would be by far the hardest decision that any individual faces in his/her life. That is, can s/he, and how, dismiss the rituals and rewards of our societies to a large, but practical, extent? With compliance, one receives all those tangible rewards of wealth, love, status, and social recognition, or at least a perception of achieving all these luring goals. None of these alluring, materialistic incentives is available to him/her once s/he steps on a new path outside the routines of conformity. It would be too difficult, if possible at all, for most of us to ignore the temptations of social extravagance, greed, ego, attachment, and power.

On the other hand, a wise, spirited decision at any age could free us from our vile habits, social problems, and negative doubts, while we build a solid life philosophy according to our positive doubts. Our new beliefs and boosted spirits turn those doubts into plausible questions about the validity and value of our existence in the perceived world. We still should tackle these questions, but they would not be as stressful and overwhelming as the mere task of living has become, nowadays. In fact, many of our new life dilemmas and decisions would feel inherently inspirational and spiritually fulfilling once we look beyond our illusions within the perceived world. Once we rebuild our beliefs and life philosophy within the realm of the real world, we can redeem our souls to be our guides the rest of the way. We can let a higher wisdom in the universe help us make all the essential decisions and mitigate our conflicts and sufferings in our journey of life.

Some of us may get the opportunity to realize and explore humans' ten *intrinsic* dimensions (inner connections) that goad another ten *auxiliary* dimensions in humans. Within these twenty finely interconnected attributes, we embrace the universe and cope better with social demands. These twenty human dimensions are explained briefly in Volume II of this trilogy in Appendix C.

Ultimately, our doubts, wisdom, and self-awareness are meant to help us organize our thoughts, appreciate the sanctity of human spirit, find our true reasons for living, develop the seven elements of 'self' noted in Vol. II, and possibly help society to develop a more viable life structure for humanity. All these fine ideals can occur naturally if only we humans think a bit deeper and embrace a simpler lifestyle outside the prevalent life structure, instead of only boosting our egoism and superficiality. Perhaps rereading this trilogy or parts of it rather regularly can help us explore our doubts with higher conviction, tackle our major life decisions more prudently, recall our commitments for an ongoing regimen of conscious learning, and liberate our 'self.' We might even get enough spiritual clues through this routine to pursue a deeper self-appraisal and therapy to unveil the evils that vanquish our spirits maliciously.

Let us do it.

www.ingramcontent.com/pod-product-compliance
Lightning Source LLC
Chambersburg PA
CBHW020349170426
43200CB00005B/103